People of the mediterranean

Library of Man

Edited by Adam Kuper
Department of Anthropology
University College London

Also in this series

Kenneth Little   *Urbanization as a Social Process*
Aylward Shorter   *East African Societies*

A catalogue of social science books published by Routledge & Kegan Paul will be found at the end of this volume.

People of the mediterranean

An essay in comparative social anthropology

J. Davis
Senior Lecturer in Anthropology
University of Kent

Routledge & Kegan Paul
London, Henley and Boston

First published in 1977
by Routledge & Kegan Paul Ltd
39 Store Street,
London WC1E 7DD,
Broadway House,
Newtown Road,
Henley-on-Thames,
Oxon RG9 1EN
and
9 Park Street,
Boston, Mass. 02108, USA
Set in Times Roman
and printed in Great Britain by
Weatherby Woolnough,
Sanders Road, Wellingborough,
Northamptonshire

ISBN 0 7100 8412 9

Contents

Contents

Tables

Figures

Map

Preface

This is a book which surveys and compares the materials collected and published by anthropologists who have worked in the mediterranean. It is chiefly concerned with the work of the last thirty years and is thus a product in which many living colleagues have unwittingly collaborated. Such merits as it may possess are the product of several years of contemplation of their merits; most of its defects are those of the author, although there are also those common to the field as a whole. One or two writers are none the less criticised with a persistence which a public acknowledgment of respect is unlikely to soften: other readers will see that no negligible person is harried.

Some colleagues have been generous enough to collaborate wittingly: Dr Peter Loizos has read most of this book at one or another stage in its preparation, has listened with true friendliness to incoherent attempts to explain perplexity and has been unfailingly wise and constructive in criticism. Dr Nevill Colclough kindly applied his acutely sceptical intelligence to some of the wilder excesses which appeared in the drafts, and may recognise that they have been modified with his help. Professor Lucy Mair read chapter 5 in draft, and the present version owes much to her criticisms. Dr Nanneke Redclift and Mr David Morgan struggled to improve chapter 3; Dr John Campbell helped to eliminate some of the blunders from chapter 6. Mr John Goy prepared the index, and Miss Sally Hewett turned a messy manuscript into a typescript which delighted the publisher. All of these are owed more than thanks, and a relationship of continuing indebtedness is hereby acknowledged.

Reine Didon   J. Davis
Carthage   July 1975

ix

This book is dedicated to the memory of Maurice Freedman, teacher, exemplar of academic and public virtue, untimely dead

1

Introduction

I The distinctiveness of mediterranean anthropology

The mediterranean attracted anthropologists almost before any other region of the world. Maine, Fustel de Coulanges, Robertson-Smith, Frazer, Durkheim, Westermarck – the roll-call of those early generals marks out mediterranean anthropology as a special case: does any other region boast such a field-staff, so distinguished by their contemporaries? One reason they were attracted was the wealth of accessible information and subsequent literary, archaeological, legal, historical scholarship which made it possible to study mediterranean institutions without visiting the mediterranean: of those men only Durkheim and Westermarck were chiefly concerned with the living, and only Westermarck visited his southern contemporaries to conduct his inquiries *en poste*. Although Mauss visited Morocco and took an interest in what ethnographers were doing there (1930) his major works refer only to classical sources. Men whose understanding of classical or semitic antiquity was of the highest order regarded their southern contemporaries as a source of charming anecdotes or as survivals (e.g. Myres, 1905, 1933, Casson, 1938).

Nevertheless, a consequence of that early interest is that the analysis of mediterranean institutions produced seminal ideas that have influenced the analysis of more remote societies, even if anthropologists in the late twentieth century are not always aware that this is so. Of course, Maine's general statement that progressive societies move from status to contract will probably be identified by most readers as based on the study of ancient mediterranean law; but would the same readers be able to trace the theory of segmentary organisation back to

1

its origins in mediterranean ethnography? The line begins with Hanoteau and Letourneaux, one a lawyer the other a soldier, whose three volumes of guidance to French administrators in Algeria (second edition, 1893) provided Durkheim with the ethnographic evidence on the Kabyle which he uses, in chapter 5 of *De la division du travail social*, to produce his theory of segmentary solidarity – whence it passed into the common currency of anthropology.

Mediterranean anthropology is not merely an intellectual quartermaster's stores, however, for it is also a museum of research strategies. Maine, Fustel de Coulanges, Robertson-Smith, each compressed an eclectic set of evidences, relating to a considerable span of time, to produce an account of some aspect of the structure of a time-island, a period of the past in which change might occur but which was regarded as more or less discrete. Frazer marshalled evidence to produce a generalised account of the fundamental processes of all human society. True, he mixed evidence from the mediterranean, as Ferguson and Millar had done before him, with evidence from other parts of the world but he began and ended in those fearful woods outside Rome where, incidentally, the walls of the temple of Diana now enclose several market gardens. Durkheim, although prepared to discuss living people, relied on his scouts in the field (and they included military men) to provide him with the data which he then analysed so brilliantly. Westermarck, unique among these early men, lived for some decades in the Villa Westermarck in Tangier and with the recognised aid of local assistants (one of whom was decorated at Westermarck's insistence by the President of Finland for his services to scholarship) conducted extensive inquiries each summer. In complete contrast to Durkheim, Westermarck performed almost no analysis on the data he collected: they are presented as a list of customs and beliefs on particular topics as they may be found in nearly every Moroccan group which claims a separate identity. His books read like a territorially restricted Frazer, but without the impetus given by that writer's preoccupation with the dark rituals at Nemi. On Westermarck, Berque's judgment is definitive: his works he says, 'ont inspirées aux chercheurs plus jeunes à la fois admiration, défiance et lassitude' (1955: 129). Fieldwork so prolonged was never so wasted. The two strategies – of structural analysis and of fieldwork – were to be combined elsewhere in other fields, but mediterranean anthropology is an almost complete museum of premodern research techniques.

These remarks are about the history of the discipline, and the use which later anthropologists have made of the substantive history of the mediterranean is a topic of such importance it has a chapter of this book to itself. There is one further point which can be made at this introductory stage. Mediterranean people have been affected, sometimes in important ways, by the anthropological works which have been written about them: for better and worse, anthropology has helped create the history of the mediterranean. The French armies in the Maghreb were accompanied by gazetted ethnographers whose task it was to investigate and record the customs and laws of the tribes of Algeria and later Morocco. The Spanish seem to have followed the same policy (see Hart, 1958). For example Montagne, whose work is still of great importance (e.g. Seddon, 1973b; Gellner, 1969; Hart, 1970; Vinogradoff, 1974b), was a *capitaine de corvette* when Mauss met him in 1930, but a sea captain with one major ethnographic study already published and a distinguished anthropological career to follow. Montagne's work, like that of his less illustrious predecessors, deeply influenced French colonial policy and Moroccan reaction to it (e.g. Brown, 1973) and it was also to some extent a misrepresentation of the facts (e.g. Burke, 1973; and see below, p. 113). Even though there is no way to show that Montagne would not have misrepresented the facts if he had been something other than he was, the direct involvement of serving ethnographers of considerable intellectual merit in military pacification and civil administration permits the student of the history of ideas to examine the fourfold relation between office, intellectual creativity, policy and government as perhaps it can be studied in no other area of the world. Moreover such a study could be complemented by an examination of the other ways in which anthropological ideas have influenced major political movements. The relation between linguistic, sociological, folkloric and physical anthropological studies and nationalistic movements has yet to be studied in detail, but it undoubtedly exists in Balkan movements against Turkish rule and would provide a contrast to the perhaps banally indignant fashion for examining the relation between anthropology and colonial oppression. In some countries the work of providing a scientific basis for nationalist claims took on such symbolic significance that anthropology ceased to be a developing academic activity altogether but was rather fossilised so that a contemporary ethnographer from France or England or America, carrying the very latest lightweight intellectual machine gun in his pack, may be suddenly confronted by a Tylorean or Frazerian professor appearing like a Japanese corporal from the jungle to wage a battle only he knows is still on. Finally, note that if Slavs might use anthropology to justify claims against Turks, the Turks themselves, when their military began the task of creating a new state, would use the work of Durkheim to inspire an official ideology of national unity (Spenser, 1958; Stirling, 1957, 1958).

Mediterranean anthropology is thus distinctive: it attracted early attention from the old heroes; it was the field in which important ideas and techniques were worked out; it is one in which it should be impossible to ignore extensive historical and literary evidence (but see ch. 6), and it is one in which anthropology has had a variety of consequences – as an adjutant of colonial policy perhaps, but also as one element in nationalist struggles for independence and in the formation of that most complex (and un-anthropological) social creation, the nation-state.

Although anthropologists in other areas have begun to come to grips with the unaccustomed problems of description and analysis which a salient and intrusive state and national government may bring, and although it cannot be said that mediterraneanists have tackled the problems with much success, nevertheless it is clear that at least in terms of opportunity the mediterranean is once again a distinctive area. For while Indianists, say, develop notions and conventions for relating the village to the state, and do so with considerable success, the mediterranean affords opportunities for comparison which are unparalleled elsewhere in the world. Consider that there are accounts of political institutions of a recognisably similar kind, from Spain, Portugal, Italy, Greece, the Lebanon and Morocco: by comparing accounts of patronage in these countries the reader may come to some judgements, interim and tentative no doubt, about the consequences of varieties of corporativism, patrimonialism, and parliamentary democracy on village politics, and may add some depth to the rather undifferentiated accounts of 'mediterranean patronage' which have sometimes been allowed to pass. It should also be possible to compare the effects which different kinds of bureaucracy may have on local politics, and to control generalisation by careful study of the interaction of state system and political system. It is the sheer variety of political forms within a sufficiently homogeneous area which makes mediterranean anthropology so promising.

II   Its failures

Needless to say the unique opportunities which the mediterranean affords may also be listed as the most significant failures of anthropology there since the Second World War. The lack of comparison has been remarked on before (e.g. Freeman, 1973) but to read ethnography after ethnography, article after article in which no serious attempt is made to compare the author's findings with those of another, is to realise the extent of the desolation. The reader may think he is in a luxuriant intellectual field, but gradually sees there is no controversy; he may think he is in the company of scientists, but finds they do not compare their results. It is a constant theme of this book that mediterraneanists have failed in their plain duty to be comparative and to produce even the most tentative proposition concerning concomitant variations, and so it need not be elaborated here: one example will suffice. The two most rightly respected English mediterraneanists have studied two communities and from the available figures it appears that one of these is the mediterranean community where resources are most unequally distributed and the other is the one where resources are least unequally distributed (the matter is exceedingly complex, see below, pp. 87-8). Neither of them in fact discusses this point at any length, but each insists that his is an egalitarian society in which every man is considered as good as every other man. The simple comparison raises a number of important sociological problems which remain undiscussed. Is it possible to say that one society is more egalitarian than another? What is the relation between considering people to be equals, and the actual distribution of wealth? What sort of institutions exist to allow people to maintain an ideology of equality when the reality is so different? In fact, because these two eminent men have not compared their own findings, or not in print, it is left to others to do so; and the conclusion in this book is that neither society is egalitarian in any sense at all. It is impossible to dispel the suspicion that the discipline might be in better shape if such a discussion had taken place between them, but it has not been the common practice of mediterraneanists to compare their findings and to draw out the intellectual implications. Even in North Africa, where the Berberologists might give some grounds for qualifying that judgement (see especially Hart, 1973), comparison generally remains of a descriptive not an explanatory kind.

Another major failure concerns history: the record is examined in some detail below (see ch. 6) and here it is enough to point to the usually very shallow time-scale in which communities have been set. It is quite rare to read, for example, about the systems of stratification which preceeded those observed by the authors of the monographs, and writers have neglected to show how a contemporary system may be related to what is known of its precursors: that it is valuable to do this is sufficiently shown by those few cases in which it has been done. Or consider family organisation. It is almost universally assumed that the rules of residence, rules of transmission of property which a contemporary anthropologist observes are ancient and unchanging. Yet to consult the studies of Le Play's followers, for example, is to read the record of forms of organisation which have disappeared in the last century; and those ethnographers who have studied records can sometimes show significant changes have occurred in the villages they studied – even if they then present this data as the decay of some family system which is itself taken to have been ancient and unchanging (as is the case with Balkan *zadrugas*). While most ethnographers of Spain and Italy will mention the consequences of post-Napoleonic tenurial reforms to liberalise landholding and to convert land to a marketable commodity, there is not one who has pointed out that the consequences are different in different places, or has tried to explain in the most cursory way why that should be so. On the southern shore the ethnographers mention the consequences of French or Spanish or Italian conquest and administration, but in many cases the authors confine themselves to a reconstruction of a precolonial era and, with only one or two exceptions, make little attempt to trace a development through the colonial era. Yet as soon as history is allied to comparison important general movements and varations emerge: it is just becoming clear for example that there was a general change in Greece and Cyprus, if not elsewhere too, from bridewealth to dowry in the course of the nineteenth century (a conference on this topic was to have been held in Cyprus by Peristiany), and some account of changes of this kind, or of the different consequences of liberal tenurial reform is clearly of the greatest importance. It is only in the last few years that people have begun to think in these terms, or to give some account of the evolution or development of institutions in the communities they study; and yet the mediterranean has perhaps the most documented and researched history of any region of the world.

It is difficult to explain these failures: some part may be a sense of professional insecurity which mediterraneanists seem to feel. Of course that is only an impression, but it seems current certainly among those who have worked in countries on the European littoral: a sense that anthropology is only anthropology if it is done very much abroad, in unpleasant conditions, in societies which are very different from the ethnographer's native habitat, very different from the sort of place where he might go on holiday. It is not uncommon, at any rate in England, to meet backwoods anthropologists who clearly convey their sense of superiority: mediterraneanists do not undergo a complete cultural disorientation such as those who work in sub-Saharan Africa or New Guinea sometimes claim to have experienced and benefited from. This book is not the place to discuss the rights and wrongs of such judgements: it may be, indeed, that experience of privation and disorientation heightens an anthropologist's sense of the problematic; and it must be agreed that mediterraneanists do often enough take for granted forms of organisation (for example, of the family), which, had they been stimulated by disorientation, they might have investigated more thoroughly. That is possible. But it remains the case that there is no necessary connection between hardship and the sense of the problematic; and the intellectual failures of mediterraneanists are therefore not solely attributable to the fact that they work close to home. Nevertheless it is perhaps a consequence of their sense of professional insecurity that mediterraneanists have tended to under-emphasise those qualities of the mediterranean which might distinguish their work and lead them to differentiate themselves from their colleagues: they have ignored or abused history, and ignored those millennia of intensive interaction which have made mediterranean societies. For that is what the failure to compare, the failure to establish simple patterns of concomitant variation amounts to.

The desire to be as primitive as every other colleague may be equally responsible for two other failures which must be mentioned here. Mediterraneanists have chosen to work in the marginal areas of the region – in the mountains, in the small peasant communities, in the tribal hinterlands of the Maghreb. It is not really adequate to explain this almost complete uniformity of choice by saying that anthropologists work alone and that they cannot therefore grasp the complexities of cities. On the one hand, it *can* be done, as the late Lloyd Fallers showed in his work in Turkey. On the other hand, even if it requires unaccustomed techniques and a willingness to abandon the pretence at holistic analysis, it is possible to investigate the relation between *bourgeois* and *villageois*. That is what M. Corbin did, for example, when she investigated the patterns of marriage and migration into the Spanish city of Ronda from its satellite settlements, using part of her fieldwork period to investigate municipal records (Corbin and Stirling, 1973). In the Lebanon alone it seems to have been impossible to ignore the ties of kinship and patronage which link the towns and the villages; consequently there are a number of excellent or interesting articles on this subject (Khuri, 1976; Nader, 1965a; Peters, 1972; Gilsenan, 1973a). But on the whole the study of the links of rural populations with urban ones has not been seriously undertaken, and there are very few city studies – even though cities derive their populations from the country, even though every mediterraneanist makes an obligatory reference to the fact that peasant societies are part societies, encapsulated in nation states.

That is the fourth weakness in mediterranean anthropology. It may be said that some progress has been made in discussion of political and administrative links between villages and their controlling communities: Pitt-Rivers's early discussion of mediation set a good example; Weingrod (1967-8) and Silverman (1965) have made important contributions to the study of patronage and the way it may, in various forms, link the village to the 'state'. However, discussion is still largely limited to the important but partial topic of the consequences of mediation for villagers and village political institutions. Loizos (1975) was able to follow some cases through from village to minister or party leader; Waterbury (1970) has a unique analysis of elite politics in Morocco, and Khalaf (1976) has a short account of political and electoral loyalties in the Lebanon. But with these exceptions the investigation of national politics is in its infancy.

Politics is only one part of the problem, and it would be wrong to concentrate on it because successes may be signalled there. At least it may be said that politics is observable: the institutions and rituals of representation can be described; decisions are or are not taken; conversations do or do not take place – politics is, in spite of the obvious difficulties, the most accessible part of a much larger problem, formulated by Redfield in terms of 'big' and 'little' traditions, and not advanced by mediterraneanists since then (but cf. Pitkin, 1959b). The fact is that all the communities of the mediterranean share in cultures which are extremely rich, contribute part of their identity, and are not coterminous with the community. A Pisticcese can listen at festivals to the band playing medleys from Verdi and Puccini, and condescend to foreigners – 'We Italians are naturally musical.' Peasants quote Dante and read Manzoni; educated men infiltrate lines of Leopardi into their conversation and watch for signs of recognition. In the same category come the Berber's recognition of the spiritual authority of the Sultanate, and the Cypriot child called Ariadne. Tokens of what is misleadingly called 'Italian' (or Islamic or Greek) culture continually appear in remote villages, and constitute a problem of explanation.

Perhaps the problem can be stated most clearly with the example of religion. Mediterranean religions are all 'of the Book', have highly developed theologies, exegetical apparatus and cosmologies. There are authorities on religion, in some cases with powers to sanction erroneous practice or belief. The religious life, customs and beliefs of villagers and tribesmen rarely coincide with the prescriptions of exegetically elaborated and sanctioned religion, and the intellectual problem is to explain the relation between the two. At an administrative level it is a matter of discovering what people in authority think and do about the 'simple faith' of their co-religionists. At another level, it is a problem of trying to explain the principles by which some 'official' religious doctrines and practices are accepted locally and others not. Campbell (1965) has described the way in which Sarakatsani recognise the sinfulness and inevitability of some of their idiosyncratic behaviour – but they are not convinced that what they do is part of the official religion, linking them into a broad community of the faithful.

Only Gearing (1968) has said that the question is one of selectivity, but his preliminary note has not yet been filled out. Clearly, in addition to an explanatory theory of selectivity, anthropologists need to discuss those elements of local religion which are purely local – where do they come from? What anthropologists have done does not meet the problem: they have described festivals and the part they play in community life (see especially Gower Chapman, 1973; Boissevain, 1965; Freeman, 1968b, 1970); they have described the roles of priests and of spiritual relationships in the political affairs of villages, but they have been singularly silent about the sources of religious forms of expression, and its relation to the standardised doctrines of religious communities. That is, incidentally, why there is no chapter called Religious Systems in this book: the information is discussed under politics or under kinship. But the problem is central to the study of religious life: by careful comparative and historical investigation it should be possible to develop anthropological understanding of

9

religion, which is traditionally derived from religious communities which are homogeneous in belief and practice. Moreover, the problems raised by religion epitomise those raised by discussion of 'national' culture: how intriguing it is that in those festivals which celebrate community solidarity and particularity, the main themes should be medleys which purport to derive from national and supranational communions.

III Assumptions and procedures in this book

The argument is not that mediterranean anthropology since the Second World War has been negligible, nor that the effort put into research there has been wasted, for there are good monographs and good articles. Rather, for one reason or another, mediterraneanists have not made the most of their distinctive opportunities – to be comparative and historical; nor have they made any particular contribution to the analysis of part societies in their relation to the other parts. This book is an attempt not only to review the literature of mediterranean anthropology but to suggest ways in which it might be improved, and this introductory chapter now ends with an account of some of the assumptions which underlie the book, and some of the limitations which it is necessary to impose.

First, it should be understood that this book is a survey of anthropological literature: it is not an ethnography which aims to cover the whole of the mediterranean using anthropological material when it is available and other kinds when it is not. There is no resort to novels and statistics to construct the missing ethnography of Salonika or Aleppo. One or two writers who are not anthropologists have crept in, because they are so good – but the exclusion of others is more or less arbitrary. Some areas are not covered as they should be: Egypt is neglected, unfortunately; and the works of the Italian ethnographers of Libya have not been consulted. Consequently there is a bias, here acknowledged and regretted, away from the south-east corner of the mediterranean. No book is excluded because it was written before any particular date, but no book which arrived to the public after 1 January 1975 has been fully incorporated into the discussions which follow: so Loizos (1975), Vinogradoff (1974b), Maher (1975) and Black-Michaud (1975) receive less attention than they merit.

Apart from decisions concerning what to include or exclude the most difficult decision has been how to arrange the material. It would have been possible to write a book with chapters called 'Albania', 'Tunisia' and so on, and to review in each of them the state of national anthropology. That did not seem attractive, and held out little prospect of helping to remedy the defects of mediterranean anthropology: indeed, the only advantage is that it avoids the necessity of the discussion which now follows. For a consequence of the arrangement of material into chapters on economic institutions or family organisation is that information about Albania may be set beside information about the Central High Atlas, and that the Lebanon and Portugal may share a paragraph. Such an arrangement violates the seamless integument in which ethnographers often wind up their data and analysis, laying them out to be admired but not interfered with. It also implies that the mediterranean is some kind of entity – that it is legitimate to set Tunisia beside Turkey because they are mediterranean, and to exclude Swat and Stuttgart because they are not. The fact is that some quite strong case can be made for classifying Morocco or Cyrenaica with Afghanistan: not simply because the methods of analysis devised for the latter country turn out useful for the other two, but because there are institutional similarities between these Islamic communities with saints and lay magnates (Seddon, 1973b). In another sense, Stuttgart, with its large numbers of mediterranean workers, also now comes within the ordinary horizons of South Italian or Turkish peasants.

In these circumstances it is unwise to insist that the mediterranean is a discrete entity, markedly cut off from other areas to the north, south and east: no such thesis is put forward in this book. Nevertheless, while it is absolutely true to say that it is interesting to compare Morocco and Swat, not interesting to compare Swat and Spain, it is also true that Spain and Morocco have been in contact with each other for millennia. It is true that, speaking a Turkic language, a man might travel from Istanbul to the Great Wall of China, and expect to be understood without too much difficulty; it is also true that Ottoman expansion brought Morocco and Montenegro under the same hegemony with Palestine and Egypt. There is some sense in which the mediterranean is a useful category.

It is too early to try to specify what sort of an entity it might be. It is clearly not possible to maintain that there was ever a primordial mediterranean culture or social order, now eroded or sharply defined in the various countries and villages of the region. Similarly, it seems necessary to suspend from consideration any such exercise as that attempted by Arensberg (1963) or Pitkin (1963): neither is concerned with the whole mediterranean, but even so they operate at a level of generality such that they stimulate no discussion or controversy and hence no development or refinement of their ideas. Nor is it useful to perform the sort of pyrotechnics which Gellner (1968) and Wolf (1969) are able to carry off by wholly individual wit and charm.

Wolf pointed to the ways in which the nexus of bilateral kinship, nuclear family households, social networks and dowry in the Latin countries contrasts with agnation, segmentary organisation and bridewealth in the Maghreb; and he also discusses the contrast between Islamic theocracy and Christian doctrinal separation of Church from State. Gellner uses the image of a mirror to contrast the Christian church (hierarchical, ritual, mediatory, emotive) and its sects (democratic, puritanical, personal) with Islam (democratic, austere, personal) and its hierarchical and emotive Orders. The weaknesses in such discussions lie in the arbitrary way in which the initial theme is selected – would patronage provide the same sort of contrast? They lie, too, in the arbitrariness with which Latin and Islamic patterns of symbolism or ideology or institutions are separately distilled from a mass of varied details: there is no part of the northern mediterranean which has not at one time or another been subject to fairly direct islamic influence, just as in more recent times French, Spanish, Italian influence has (to speak mildly) made itself felt on the southern shores: so what is the justification for the contrast between north and south? Would it not be distinctly odd if the only relation between the patterns was one of opposition, of a 'mirror image'? Moreover, the process by which Islamic or Latin patterns are distilled is itself obscure, dependent on secret retorts within the writer's mind: that is sufficiently suggested by the marked differences between the essences distilled from the same material within a single year by those two authorities Gellner and Wolf – what decoctions could lesser men create? Finally it is important to be precise about the relation between the (arbitrary) patterns on an (arbitrary) theme: it does not help successors to be told it is one of contrast, or of opposition, or of reflecting as if in a mirror. (Do they reflect each other? Where is the mirror as if?) People must be brought to ask – how is it possible to talk about the similarities and differences among the societies of the mediterranean in a *productive* way?

Neither the broad identification of a culture area (a certain kind of agriculture, a certain respect for towns, a climate, a type of plough and a couple of syndromes) nor the arbitrary charms of doing it with mirrors are appropriate ways to identify whatever it is that 'the mediterranean' may be. Make no strong claims: admit that the people who live here are of markedly different kinds – Muslims, Christians, Jews; shepherds, farmers, factory workers and bankers; corporatists, communists, Arab socialists and parliamentary democrats. But then recognise that they have been trading and talking, conquering and converting, marrying and migrating for six or seven thousand years – is it then unreasonable to assume that some anthropological meaning can be given to the term 'mediterranean'?

Maunier has written of the Kabyle institution *taoussa* (1927) – a system of exchange, indebtedness and competition which his training by Mauss allowed him to identify as a kind of *prestation totale* whereas formerly it had been likened to mutual aid societies (see pp. 18, 161). His contribution to the present discussion is that when he found institutions similar to *taoussa* in Egypt, Provence, Morocco, he elevated it to the status of mediterranean social fact (*un grand fait méditerranéen*): it was not merely Kabyle, circumscribed by locality, for its reappearance in modified forms in different societies suggested something about a mediterranean social order. It is likely that the candidates for such a status are relatively few: collective oath in Morocco and Albania; towers in Italy and the Balkans; perhaps godparenthood; perhaps honour – the list is short, and none of the institutions is universal within the mediterranean nor exclusive to it. Nevertheless, to investigate the institutions which are or were widely diffused may be one way to give substance to the notion that these numerous different and changing communities have been in contact with each other for millennia.

Mediterranean social order does not therefore refer to an aboriginal society, the institutional equivalent to the grunts and glottal stops of some primordial language. Nor was it ever a complete social order, in the sense that there was a complete and uniform range of social institutions (a mediterranean family, a mediterranean economy, polity, religion). It is, rather, those institutions, customs and practices which result from the conversation and commerce of thousands of years, the creation of very different peoples who have come into contact round the mediterranean shores.

Within the mediterranean there are lesser regions where it is possible to speak with some confidence of a common culture. Consider, in this respect, Freeman's defence of her decision to do fieldwork in Valdemora: her friends took her to task because that hamlet has only ninety-odd members – was it really representative of Castille? Her reply is partly contained in an article (1968a) in which she establishes that small communities in Castille are often organised in much the same way as Valdemora, which thus becomes representative of a category of settlements. But she also argues that Valdemora partakes of Castillean, even of Spanish, culture: 'Valdemora is not simply an extreme in Spanish culture but is as legitimately a *version* of that culture as any other [community]' (1971: xiii-xiv). By that she does not mean simply that Valdemora is part of a whole and to study it is to contribute to the study of the whole, for she adds that some features of Castillean society can be better studied there because they are thrown into relief: in larger towns where hierarchy and dependence are thrust before the observer to occupy his field of vision, institutions and ideologies of equality although present are lost to view or misunderstood. In Valdemora they are plain to see (ibid.: xv) – but they are still no less than versions of something which is common to all Castille, perhaps to all Spain.

Freeman's defence is against a charge of unrepresentativeness, but the idea can be used more widely. At a regional level it is not improbable that it makes sense to speak of general social characteristics which are present as versions in each of the communities. It is these areas, with an identifiable type of institution, language and culture which may be said together, in the interaction of individuals, to produce a national society and culture, where these regions coincide with boundaries between states. In the remoter interactions, at longer term, a mediterranean social order may emerge, created from the contact of individual representatives engaged in trade and conquest. 'The mediterranean' in this sense is not 'a society' or a generalisation at a remote level of abstraction about the characteristics of its component societies: indeed it seems unlikely that it is possible to generate an abstraction which would subsume all mediterranean societies and yet exclude the rest of the world. Rather, the mediterranean must be understood as the result of the interaction (for various purposes) of people from diverse societies: those institutions and processes which have been created to facilitate interaction; those relics which were created by it and now appear diffused in certain zones, if not throughout the area. Mediterranean social facts are the product of the interaction of people of diverse kinds from time to time in a period to be counted in thousands of years, and they are to be investigated historically and comparatively.

Enough has been said about the possible future product of comparison. It remains only to point out that the process of comparison is not carried out in a single consistent way in this book. Sometimes it means no more than putting evidence from one place alongside evidence from others to show what kind of evidence is required if the accounts are to be comparable. Future ethnographers may be advised by it, and others may be inspired to reopen their notebooks. In other cases it has been possible to suggest very tentative sets of concomitant variants, for example in those passages on the transmission of property and the kinds of relations between and within families. In other cases, such as the discussion of politics, comparison has entailed the rather brutal imposition of a set of categories on to the available material in order to insist that comparison cannot be carried on at a holistic level. In one or two cases, most notably that of honour, it has been possible to suggest that where an author has contradicted himself or been inconsistent, one of his views is to be preferred to another because it is more conformable with what is known of other mediterranean societies. Finally, comparison has sometimes made it possible to perceive gaps in the ethnographic record and to produce a list of notes and queries with a plea for conformity to certain norms of reporting. Thus there is no theory of comparison which is created in this book: it is an activity which is carried on in a number of ways, as seemed best suited to the material available.

A final note of apology, perhaps of exculpation, appears to be in order. It has seemed inappropriate to append any chapter called 'Conclusions' to a book which is so clearly a report on an unconcluded affair, or to attempt to present in summary form the judgements which are made from time to time in what follows. The main criticisms of mediterranean anthropology which inform this book have already been stated in section two of this chapter and are substantiated rather than qualified in the rest of the book. Moreover, it could be rather pretentious and rather daunting to attempt summary judgment on the whole of mediterranean anthropology. Pretentious because (as already noted) the whole of mediterranean anthropology is not covered in this book. Daunting, because it could suggest to future students that they are expected to be complete mediterraneanists – historians, theologians, political scientists and economists as well as anthropologists. That is not the message; it is simply that if the unique characteristics of the mediterranean are to be recorded and analysed then each ethnographer who pursues knowledge within his area of interest should pay attention to what his predecessors have done and what his successors will require of him: from the intention to be comparative, and from the willingness to provide materials for comparison, flows the need to use history, to evolve a theory of the relation between parts. That is the conclusion of this book. It is also the beginning.

2

Economic anthropology of mediterranean societies

I General survey

The societies of the mediterranean have not generated any major debate within economic anthropology. That is partly because anthropologists have in some sense taken mediterranean economic institutions for granted; partly because none of them has been a determined contributor to theoretical debate; and partly because their method of work, in small communities where they have emphasised isolation and have tried as much as possible to conduct an island investigation, has concentrated their attention elsewhere. So for example the world of market places has been investigated only in Morocco and, with three exceptions (Benet, 1957; Mikesell, 1958; Waterbury, 1972), not since the studies by Westermarck's protégé Fogg in the late 1930s. Fogg worked through interpreters, and because the Spanish Zone of Morocco was closed to foreigners from 1936 he seems to have conducted most of his investigations without leaving the Villa Westermarck in Tangier. His articles are full of detail, and interesting, but not much referred to nowadays. Otherwise the economy is generally taken for granted and the reader is allowed to assume that, on the whole, it is really very like the economy he knows and understands from personal experience – except that one or two things need to be explained about the economy of sheep or olives or whatever; and those dim fruits of technical lore come retail-ed in the guise of constraints to account for such minor divergences from the wholly familiar as there may be. Yet even if there was complete consonance between village economy or tribal cantonal econ-omy and the familiar, supposedly uniform, economies of the more

17

industrial societies of Europe, that would be no good reason for failing to investigate and record. It is likely that if any of the anthropologists who had worked there had been determined to contribute to theory, the differences between the mediterranean and 'the market economies' would have been emphasised, perhaps even to exaggeration. Certainly the institutions are there and could be depicted in relief: quirks of labour recruitment (Sanders, 1955); the use of lotteries to determine the allocation of resources of wood (Kenny, 1961), of water (Berque, 1955), of office (Freeman, 1970), or to divide an inheritance (Levy, 1956); the symbolism of food and the sexual division of consumption (Ferchiou, 1968) – any of these institutions might give pause for thought. Indeed, Maunier, in his essay on *taoussa*, finds traces of it from Kabylia to Provence, and considers himself in the presence of *un grand fait méditerranéen* (Maunier, 1927). Doubtless the discovery of *grands faits méditerranéens* is a shaky enterprise requiring boldness and even a certain indifference, on occasion, to the weakness or absence of evidence; but the institutions, *taoussa, adra,* are there and could be the basis of economic investigations which, of course without question far too venturesome, nevertheless had the virtue of presenting data on economic activity and of not assuming that it was, in these peasant societies, just an inferior version of the anthropologist's own rational, profitable, commerce.

Anthropological work in the mediterranean has two defects: one is a recurrent theme in this book and it is that mediterranean anthropology is not sufficiently comparative, that there is not enough determination among the anthropologists to make comparisons of their own data with those produced by others. Comparative intent does not entail a Maunier-like activity – although that, too, is a product of comparison; but, for example, a simple desire to say or, by presenting data suitably, to allow others to say, 'Property in this society is distributed more unequally than in that other.' The second aspect is that the linkages between village or tribal communities and the nation-states are rarely explored. In political anthropology this is manifest in the general inability to cope with national processes – in the lack of theoretical concepts for analysing the articulation of politics from, as it were, parliament to parish council. As the reader who penetrates so far will see, political anthropologists have tried to remedy this lack, but in the discussion of economies there has been no such attempt and the impression is of an anthropological mediterranean composed of

agricultural, occasionally pastoral, communites each isolated from
every other. This is so untrue to the facts of the case. Braudel for
example is able to say that the mediterranean is essentially an area
dominated by towns, cities and the roads linking them, along which
people are in constant movement (1972: I, 278, cf. Pitkin, 1963: 120).
That perhaps goes too far: in Italy one of the things which explains the
different evolution of north and south is precisely the variation in
domination by cities; for while in the north there were fifty or so
mercantile, administrative, artistic provincial centres, in the south
there were no more than three major centres (Palermo, Naples,
Rome); they were remote from the greater part of the population and
superimposed almost directly on villages and agrotowns without
acceptable pretensions to represent civility or commerce. But even if
the Braudelian emphasis on cities and movement requires qualification it is none the less true that anthropologists' concern to study small
communities as if they were isolated has led to a false picture. Few
anthropologists have studied towns (Brown, 1973; Gulick, 1965b)
though some have done research in them (e.g. Parsons, 1962, 1964)
and others have written in general terms (Carlo Baroja, 1963; Benet,
1965). Further it should be noted that any claim that there is a mediterranean area at all must, to be sensible, be based on the fact of
movement – of traders, of armies, of nomads, of migrant labourers, of
immigrants. There have been massive movements of population from
one part of the mediterranean to another. Families and small groups
of families have also moved, retaining connections with their points
of departure. The Halefoglu family in Antakya is Albanian (probably
Tosk, see Whitaker, 1968: 276) and claimed a branch still there. The
Karabey family in Hassa has connections in Syria, Yugoslavia and
Adrianopolis (Eberhard, 1970). The original settlers in Osmaniye
included a group of 'gypsies' – Albanian-speakers (Eberhard, 1953a).
Under Ottoman rule there was considerable movement of elite
groups as well as of tribal and nomadic masses. If there are any
common characteristics, these must be the product of contact,
exchange – they must be created by human interaction. To read the
work of an historian, Braudel, say, or Bovill (1968), is to notice above
all movement, contact, exchange; yet to read the work of an anthropologist is to receive the overwhelming impression of settlement and
self-sufficiency, with token references to merchants and landlords
living in cities, with occasionally illuminating references to relations
of peasants to metropolitan centres, but little more. True, Campbell

19

has written of transhumant shepherds (1964); Marx (1967) of the movement of Bedouin in Israel. But in Peters (1960, 1965, 1967, 1968) the semi-nomadic Bedouin scarcely seem to move, frozen in the desert. Gellner's Saints (1969) depend on others moving around them, but little more is heard than the distant passage of a few sheep. Who remembers that Vasilika was founded by the grandfathers of Friedl's adult informants (1963a: 7)? Or that it is close to one of the great routes across the Boeotian plain? It seems that anthropologists are happiest, in the mediterranean, with sedentary peoples, as isolated from external influences as they can be made out to be. But this is a false picture: no cities, little immigration, little trade, always very little about the sea itself, scarcely anything about industrial or craft activities: anthropological studies of mediterranean economies are circumscribed, limited, misleading (see Appendix 1 at the end of this chapter). Favret has remarked that anthropologists have neglected modernisation 'en faisant comme s'il y avait deux sociétés – l'une moderne et l'autre traditionelle – exactement comme il y a deux disciplines dans le département des sciences sociales . . . l'anthropologie et la sociologie' (1966: 6). That is perhaps not strong enough: with the exceptions noted, anthropologists have neglected traditional cities and traditional movement.

The state of affairs is so grave it is impossible to set out to remedy it with any confidence and the most that can be attempted in this chapter is a succinct summary of the main studies. It begins with an account of nomads and pastoralists, continues with a discussion of migrations, and then farmers, merchants and traders. The last section is devoted to development schemes and their effects on local systems.

II Work on pastoralists

The movement of pastoralists is generally determined by the needs of animals and by the seasonal availability of grass. Two anthropological studies of mediterranean pastoralists are by now well-established texts in the field: Campbell on the Sarakatsani of Epirus, Marx on the Bedouin of the Negev. Neither study provides an account as detailed as Barth's exquisite timetable of land-use in South Persia (1959-60); but each shows the effects of what Campbell calls the 'physical and political environment' (1964: 24) on the social and economic organisation of the groups. A third, much more recent study, is by Vinogradoff (1974b) and it contains valuable information on the effects of

French colonial policy on the tenurial system of the Ait Ndhir in Morocco (especially pp. 93-105); it is less informative than Marx or Campbell on the details of production, comsumption and exchange.

It must be said that mediterranean pastoralists are constrained as much by government as by grass: they are not free wanderers, not independent transhumants, but minorities, regarded as untidy nuisances by administrations who have consistently attempted to make them settle. Government policy often results in a blurring of the familiar distinctions. Aitken (1945) remarks that Spanish shepherds could travel to pastures 400 miles distant, and that ' . . . the cañada were not so much routes as "elongated pastures" . . .' with tax collectors established at bridges and passes. He intends his readers to see that government control can almost convert transhumants travelling rapidly from only one place to only one other, into nomads wandering on one pasture – of, it is true, a peculiar shape. Moreover, Greek shepherds, Bedouin herdsmen have a culture which 'is not the predominating culture in the geographical area inhabited by them. This area is characterised by the presence in all its parts of a much more numerous sedentary agricultural population . . .' (Patai, 1951). Pastoralists are surrounded by dominant peasant communities, and they may change quite suddenly from a state of pastoralism to a state of peasantry. So Cohen reports that some of the Arab villages in the Triangle in Israel were the winter settlements of transhumants from the Nablus mountains. Cut off by the 1948-9 war and the fairly secure international boundary which followed, they became peasants and industrial workers (A. Cohen, 1965: 10). Under an earlier regime apparently settled and secure peasants might, when Ottoman control was weak, escape into nomadism to avoid tax and conscription: 'They did not have to go far . . . to become nomads' (ibid.: 7). The status and personnel of agricultural and pastoral production were not sharply distinguished; in the Alps men were farmers and transhumants and migrant labourers (Burns, 1963); in Epirus, Sarakatsani are reported to have settled quite readily (see below, p. 22). The archetypal conflict between herders and tillers, widely reported from the European mediterranean, might thus take on an added dimension of bitterness: the herder whose flocks damage crops is a neighbour and rival, a temporary apostate from the settled misery; the irate farmer is a renegade who last year saw no harm in allowing his herds on to other men's fields. However that may be, the accounts of mediterranean pastoralists show they are in frequent conflict with settled farmers;

21

they are under constant pressure to settle; they are dependent on outsiders for access to pasture and markets. The gross effect is to increase the internal differentiation of the pastoralist groups.

The Sarakatsani of Epirus are entirely dependent on animals; they grow nothing, but herd sheep and goats. They are, properly speaking, transhumants – men and women who move with their flocks from one defined area to another (Campbell, 1964: 28-9):

> . . . the journey itself is not pleasurable for the shepherd. Particularly in recent years it has become difficult to find grazing on the road and there are hostile and sometimes violent encounters with villagers and agricultural guards. The sheep travel eight to ten miles each night on a road which is often congested with flocks of other *stanis*. . . . After a journey of perhaps ten days they finally reach their homeland, the high mountains of Zagori.

Sarakatsani own no land, but they can get pasture at a cheaper rent from the council of the village where they are officially resident: a regulation of 1938 also made them choose to be resident in only one village. Most Sarakatsani seem to have opted for a village in the area they use for summer grazing, although some are reported to have settled. The sedentary Sarakatsani encountered by Sanders near Volos, and the semi-sedentary (women working the land, men herding the flocks) ones near Kalpaki were presumably men who had opted for official residence in winter grazing areas and had acquired arable: 'This tendency of the Sarakatsani to turn to agriculture where land becomes available to them was evident in several places' (1954: 124-6). The Sarakatsani who continue to herd thus move from an area of relatively cheap and plentiful grazing in the summer mountains, to an area of more costly, scarce and scattered grazing on winter plains and foothills. The flocks consist of goats, which can graze most terrain, and sheep: rams, lambs, yearling ewes and mature ewes. The mature ewes are covered in August, drop their lambs in December or January, and are in milk until August although the quantities produced diminish acutely after May. During pregnancy and while they are in milk the ewes need good grazing: in the winter plains this is scarce, so the flocks are divided. Sarakatsani reserve the best grazing for the pregnant ewes and for the lambs after January. Yearling ewes, which need strengthening as they approach their productive period, are grazed on the next best land, while the rams and sterile ewes graze rougher and tougher pastures. Goats get what remains. Sarakatsani have to divide their flocks because good winter grazing is so scarce: if there were no encroachments of arable, presumably they would not object to putting sterile ewes or goats in to richer pastures. Because the flocks have to be divided, the owners have to amalgamate. That is for two reasons. First, most households do not have enough men to look after four flocks, and by combining sheep of different owners they can disperse the flocks of different productive categories. Second, during the winter months the Sarakatsani sell their milk to merchants who convert it to cheese on the spot. The technical requirement of milk-processing are such that it is uneconomic to set up a cheese-making station unless there are at least a thousand ewes in milk: it is very rare for there to be so many in the ownership of a single household. The calculation is hard to make from Campbell's figures. However, from Appendix III it appears that between 55 and 60 per cent of a herd is likely to be ewes in milk. So, to provide 1,000 of them the herd would have to be of about 1,750 animals. From Appendix I it is clear that no household, and only one company (*stani*), had so many. The merchant sets up his cheese station with a large group, and other nearby groups bring their milk in. Benefits are got by being in a big company, therefore, even if it is not so big as to occupy a cheese-maker: some labour is saved perhaps; but more important is the association between a particular Sarakatsani company and a cheese-merchant – an association which is strengthened, presumably, if a cheese-maker is resident with the company.

Association with a merchant is important to the Sarakatsani because a government regulation imposes on the shepherds a need for cash which is out of phase with the annual cycle of productivity of the herds. Sheep produce most in the winter and spring months, when their milk, male lambs and surplus wool can be sold. The government regulation requires all transhumants on the move to possess a certificate from the village president whose territory they leave, to the effect that they have paid their dues and are not in debt for rent. The Agricultural Bank similarly makes loans, on an annual basis, which must be repaid in full with interest for at least twenty days between 1 July and 1 October. Campbell does not say so, but the timing of this requirement seems to meet the needs of farmers: it is, after all, an *Agricultural* Bank. Therefore Sarakatsani shepherds need to have cash at the time of year when they have least income, and they therefore take an advance in August from the cheese-merchants against the winter milk; with this money they can settle their debts before leaving for the plains in early November. The advance is settled in the accounting after the spring, in April or May. But then the shepherd again needs cash to get his certificate from the president of his winter village and if the income from milk, lambs and wool is insufficient, he may apply to his merchant for another smaller advance against the summer milk.

Merchants ordinarily and willingly provide such credit. They need secure supplies of milk and that is the way they achieve them. But the Sarakatsani require more of their merchants than this normal support: they may need further loans in the winter because they have had a bad year, or because they need to spend their cash on manufactured feeds: Campbell's Appendix III ('A specimen family budget') shows that the family's expenditure on cottoncake was a quarter of all their expenditure, and rather more than their total expenditure on rent for grazing land. To get these credits, as well as to get help in dealing with government officials and village authorities, the Sarakatsani try to create special ties with merchants and to reinforce them with spiritual sanctions (see pp. 144-6). But to do this they have to identify themselves as outstanding Sarakatsani – not merely wise, honest, reliable, but men who command a following in their community and to whom a merchant can be bound without too much fear of loss. So a shepherd who can get enough men together to create a milking-herd of 1,000 sheep thereby establishes the basis for a close association with a cheese-merchant; and even if he is merely the host to a cheese-maker serving a number of flocks that is still the basis for claiming special consideration from the cheese-maker's employer, the merchant. The shepherd who can acquire a substanial following is distinguished from other heads of household by the term *tselingas,* leader; the group of men who, reluctantly, accept his leadership is called *tselingato.* 'Le tsélingato n'est qu'une co-opérative de famille d'ordre économique surtout. . . . Le noyau central de cette co-opérative est une famille élargie, riche, dont le chef devient le chef-gérant de la co-opérative' (Kavadias, 1963). But Campbell's evidence makes it clear that non-kinsmen might be attached to the core family, as well as distant kinsmen: the *tselingato* was not a kin-group, exhaustive and exclusive. Campbell says that in the nineteenth century there were larger flocks, more men with the appellation *tselingas* than there were in the 1950s (1964: 16).

The seasonal movement of flocks has been fitted into an administrative framework which demands cash when the Sarakatsani have little. The official provision of credit is based on regulations designed to suit farmers harvesting in the summer. The requirement that the Sarakatsani should be officially resident somewhere has made it more difficult for them to find winter pasture. The result of these three things is that Sarakatsani are now dependent on cheese-merchants if they are to maintain their traditional way of life (ibid.: 255); and if they are to be secure in their dependence they must struggle to differentiate themselves from other Sarakatsani.[1] In this case, which is the only study of mediterranean people who do no farming at all, it is quite clear that the economy is not independent of towns, cities, governments, merchants. Indeed, it is the twice-yearly movement, which at first sight creates the illusion of detachment, of a population and its herds slipping through the interstices of a sedentary farming community, which really brings the Sarakatsani into constraining contact with the world. The same is true of the Bedouin tribes of the Negev, described by Marx (1967): his is the only other study which gives much detail of the economy of people who consider themselves pastoralists. Even though they are farmers, even though 'most men regard farming as their economic mainstay', Marx says the Bedouin regard themselves as camel herders by nature, and, indeed, he gives this identity prominence in his explanation of their economic behaviour. The Arab population of the Negev amounted to about 16,000 Bedouin and peasants. The Bedouin are the remnants of some ninety-five tribes, formerly grouped in eight confederations which had grazed their flocks in an area covering the Negev desert and the northern Sinai peninsula. The peasants are the descendants of landless farmers who, during the period of British rule (1917-48), moved into the Negev from Gaza (Marx, 1967: 10, 63). They acquired ownership of some land (ibid.: 75) and sharecrop more on annual leases from Bedouin landlords. Peasants, Islamic, Arab-speaking, form separate groups which are attached to one or more Bedouin groups – they are dependent politically and economically on Bedouin (ibid.: 79); they may in some cases outnumber their Bedouin landlords (ibid.: 75), and they maintain their own feuding co-liable groups (ibid.: 79) and do not intermarry with Bedouin (ibid.: 114).

In the war of 1948 the Bedouin had mostly withdrawn into Sinai or Jordan: those who remained were poised for flight should their worst expectations of the new State of Israel be confirmed. But in fact, in

1953, they were granted citizenship and confined in a reservation under the Israeli Military Administration. As a result of these political changes four distinct categories of person lived in the Negev reservation when Marx studied them in the late 1950s. These were the peasants, already described; and then those Bedouin who were in possession of land in 1948 and who were self-sufficient: these, with their peasant leaseholders, numbered five tribes and 5,500 men. Two further tribes had insufficient land to achieve autonomy and leased land from the government: with their attached peasants they numbered about 4,700. Finally, fragments of eleven tribes lived wholly on land leased from the government (ibid.: 244).

Marx never informs his readers how much land the people in these various categories hold. The state owned about 38 per cent of the reservation and leased it to the tribes with too little land (ibid.: 42); and about two-fifths of that land was arable (ibid.: 54-5). Arable land constituted 36 per cent of the total area of the reservation (ibid.: 14-15). In fact the land was by no means homogeneous in quality: the reservation sits squarely on the 200 mm isohyet, generally taken to be the line dividing viable from non-viable farming land: since the isohyet indicates a mean, and since rainfall is extremely variable from year to year, and almost from field to field, it would not be sensible to set up farm close to the isohyet. But in fact Bedouin and peasants do grow barley and wheat throughout the reservation: simply, they trust less in barley in the arider zones. As the land becomes less valuable in the south and east, so property rights are less clear (ibid.: 135), and anyone may pasture his flocks (ibid.: 94). What is important is water, which is stored in cisterns found in wells and used for watering animals rather than irrigating fields. The owner of a cistern is a desired affine, and Marx shows that the Bedouin use some of their stock of marriageable children to create claims on water in as many areas as possible. Thus the Sarāi'ah with land in the west have four affinal alliances with cistern-owning Sarāi'ah sections in the east, and in each case they took women, paying brideprice. The western Abu Gwe'id have five such links in two generations: three were created by exchange marriage (ibid.: 134-8). A similar use of marriages is noted by Peters: Bedouin in Cyrenaica use marriage alliances to get access to water in times of local drought (1967: 264; 1968: 267, below, pp. 213-16). Vinogradoff says clans in the plateau part of Ait Ndhir territory were paired with clans in the plains part (1974b: 39-41, 69). Both Peters and Vinogradoff say that these economic alliances were also political. Marx distinguishes the Negev alliances – only some were economic.

About 16,000 people live in the Negev reservation. They grow barley, and herd about 70,000 sheep and goats, about 10,000 camels (ibid.: 75). Neither farming on its own, nor herding, nor indeed both together, is adequate or secure. There is never enough grazing within the reservation, not in any year; and the Arabs survive extraordinarily by government relief, more ordinarily by grazing flocks outside the reservation and by working for a wage, again outside the reservation.

The farming year begins in November when arable in the plains and valley bottoms is ploughed and sown. It can then be left, for the herds are led eastwards into the hills to the winter pasture and kept there until April when the first dry summer winds burn up the grass. At the end of April the herds are moved to the north and west, passing through the grain fields, to press against the reservation boundary until the Israeli Military Authority grants permits to allow the herds on to the harvested fields of the Jewish settlements. Only one herdsman may go with each flock and he may not raise a tent. Other men harvest the grain, others still go to work for wages. In September the movement eastwards begins again: the animals are fed on the straw carefully reserved from the harvest and arrive in the eastern hills in October or November; if they are lucky the rain arrives at the same time, and the pastures are ready for them.

The agricultural cycle thus meshes with the pastoral, and fields are cultivated almost *en passant*. Government regulation of herding outside the Negev also releases some men for wage labour: Marx calculates that about 13 per cent of the labour potential was engaged in semi-permanent or seasonal work in agriculture in the Jewish settlements in 1960-2. The Bedouin are thus not true nomads: they do not move freely within a territory; they are partly dependent on wage labour, and on agriculture. Nevertheless it is sensible to include them here: they feel themselves to be nomads. Bedouin and peasants are dependent to roughly the same extent on animals and on farming, yet Bedouin move much more than peasants do and Marx explains that by invoking their sense of nomadic identity. 'The Bedouin's ideology focuses his attention on his pastoral pursuits, and that of the peasant on his farming; and thus historical factors prescribe their respective cycles of movement' (1967: 99). Indeed, if Bedouin did not feel as they do, government policy might not have had the effects which it did. At first the government leased land only to Bedouin, who promptly sub-leased portions to the peasants on a sharecropping contract: the Bedouin are *landlords*. Governments policy was, too, that the leases should be granted to leaders, sheikhs, because that would be easier than dealing with a mobile uncontrollable crowd of unknown herdsmen: here, as elsewhere (Eberhard, 1953a, 1953b), the leaders used their position as intermediaries to increase the economic differentiation between themselves and their followers. Ordinary Bedouin thought such men better able to persuade the IMA to grant permits to graze outside the reservation.

In short, nomads, transhumants, always exist in an 'artificial' state in the mediterranean: they seem from the published studies to be always subject to a government which seeks to control their movements, to tidy them up. While A. Cohen can say of the resort to nomadism under the Ottomans that it was 'a method . . . whereby the [sedentary] population protected itself against excessive . . . insecurity and exploitation' (1965: 7 n.3), that is no longer true in the mediterranean world after the Second World War. In Israel the controls were strict because national security was involved and because the loyalty of Arabs, whether Bedouin or peasants, was questioned. That they were confined to the reservation may perhaps be attributed to the particular political circumstances, but the attempt at control is part of a more general phenomenon: governments always try to limit the movements of herders, whether through setting up boundaries to contain them, as in the Negev, by requiring certificates, as in Epirus, or by specifying routes and demanding tolls, as in Spain (Aitken, 1945). Nomads and transhumants damage crops, they are untidy in a state where citizens have addresses and pay taxes and vote. Such evidence as there is seems to show that one consequence of government intervention is to nurture the plant of hierarchy: Sara-katsani, Bedouin of the Negev, Eberhard's Turkish herdsman have all, in their different ways, become more differentiated. Even though, as Eberhard points out (1953b: 33-4), nomads and possible trans-humants are never completely unstratified in their pure state – if such ever existed – none the less there is little doubt of the effect of government regulation: they become more differentiated. Government control creates what Campbell calls 'the physical and political environment' (1964: 24), and there are no studies of wild egalitarian mediterranean pastoralists; they are always profoundly affected by the encompassing peasant-settled populations and their rulers, to whom it is now necessary to turn.

III   On migration and labour migration

It would be a mistake, however, simply to contrast would-be mobile pastoralists with sedentary peasants. For it is a condition of the survival of peasant agriculture that surplus population should move off the land. That, too, creates movement – movement, however, which is not much studied by anthropologists. Migration is another relatively neglected mediterranean topic.

The first point to notice is that some mediterranean communities push out surplus population even if the places they go to are not utterly attractive. In general discussions of peasant communities people often say that that is the function of inheritance: if one son inherits immovable property and brings his wife to it, then the landowning population is kept at a fairly constant level, and an established ratio of men to land is maintained. It is hard to know why this is not common in mediterranean countries. Those who believe that rules of impartible inheritance were imposed by an upper class anxious to maintain taxable units at an economically satisfactory level may point to the absence of a developed manorial system in the mediterranean but, however enticing that suggestion may be at first sight, it does not withstand the weight of detailed evidence. In a characteristic and lucid passage Wolf (1966a: 73-7) remarks that impartible inheritance of immovable property is common in the mountain fringe of the European mediterranean – where he himself had worked (e.g. 1962) – where the technical requirements of agriculture rather than any conceivable class interest demand that surplus population should be pushed out (see also Burns, 1963; Callier-Boisvert, 1968; Cole, 1969; Douglass, 1969). It is not even always the case that impartible inheritance is associated with ownership of land, for in Puglia, in the nineteenth century, a diligent follower of LePlay recorded that rule observed by landless labourers (Santangelo-Spoto, 1892; Davis, 1976a). Moreover, population can be exported by other means than an inheritance rule: landowners who employ labour, who put land out at rent or have it sharecropped get indirect means to control the size of populations in rural areas. Therefore it is not surprising that the areas of big estates in Italy, for example, are also the areas with a multitude of small cities. But there are no anthropological studies of migration in these areas. The poorer rural areas of the mediterranean were relatively underpopulated until the nineteenth century and population growth could at first be absorbed by technical improvement and investment. Certainly the sale of church lands and the abolition of feudalism in the north-west mediterranean at the beginning of the nineteenth century brought vast amounts of land under cultivation: most monographic studies mention the local effects, even when they ignore the fact that this was a more general revolution. It may be that these Napoleonic measures, together with sales of common lands later in the century, explain why there was no steady exodus from the land – why the simplest indigenous method of pushing out surplus population was never widely adopted in those areas.

All other migration from rural areas in the mediterranean is most commonly explained by the relative attractiveness of the places to which people went. The really huge movements of the nineteenth century to the Americas and Antipodes, the mass movements into the cities which began then and continue now, the growth of the Jewish population of Israel through immigration, the sudden expansion of labour migration after 1957 – all these are explained by the attractive power of the receiving countries compared with the conditions and lack of opportunities which men suffer at home. The exodus from the rural areas to the cities, to mediterranean ones as well as to those of Northern Europe, the Americas and Australia, is distinguished by its permanency: the men and women who go intend to find a new life, even if they return after a few years; even if they return to their native territories after decades, buying land and settling down to die. Labour migration, mostly though not exclusively to Northern Europe, is distinguished by the fact that migrants appear not to want a new life away from home, but to maintain standards or to achieve prestige in their native communities: the impulse and orientation are thus often 'traditional'; foreign wealth is accumulated to a target. Migration to Israel is a special case: it is usually definitive and the migrants often move into the agricultural sector. Moreover, it is highly administered, and thus contrasts with migration to cities and with the slow movement of tribal populations in the Balkans (see e.g. Andromedas, 1968; Durham, 1909, 1928). The vastness of scale of Israeli immigration, finally, distinguishes it from earlier government-controlled movements of population in Morocco (*guish* tribes: Schorger, 1969; Vinogradoff, 1974b: 85 (map)), or of Turks to Cyprus (Beckingham, 1956: 126-7; 1957: 171-2).

Of these three kinds of migration – none of them homogeneous – only the first has been studied by anthropologists in any detail, and even within that category transoceanic migrants are largely ignored. (But see Gulic, 1954; Tannous, 1942; Khuri, 1967; Sweet, 1967 – all on the Lebanon; Cronin, 1970 – on Sicily. The classic work on southern European emigration to Australia is C. A. Price, 1963.) So far as internal migration to cities is concerned Friedl (1959b; 1963a; 1968), Lineton (1971) and Kenna (1971, 1974) have written about Greek villagers moving to Athens or Piraeus. These accounts are sufficiently similar to allow comparison and are used here to provide the main thread of the description: other books and articles are noted from time to time they appear. Friedl has given an account of migration from Vasilika in Boeotia: 216 people lived there in 1955, and it seems to have been relatively prosperous. Kenna describes the movement of people from Nisos, an island in the Dodecanese with a population of 394 in 1966; in 1973 there were 354 members of the Association of Nisiots living in Athens, and not all Nisiots there belonged to it. Lineton writes about the connections between Mina, a commune (*kinotis*) of 1,400 people in 1956, of a mere 400 in 1966, and Piraeus.

Vasilikan parents, anxious to set up their daughters in a way which adds to their prestige, try to provide dowries – a house or house site in Athens – which will attract educated town dwellers: Vasilika exports brides for the clerical class. Friedl does not give very precise figures, but it is clear that the wealthier families in Vasilika had in fact successfully exported their daughters to be wives of respectable men in provincial cities or in the capital: a considerable amount of savings goes with them, in the same way that income, discounted against inheritance, is spent in towns to get an education for sons who are deemed brainy enough to warrant such expenditure. Money and people leave the village (Friedl, 1963a: 73-7). The same point is made by Lineton: house sites in Piraeus, costing £2,500-£5,000 in the late 1960s, were the most acceptable dowry. Kenna does not emphasise the movement of women at marriage, and it seems that although Nisiots established in Athens may send home for a bride, the more prosperous women marry and stay on the island even if their husbands work as migrant labourers for a season or two in the first years of marriage (1974). It is often enough said that emigration and labour migration are considerable costs to the sending communities: remittances do not outbalance the costs of unbringing, education and support; the younger people, those with most initiative, are the ones who can perceive the opportunities and summon up the courage to endure the often unpleasant conditions in the cities, and that creates cumulative deprivation in the villages. There is a net loss of wealth and of people, life becomes even less pleasant, and so more people leave (e.g. Reiter, 1972: 41-2; Capo and Fabbri-Gaggi, 1964; Evelpidis, 1968). Both Friedl and Lineton, however, point to considerable export of savings from rural areas to the cities: it is a manifestation of town-country relations which is not often remarked upon.

The flow of people to the towns, accompanied by parental savings in the form of dowry or expenditure on education, creates ties between towns and villages of a more intimate kind than those between merchants and producers or landlords and labourers which are so often adduced to illustrate the peasant-townsman relationship. Lineton, for example, says that Mina seemed to him, at times, like a 'distant and disadvantaged suburb' of Athens or Piraeus – where there is an urban village called Maniotika (1971: ch. 3, s.8). City dwellers owned half the olive trees in Mina and were two-fifths of the membership of the co-operative (ibid.: ch. 3, s.7): life in Mina could not be understood without reference to relationships in Piraeus, nor Maniotika be discussed without analysis of Mina. Andromedas confirms Lineton's judgment. He refers to the 'colonies' in the metropolis as 'urban extensions' of Mani and tells the story of a vengeance killing which he heard in Mani: the informant described the origin of the dispute, and then the killing, in graphic detail. It was only when he described the dying victim grasping for support at a nearby *lamp-post* that Andromedas realised that a rural quarrel had had an urban end: his informant moved from one environment to the other without so much as mentioning the transition (1968). Maniots return to the village in the summer for the festivals if they can – even a despised communist ex-prisoner who spoke to no one while he was there. Kenna describes the Nisiots in Athens, who now are settled in Dafni having moved out from their original Quarter, Nisiotika. (In 1973 Nisiotika was a picturesque slum whose drug-crazed American expatriate inhabitants carried on a conservationist campaign to preserve their putrifying dwellings from demolition by a xenophobic Department of Antiquities anxious to re-discover the classical ruins underneath the nineteenth-century houses built in distinctive Nisiot style (Kenna, 1974): by comparison Dafni was a wholesome Athenian suburb.) Nisiots return to the island in the summer, and may be in weekly contact during the rest of the year: there is a licensed messenger, the *tachydromos,* who travels between Athens and the island, carrying parcels and messages: islanders send oil, cheese; city dwellers send white bread, tomatoes, melons and medicines. Part of the island's exported goods is rent since, as in Mina, many of the Athenian colony still own land on Nisos. People whose parents have died on Nisos return annually to perform rituals for them, part of an elaborate cycle to ensure salvation; and most Nisiot emigrants return for the annual festival at the island's monastery; some do not, saying they cannot afford the numerous gifts which they are expected to bring with them. Nisiots are thus bound to their island by economic interest, by ritual obligation and by loyalty and affection for a place. These interests, obligations, loyalties are kept alive by the Association of Nisiots Everywhere. (But in fact Dr Kenna is the only member who does not live in Athens.) Founded in 1924 the association had 354 members in 1973 who were broadly speaking of two kinds: the Athens-born children of early emigrants from Nisos had got white-collar jobs, which was their parents' desire; later emigrants, arriving after the Second World War and become prosperous in the building trade, seemed not to want clerical or professional jobs for themselves, nor for their children. The committee was composed of representatives of both kinds. The purpose of the Association is to aid Nisiots in the city, to arrange social events and, above all, to shower improvements on the island. Members have collectively provided an extension to the island school, a war memorial, annual prizes for some school children and sweets for all of them, and so on. In 1973 there were proposals to build chalet houses and public lavatories on Nisos, but at this point the islanders objected on the ground that the city men were too preoccupied with their own comfort.

Friedl does not write so much about the social relations of migrants and villagers. Perhaps this is necessary in a short book; perhaps it is related to the recent foundation of Vasilika, to the lack of any developed religious cult associated with the village, to the fact that most emigrants appear to be women who, with their wealth, are rapidly absorbed into an urban community. The population of Vasilika is of course smaller even than that of Nisos; young men do not flock to the city to look for a new life, and Vasilikans have no Association or Quarter there. Contact between the village and the city is at the level of families or individuals, who consult about dowries to be paid, land to be sold, houses to be built. Friedl doubts that kin relationships are maintained at any great intensity after the first generation (1959b).

At a more general level she discusses some aspects of village life and attributes them to an imitation of ways which are deemed by villagers to be typically metropolitan. Why are Vasilikans always late for appointments? Why do the men wear lounge suits when they work in the fields? Why do they aspire to occupations such as law, medicine, philology for their children? Her answer is that Vasilikans imitate an idealised city way of life which is out of date: they have discovered Sjoberg's pre-industrial city, and taken it for real. It is possible that Friedl is right, even if she does have preconceptions about the clothing and manners suited to the horny-handed sons of toil. There is no necessary incompatibility of agriculture and a concern with etiquette; but the obsession of peasants with city ways is well attested and at the simplest level it is manifest in admiration for linguistic ability. South Italians, to indicate the highest pinnacle of intelligence and urbanity, say of a man that he can speak 'the seven languages', although significantly they do not always agree which seven confer such status. In Pisticci philology was a preferred profession – as it was in Kalo until recently (Loizos, 1975). Cutileiro records the remark of a Portuguese police corporal in Vila Velha; the most intelligent man he ever met was a Lisbon sergeant: 'He was so clever he could write with both hands at once' (1971: 197; cf. Berque, 1957: ch. 5). Friedl suggests that the old-fashionedness of peasant images of the city is a consequence of the kinds of contact the villagers have with administrators, teachers, lawyers, doctors. Certainly that is not a universal phenomenon: Kenna for example makes it clear that Nisiots now no longer look to the traditional high-prestige occupations in cities, but see the greater opportunity for their children in the building trade, and in the possibility of becoming a contractor. However, even these men travel to work in their best clothes, changing on site, in order to appear clerks (Kenna, 1974).

The connection between migration and stratification is a close one in the following ways. First, it is clearly important to consider the social standing of the peole who move: in Vasilika it appears to be the wealthy, in Nisos the poor. In Kufr al-Ma it is apparently high-status men who move out, into the army and professions (Antoun, 1965). Nader also implies this describing the patronage (*waasta*) relations of villagers with ex-villagers. Khuri's study of two villages in the Lebanon, one Shi'ite, one Greek Orthodox, makes the point that the Christian villagers have better educational opportunities, and can thus capture better jobs (cf. Gulick, 1954). Second, it is clear that in Vasilika a man acquires the prestige of being a good parent when he can set up his daughter in town: migration, in this sense, has consequences for the location of individuals in the social hierarchies of the sending communities. This is quite apart from any consequences which follow from the support which emigrants may give to their families at home. Lopreato for example argues that social mobility can be achieved by members of the migrant's family provided they spend remittances in traditional ways (1967: 213-16); he also argues, and this is a slightly different point, that the profile of the stratification system in Franza has changed – there were, in 1959, more families in the higher strata than there were some years before (ibid.: 210). And that has consequences for how people perceive the system as a whole: he found a positive correlation between contact with emigrants and reluctance to accord respect to social superiors (ibid.: 233). The reader may be advised to treat Lopreato's data diffidently. The argument of his book is based on statistics which he collected himself but which do not go into much detail about the material bases for stratification, and anthropologists could be more at home with arguments which are merely illustrated with figures. His ethnographic comments, in his book and in his articles (e.g. 1962), do not give any ground for confidence in his ability to represent the quality of life in Franza. Fourth, as Lineton remarks of Inner Mani, emigration is one consequence of the incorporation of depressed rural areas into wealthier nation-states: the evacuation of Maniots is an expression of the disparities of wealth and status between urban and rural districts. Integration makes rural communities poor by comparison with the urban centres of the wider society which therefore are able to attract the good things, the assets from rural areas: brides, savings, vigorous young men. If it is right to think that Vasilika is a rather more prosperous village than Mina, then it is perhaps possible to understand why the pattern of emigration is different: men in Vasilika may get a satisfactory income from agriculture, so it is not worthwhile to emigrate unless there is also the possibility, through educational achievement, to move into an occupation associated with higher prestige.

Finally, before leaving this topic, it is worth mentioning the paucity of information about immigrants' associations in cities. The Nisiots in Athens have been mentioned; Suzuki (1964) has an interesting account of emigrants from Ortakoy employed by an American academic institution in Istanbul. Otherwise, Boissevain (1970) describes the various forms of association among Italians in Montreal, while

Khuri has presented material on the slightly different but related topic of family associations (1976). His study of the comparative failure of Beirut politicians to mobilise 'families' might be set beside Waterbury's description of the solidarity of Swasa grocers in Moroccan cities (1972, and below, pp. 61-3).

Consider, now, short-term labour migration. Although it is usually said to be a recent phenomenon, a consequence of the opening up of European labour markets after the Treaty of Rome,[2] the movement of labour from mountains to plains at harvest is ancient; short-term labour migration is reported in Morocco from about the 1840s (Waterbury, 1972: 13, 38), and was characteristic of the early stages of contact between Mani and urban Greece (Lineton, 1971: 276-82). Such movement has become much more common since the mid-1950s, but it is not new. The sharpness of the distinction between long-term emigration and short-term labour migration is of a different kind: it resides in the intentions of the migrant. A man or woman who goes to live in Athens, Turin, Madrid, goes to set up in a new life. A man who goes to work in these cities, or to Stuttgart, Hamburg, Basel, Lyons, Grenoble – that man aims to improve his life but not to live in a different way. In Pisticci, for example, where total family incomes are derived from a variety of sources, the possibility of working in Stuttgart or Hamburg is added to the range of openings, none of them entirely adequate in itself, by which a man may meet the obligations which being a Pisticcese imposes on him: to earn a dowry for his sister or daughter; to buy sumptuary equipment which a rising standard of living and increasing penetration of the local economy by northern industries have made essential to a self-respecting household.

Labour migration is thus one fragmented opportunity by which people achieve a particular target. Moreover, among opportunities, the one which requires a man to leave home for a year or two, to live in employer's barracks, to eat strange food – that one is not highly regarded, and it is seized only by men who cannot get sufficient income any other way: young men leave to save the prestige of their families when prestige is in doubt. They are marginal men, teetering on the brink of downward mobility, and struggling to keep up. Their remittances are not used in ways which innovate within their communities, but in traditional ways – dowries, settlements, prestige-giving sumptuary goods. Nor are they people whose voice is heard in the councils of the secure and the old, of men who need to struggle less.

Village-imposed needs are a commonly reported motive for labour migration: Kenna distinguishes the poorer Nisiots who emigrate to Athens from the wealthier married men who plan to work only for a year or two: the latter are careful not to get involved in relations with urban Nisiots, where they would acquire too many obligations (1974). Waterbury (1972) records that Swasa traders are usually village-oriented unless they become extremely successful. They take up business in order to compete with their fellow tribesmen in their homeland: to buy a gun; to acquire more beautifully embroidered slippers – eventually to build a villa bigger and better than any other man's. The emphasis once again is on competition and struggle, though it should be noted that the Swasa struggle to be supreme, unlike the Pisticcesi who struggle to keep up. An argument can thus be constructed which emphasises the lack of benefit to rural areas: it is not merely that remittances are insufficient to repay the costs of nurture; nor that remittances are spent in unproductive ways – but also that labour migration results in no particular ideological gains: *Gastarbeitern* are segregated abroad, insignificant when they return home. Against this must be set the description by Stirling (1974), based on a short return visit to his two Turkish villages (1965). Stirling concludes that in the period after 1950 really very important and far-reaching changes in knowledge, skills, and values had occurred as well as in standards of living and possession of consumer durables. Religion, child-rearing and marriage seemed relatively unchanged, but the independence children got by earning, the knowledge they acquired from travel, from the wireless, had, he says, introduced significant change. He does not separate the particular influence of migration still less of labour migration or emigration to cities; and he gives little indication of the rank of the persons involved. Nevertheless, he clearly intends that migration should be given considerable causal weight in the analysis of social change. Stirling has the advantage over other anthropologists who have written on this topic, that more than twenty years intervened between his original fieldwork and his short visit in 1973: the changes were perhaps more apparent to the eye. On the other hand, his later essay does not identify the migrant labourers very precisely, nor does it distinguish the influence their experience and ideas have had on the community from the influence of wireless, schools and local industry. Stirling, therefore, is not profoundly inconsistent with Abou-Zeid who has argued that young men in Kharga got the need for cash by first building the railway on which they shortly departed: '. . . the introduction of money into the Oasis has been in large part responsible for labour migration' (1963: 46-53).

One of the most interesting consequences of labour migration, and also one of the least studied, is what happens to those members of the family who remain. It is not unreasonable to suppose that the suffering of the migrant is matched by his family's; moreover, the accommodations which women make to the absence of their men should be of particular interest in communities whose anthropologists so often emphasise the protection of women and their customary dependence on men. Callier-Boisvert, writing on northern Portugal, says that the women have created a self-regulating and autonomous community. They are almost entirely responsible for all farming, they neglect traditional women's tasks such as embroidery, and are poor and unimaginative cooks. At the same time they maintain strict standards of sexual behaviour (1966). Soajo may be an extreme case: Callier-Boisvert gives no figures, but it seems that most men are away, and that some of them, far from being temporary migrants, remain abroad for decades. Nevertheless, Sweet hints at something of the same increased autonomy in 'Ain ad Dayr (1967); and it may be that Alport's article on the Mzab (1973) can be re-read in the light of these two accounts (see also Maher, 1975).

Consider finally the one case of a mediterranean country which has become a centre for massive immigration. Israel's population of 2.5 million in 1965 consisted largely of Jews who had immigrated in the previous seventy years, one million of them arriving after 1948.[3] Of these some 130,000 came from Morocco, 130,000 from Algeria, 82,000 from Tunisia, and 70,000 from Egypt. Oriental Jews also came from the Yemen (P. S. Cohen, 1962).

The Jews in Morocco were descendants of refugees from Roman oppression, pre-Christian and pre-Islamic, in Palestine, together with those of their Berber converts who did not adopt Islam after the Arab invasions, and some Sephardic Jews who took refuge in Morocco from Catholic persecution in Spain. These latter were almost invariably urban, retaining a special language (Haquitilla) well into this century (Bensabet, 1952), and proving responsive to French influences after 1930. The others lived in the Atlas mountains as well as in the towns. Some idea of the scale of Jewish settlement may be got from Willner and Kohls, who cite Flamand to the effect that in 1949 there were 155 Jewish settlements between Marrakesh and Mogador

(Essaouira), and that there were a further 34 abandoned settlements (1962:n.5). Jews were more likely to move to the towns than their Berber neighbours. This was because they were officially disbarred from owning land, though they might acquire use-rights in lieu of repayment of loans: they practised crafts and commerce, and with unremarkable exceptions lived in ghettoes (mellah). Chouraqui (1950) gives an account of their legal disabilities: Moroccan Jews had no citizenship and, more or less like women, lived in the status of perpetual protégés but able to change protectors without much trouble. Dunn, for example, thinks that the Jews of the Ziz valley accepted the Ait 'Atta conquerors without hesitation (1973). Jews in the cities were protected by the Sultan – he alone had the right to plunder them – while those in rural areas, supplying clothing for example to the local markets, were protected by more local potentates. In fact, plundering was intermittent and, with their own community courts, religious magistrates and communal finances, Moroccan Jewry constituted 'un état dans l'état' (Chouraqui, 1950: 179); or rather, since it was only in 1945 that the French instituted an overall council drawn from local community councils, several states within the state.

Chouraqui (1950, 1952) provides the most accessible account of Moroccan Jewry *in situ*. Rosen (1968) has a short account of city Jews just before they emigrated, which illustrates the 'symbiosis' – a commonly used word about this connection – between Berber and Jew in the Atlas. When the 1967 war broke out a Jewish merchant was visited by a Berber from the village in which he had been brought up. Some decades before, in the mountains, the Jew's father had sacrificed a sheep to the Berber's father and had been granted protection in perpetuity. The Berber arrived to annouce 'that no matter what happened in the Middle East they and all their family had no need to fear for their own safety'; and he offered to protect them in the city. They declined, thinking there was no need. Rosen points out that while Jewish and Muslim cultures overlapped, the two religious communities were socially segregated in such a way that members of one did not compete with members of the other: Jews were useful clients, allowed to make alcohol, for example, or to take interest; when Arab nationalists tried to organise an anti-Jewish boycott in Morocco, the Berbers' traditional dissidence led them to side with 'their' Jews rather than with the Arabs in the capital.

No study of oriental Jews follows their emigration through from their country of origin to their place of re-settlement, although several attempt a reconstruction of the conditions of Jewry in Morocco. These include Willner and Kohls (1962); Deshen (1965); Weingrod (1960); Willner (1970); Shokeid (1971). Willner (and Kohls) reconstruct the life of the Jews of Ait'Adrar, in the Atlas south-east of Marrakesh, from statements made in Ometz after immigration to Israel. Deshen reconstructs relations between two groups or factions of Jews from the island of Djerba, as far as they are relevant to their relations in Moshav Yatziv, where they were grouped with ten families of Atlas Jews. Weingrod has a more general account, for he studied immigrants from Casablanca, Meknes and B'Nimilal re-settled in Oren. Shokeid's account is of a group from Amran, in the Atlas, some of whom eventually settled in Romema. It is fair to say, indeed to echo Gluckman (1971), that these are disparate studies: the earlier ones were made while the official policy was to create an Israeli national culture, and seem to concentrate on the strains which that placed on the officials to whom this task was entrusted. That should not be understood to mean they were uncritical of melting-pot policies. Willner and Kohls, for example, report that 'Only after an intensive campaign of infant care and cleanliness by the (Israeli) instructress ... were children (of Moroccan settlers) ... ever heard to cry in the village' (Willner and Kohls, 1962). If Weingrod's account, too, concentrates on the administration of community in Oren, that may be in part because communities were, in the 1950s, still heavily administered. It was not until the end of his period of fieldwork, begun in 1957 and continuing with intermissions until 1962, that the authorities began to relax control. It is characteristic of these changes that Shokeid, who first visited Romema in 1961 and then returned for eighteen months from 1965, is able not perhaps to disregard officialdom altogether, but at least to explore the extent to which Romeman politics and economic initiatives were autonomous – were related to their traditions about their relationship in Morocco. Shokeid's approach should be sharply distinguished from Deshen's (1965): Shokeid is sceptical about the historical status of these traditions, and he uses them, as some anthropologists might use myths, to explain contemporary alignments and allegiances, whereas Deshen was not then wholly detached from Eisenstadt's notions about predispositions (1953).

In these circumstances it is hardly surprising that no over-arching generalisations can be made with security about the response of oriental Jews to the new framework of opportunity created to receive them – in their hundreds of thousands – in Israel. It is worth noting that they arrived from countries where they had no citizenship to one where they resumed ancient rights (see especially Shokeid, 1971: 134-5, 158-9); from countries where they were excluded from an agriculture which was mainly for subsistence to one where they were slotted in to a national agricultural cash-crop production plan (Shokeid, 1971: 48-61; Weingrod, 1960: chapters IV, V); and from countries where they marketed in market-places, to one where they sold mostly through a government agency, into an international market.

The study of Israeli Jews has been undertaken mostly by sociologists, and is therefore beyond the scope of this book. With few exceptions the anthropologists who have worked in Israel have studied Arabs, and their findings are noted from time to time. Because Ashkenazi Jews come from outside the mediterranean, and because as they cross the frontier of their country they also cross the boundary between disciplines, their immigration is not discussed here.

IV   On agriculturalists

North Europeans think that the mediterranean climate is ideal. In fact it varies; it is liable to produce droughts and floods, frequently requiring elaborate investment in drainage and irrigation; precious rain falls unjustly on one neighbour's fields, and is inexplicably absent from the other's. From one year to the next the rainfall may vary by as much as 300 per cent (A. Cohen, 1965: 19-20). He who reads the monographs must be impressed by the preoccupation with unpredictable weather, and the resentment of climate which it produces. Take Cutileiro as fairly typical (1971: 4-5):

> April is a month of great irregularity. Since it is then that cereals
> need rain for the grain to develop, the quality of the harvest
> hinges on the April rains. . . . The hot, dry period of the yearly
> cycle lasts from May to September. . . . October is a very irregular
> month and, if there is heavy rainfall, cereal seeds may be washed
> away or sowing delayed.

(Blok, 1974: 17-19; A. Cohen, 1965: 19; Davis, 1974a: 161-5; Gubser, 1973: 8-12; Lopreato, 1967: 54-8; Marx, 1967: 27-30; Sweet, 1960: 12).

Mediterranean agricultural land can be good, rich and fertile but

41

most anthropologists have studied relatively poor areas. Friedl (1963a) is an exception; Berque (1957), Pitt-Rivers (1961), Lison-Tolosana (1966), Freeman (1970) and Loizos (1975) have studied villages in which there is some irrigated land, and the vagaries of rainfall are corrected. But the majority have studied people who cultivate dry land under wheat, barley, oats and some pulses, together with fruit and vegetables for household consumption. The fertile volcanic soils of southern Italy, the peasant settlements on the plateau of Cyrenaica, the Lombard plain and Po Valley – these are ignored: anthropologists have sought out the extensive farmers.

The chief characteristic of extensive farmers is that they spend little time working the fields. As a guide, consider the figures produced by De Benedictis and Bartolelli (1962; see also Davis, 1973: 99, Appendix IV). The average figures for labour hours on one hectare of grain in the Metaponto are as follows: in October or November ploughing and sowing require thirteen hours' work; in January, a further eight hours must be spent harrowing and fertilising; in March, sixteen hours to apply weedkiller; in June, fifty-eight hours for harvesting; in July or August, sixteen hours on the first preparatory working of the soil, and then another thirty hours in September for the second preparation. That is a total of 141 hours, less than twenty man-days in the year. In addition, women put in five hours at the harvest. These are of course merely indicative figures: not all mediterranean farmers use fertilisers or weedkillers; and if they thresh grains under the feet of a mule, and winnow by human hand, they may put in rather more than fifty-eight man-hours at harvest. Flat land, moreover, requires rather less time to cultivate than sloping or broken land. For these reasons the figures do no more than remind the reader how little labour is required for one hectare of wheat. The production of other crops of course requires more work, but nevertheless Stirling's anecdote is reasonably typical of mediterranean peasant extensive farming (1965: 48):

> One villager, unsolicited, told me that the peasants only work for four months a year – a month in the spring, a month in the autumn, and two months in the harvest. He was overstating his case and, as someone commented, in two months' harvesting they do four months' work; but the idea of having to work for wages day in day out all the year round was greeted with horror.

Similar remarks are common enough in the monographs. In Pisticci,

'There are long periods in the winter when there is little to do; and many people are unemployed for a large part of the year. . . . People work extremely hard for part of the time and then have little farmwork to do' (Davis, 1973: 93; cf. ibid.: 11-12). In Belmonte de los Caballeros: 'Work is especially concentrated in a few weeks when specific tasks have to be done' (Lison-Tolosana, 1966: 33). In Al-Karak half of the workers in the construction industry alternate between construction and agriculture (Gubser, 1973: 33); 'Farming is extensive, with little capital investment or labour. Cereals (wheat and barley) . . . are still the principal crop' (ibid.: 35). Broegger is the only writer to claim that there are long periods of continuous work: 'There is a period of comparative leisure from the end of August through September, and a peak of activity in October and November. The rest of the year requires a fairly stable input of labour.' But his data are unreliable, not supported by figures for farm size or land use. For example he shows that three months are required for hoeing vineyards; that may be what his informant did, but he was a specialist in vines, and farmers with smaller vineyards would not have been so busy (1971: 41-8; cf. 37-8).

It is of course quite simply not the case that extensive farmers never grow anything but wheat; however, the vegetables, olives, fruit which are grown are mostly for household consumption and not for market: they too require work, but olives or citrus are rarely planted in sufficient quantities to merit the term grove or orchard; and the division of labour between the sexes, often excluding one or other from all agricultural activities except at harvest, is usually ill-adapted to the introduction of cash crops – tobacco, cotton – which require a heavy amount of women's labour on routine work during the growing period.

Anthropologists often associate restriction of women's work with restrictions of their sexual activity. Certainly, such restrictions keep the labour input low. The ideal may be that women should do no work at all in the fields, or that they should only work on their family's land at harvests, or that they should never work for other men; but whatever the ideal, some fail to attain it and they and their men consequently lose prestige. The range seems to run from Soaja, where farming is 'entièrement confiée aux femmes' because there are no men or very few men to do the work (Callier-Boisvert, 1966), to Sicily, where 'women are virtually excluded from agricultural work' (Blok, 1974: 49). In Bint el-Huḍūd about 150-200 women did go to work on

Jewish farms every day, travelling by lorry, and recruited to work in lineage-based (*hamula* – see pp. 111-12) gangs (A. Cohen, 1965: 39). In Albania in the early years of the century women often worked in the fields because it was not safe for men to do so: women were exempt from reprisal for homicide (Cozzi, 1912: 313). In Turkey women worked in small walled gardens near the villages, never in the open fields except at harvest (Stirling, 1965: 45, 47; Alberoni, 1961 – an Italian case). The evidence is voluminous for the middle-range: women should not work in agriculture, but some do: 'Economic circumstances may force [women] to hire out for work or to run their own errands, but as far as possible, they maintain a certain amount of isolation from men' (Gower Chapman, 1973: 38-9; Pitt-Rivers, 1961: 84-7; Freeman, 1970: 187-91; Lison-Tolosana, 1966: 86; Davis, 1969a, 1969b, 1973: 103-6; Loizos, 1975: 54-6). The effect of a prohibition on farmwork is that the most properous farmers (who are able to maintain a family complement of women in purely domestic activities) are those who are most inhibited from making innovations in their product mix, for, where they might be able to sustain the investment and to produce a cash crop on a large enough scale, they cannot supply the necessary labour. It is important to realise the amount of labour required for cash crops. Remember (p. 42) that a hectare of grain requires 141 man-hours and 5 woman-hours of labour, and compare that with the labour required for tobacco: one hectare requires 1,497 man-hours and 1,170 woman-hours – about 10 times the man-hours and 235 times the woman-hours for grain (De Benedictis and Bartolelli, 1962; Davis, 1973: Appendix IV). These figures assume land of a particular kind and a local division of labour, but the proportions may be taken as broadly indicative. Labour inputs of this size, if they are to be met from within the family, do require women's work; but the only women who work in fields are ones from poor families which do not possess capital resources to switch to cash-cropping. Indeed there are reports from Islamic communities of poor men who leave the land and become wealthier, seclude their women and veil them (e.g. A. Cohen, 1965: 35). It is remakable that where women are permitted to work their family land there are signs of greater innovation in agriculture: Vasilika (Friedl, 1963a) and Kalo (Loizos, 1975) are communities in which tobacco and cotton and citrus production have all been recently expanded to a commercial level. Finally, on this topic, it is interesting to call attention to Silverman's short essay (1967) on the position of women in Colleverde. She there contrasts the farmstead-dwelling women of extended families whose capacity for work is highly valued, and town-dwelling women of nuclear families whose chastity is highly prized. To some extent the contrast is similar to that reported from elsewhere between rural-dwelling people and those who live in a central settlement: but attention should also be paid to the fact that, under the sharecropping system, 'an expanding family can contract for a larger farm' (Silverman, 1967: 134; see below, p. 172). 'Farm tenancy permits peasant families to change farms as the family's size and its labour resources vary' (Silverman, 1968b: 71): agriculture is often intensive in this region and, where men can get access to resources by increasing the labour force, there seem to be no restrictions on women's labour; moreover, women's sexual activity does not appear to be as controlled as it is in Colleverde town. But little is known about the internal organisation of Italian extended families, and it would be rash to argue, now, that women have greater freedom because they make a greater economic contribution. Women work hard in agriculture in the Balkans, but do not have much sexual freedom – it might almost be said that their only freedom, at least in Albania, was the right to declare themselves not women, to swear perpetual virginity (Hasluck, 1954).

'A nomadic tenor also characterised the life of the peasant cultivator', Blok writes (1974: 46); and he explains that scattering of holdings, the variety of supplementary jobs, the instability of contracts – all these made it sensible for peasants to live in concentrated settlements and to travel to work the land. The monographs are not rich in details of the relation between settlement and land system, the account of Pisticci remains the most complete (Davis, 1969b, 1973: 9-11, 157-62), but it is clear that some of the communities with intensive agriculture also have concentrated settlements, necessitating daily journeys. These include Vasilika, a concentrated settlement where cotton and tobacco are cash-cropped: Friedl gives an evocative description of movement through the village (1963a: 14-17). In Belmonte de les Caballeros some but not all owners of irrigated gardens live on them (Lison-Tolosana, 1966: map, p. 3). Pitt-Rivers says that 23 per cent of Alcaleños live on their gardens and are proper country dwellers (1961: 3-4, 6). With these cases in mind it may be considered unwise to grant any causal status, of land tenure on settlement, or of settlement on land tenure. So, although Lopreato's compassion is luminous, it cannot be said that he has been sociologically very discerning: under the heading 'Arduous leisure' he writes (1967: 59):

> [the peasant] spends several hours a day walking to and from his
> tiny strips of land, carrying his ancient hoe, a water receptacle,
> and a lunch bag. . . . When he arrives on the land, his body,
> already weakened by burden, disease and starvation, is exhausted
> by the long march in the mud or the dust.

Lopreato goes on to discuss exploitation by landlords, so perhaps
intends his reader should see the settlement pattern and tenurial
system in the wider context of contractual relations; but his account is
not one which makes the connection immediately clear. Cronin
(1970: 38) is more definite in her implication: 'One man's holdings are
often split and veer off in all directions . . . most men spend from one
to three hours travelling. . . . The time required from town to the land
. . . is great and the energy lost using their primitive modes of
transportation is [very great].' If these passages suggest that farming is
extensive because men are tired when they get to work, they should be
supplemented with information about the security of tenure, the
possible advantages in spreading risk, and the need to acquire other
jobs from time to time as land becomes available, for which residence
in a centre is desirable. It is in a centre, too, that men can most publicly
seclude their women, and make it plain that they withhold them from
work. The two themes are related: travelling men and secluded
women are both ways in which labour is removed from productive
agriculture.

It is convenient to treat the two topics of labour recruitment and
access to land together. It is rare to find an individual or household in
the mediterranean getting access to land in only one way. If the reader
will allow a typical figure, he is a man with a little property, and a
small tenancy, a little land sharecropped, who sells his labour from
time to time and, especially if he has a special skill, does favours for his
friends or helps them out when they need it; at harvests, if he cannot
get enough manpower from his family and kin, he employs labourers.
In some areas, where local economies are reatively diversified, men
may also work as industrial labourers – in factories, in building, even,
in Israel, on more industrialised farms (Burns, 1963; Bailey, 1973a;
Davis, 1969b; J. Schneider, 1969; A. Cohen, 1965: 27). Even when
property is extremely concentrated (or said to be so by an ethnographer – see below, pp. 86-9), and most tillers of the soil till other
men's soil, it is rare for the population to be divided neatly into land-

owners and a homogeneous mass of labourers. So Block – one of the few anthropologists to work in an area of big estates – says that the landowners' agents and major tenants (*gabelloti*) characteristically offer land to the peasants on a variety of different sub-leases, and grant some land contracts to men who are qualified to receive them because they are also employees (Blok: 1974). Categories are not discrete. Men rarely have got one single means of access to land; and the men who work on a particular field in the course of a year are likely to be recruited in different ways. In these circumstances it does not aid analysis to distinguish men who pay for the right to work land and those who get paid for working it. To take a village or a region or a country and to count the amounts of land farmed by wage labour, by tenants, sharecroppers and owner-cultivators puts facile emphasis on the relation of men to land. If anthropology has anything to contribute in this area it must surely be to observe that land tenure is one aspect of relationships between men. They are relationships about land, to be sure, and perhaps they have some specific characteristic because of that: but the starting-point must surely be the complexity of social relationships. It is common to read non-anthropologists who write of the distribution of land and of land contracts and who pass by some glassy intuitive leap from tenure to protest and revolution. That is a procedure so transparent it reveals assumptions, not ignoble ones, about justice and oppression, which are not always shared by the people they discuss. Anthropologists generally take a broader, more opaque view; but they should therefore be able to say that land rights – in some cases, water rights – cause conflict in every mediterranean society. Conflict is a specific characteristic of relationships between men about land. In some cases the relationship of landowners or landlords to the men who work their land may acquire a revolutionary charge, become the object of class struggle. In other cases land relationships are the basis of systems of family and kinship; and it may be said that families in the mediterranean quarrel more about land than classes do. Anthropologists, then, should show that rules about land govern relations between people, and that in the mediterranean they appear particularly complex and fluid. With that as a base, attention can turn to the consonance of rules about land with rules about other things, and to the very difficult questions about the relation of particular kinds of rule about land to the performance of local economies. It is not always the case that large estates are more efficient than small ones; it is not always the case that it is more profitable to employ labour than to put land out for sharecropping. Most ethnographers pass these last two questions in silence; those who do not (e.g. Davis, 1969b, 1973) tend to argue that the rules people may have enabled them to exploit an economy in the most sensible manner: the economy may be absurd, but what people do is reasonable in the circumstances.

Consider the possibilities. First of all, communal tenure which is in decline throughout the mediterranean. In south-west Europe common lands were eliminated in the name of liberalism during the nineteenth century. They were for the most part lands which co-existed with private property, and were used for grazing: members of the community usually also had rights to collect wood and wild fruits (cf. Chiva, 1963). In Italy, for example, such rights also extended to some property which was nominally individual – promiscuous rights, they were called, and liberal revolutions, in effect converted promiscuous rights into promiscuous persons, of the kind described as 'typical' a few pages ago. In the Maghreb communal ownership has a rather different connotation. Men had rights to land in Morocco by virtue of their membership of tribal groups and sections: that was all the land they had rights to. Some variation existed: the Seksawa recognised individual property in plots of irrigated land, held dry farming land in common, while property in forest and pasture was 'seulement reglée par les droits politiques' and the balance of power between Seksawa and their neighbours (Berque, 1955: 126-8). The policy of the French was to define rights or, as Vinogradoff caustically puts it, to identify who had the right to sell the land to *colons* (1974b: 93-105): so far as the Ait Ndhir are concerned she seems right to cast a sceptical eye over the claims of benevolence and concern for the natives expressed by, say, Montfert (1934; cf. Guillaume, 1960). On the evidence available communal property is in decline in the Maghreb, and in any case is or was a characteristic of people who lived in tribal groups and who had an ethnic identity defined in part at least in contrast to a colonial power.

In the area of private property the possibilities range from complete cultivator-ownership to complete landlordism, in which the cultivating population gets access to land only by accepting a wage. In between is the possibility that the cultivators may pay to get access to the land, and then hope to extract from it more than they pay for it. In most real economies cultivators get access to land in all three of these ways, but have the first only as their ideal. So peasants are often said to value independence, and what is meant by this is that they seek to achieve a condition in which they need to accept neither a form of tenancy nor a wage in order to live.

In some communities there is a fairly wide distribution of adequate amounts of land. Typically, men get access to land through inheritance and through endowment at marriage (see ch. 5). Although these may appear the least oppressive ways (since they seem not to give rise to any permanent differentiation) none the less they are not conflict-free, and the fact that family relationships carry an economic load is associated with quarrelling between co-heirs, or between generations. Surplus labour in these societies may be sold (Friedl, 1963a: 20; Davis, 1973: 46), and the ability to sell labour may affect family relationships: it is rare, but there are instances of fathers paying a wage to their sons for their labour on the family farm (Pitt-Rivers, 1961: 100; Freeman, 1970: 72-3). Similarly, the demand for labour at peak periods may be met by employing outsiders who are sometimes brought considerable distances, even in societies where land is fairly widely distributed (Friedl, 1963a: 23-4). When there are tasks which are not urgent and which permit sociability people may exchange labour (Sanders, 1955; Davis, 1973: 102-3). There are reports of quite large gangs established in this way when the techniques of production or the mode of distribution requires it. Sanders has noted the way gangs of kinsmen and women are recruited to lift potatoes when a merchant arrives to take up a crop (1955). In Pisticci machine-threshing is a service provided by garage owners and merchants: they travel round the countryside, visiting, threshing and moving on. The costs are higher the more travelling the machine has to do, and so a farmer who wants his grain threshed quickly combines with others to amass a full day's work for the thresher. The *ad hoc* groups usually include neighbours, who may not be on particularly good terms: although they may seek to sink their differences, quarrels often break out (Davis, 1973: 102-3). That may be conncected with the way work is organised on these occasions: the whole group is supposed to stay together for as long as it takes to finish the amassed grain, and no payments are made. Since men put in equal amounts of work but usually have unequal amounts of grain to thresh, good-neighbourly co-operation, often achieved with difficulty and only under the spur of self-interest, may break down. Pisticcesi do not often work together in large groups, and they have no methods of equalising the accounts. In Veliko Selo no one can refuse to help, if asked, but unrelated men are paid a full wage, distant kin a part wage, and close kin give their labour in exchange for labour in the future (Balikći, 1965: cf. Lineton, 1971). The Seksawa harvest almonds communally and only divide the crop among lineages and then among owners when all the work is done (Berque, 1955: 169). Finally, and with no guarantees offered, it is pleasant to cite Cozzi's account of 'free' gifts of labour in the Albanian highlands: poor men without a yoke of oxen could ask a richer man to plough for them, which they would do *gratuitamente,* usually on feast days; in return they were entertained *profusamente* to supper. Supper was also the reward for men who joined hoeing gangs (Cozzi, 1910b: 40).

The characteristic of peasant ownership which distinguishes it from other kinds is that of fragmentation. This is often described as if it were an automatic inevitable disaster, a state of affairs resulting from the application of irrational rules of inheritance. So in Nicuportu '. . . the rocky arid soil and the Italian rules of equal inheritance have combined to render farming difficult and unprofitable' (Cronin, 1970: 38). Friedl, no doubt in an aberrant moment, states this as a general principle: 'With limited land resources . . . [a bilateral partible] system of inheritance in each generation would, in and of itself, lead to the fragmentation of holdings beyond the point of economic value for any household' (1963b: 115). But the size and scale of holdings can be affected by things other than inheritance rules, for example by sale and purchase, or by general rises in the acceptable standard of living (so that formerly adequate holdings become 'too small'). It is important to remember that no inheritance system whatsoever results in general diminution of plot size unless the population increases (Cuisenier, 1967; Davis, 1973: 108-11). That said, it must be admitted that in the years up the the 1950s the mediterranean populations had generally been increasing for a century or more, with interruptions during the years of war (e.g. Stirling, 1965: 140). But it is still necessary to be fairly cautious in ascribing poverty to fragmentation, and in turn ascribing fragmentation to inheritance. There is, true, a certain helplessness about dead people which permits the unwary to cast them in the role of victims of forces beyond their control. However, it *is* unwary to do this without first checking how much land is transferred at death, how much conveyed *inter vivos:* in Pisticci it seems that the most land was conveyed *inter vivos* (about 61 per cent); of all land transactions involving close kinsmen only 19 per cent involved a dead close kinsmen (Davis, 1973: 107-18; cf. Pitkin,

1960). Such figures cast doubt on any suggestion that fragmentation is always the result of impersonal forces or is an unintended consequence of something, and they should lead anthropologists to look carefully at transfers of land in communities in which marriages are endowed with the parents' property (see ch. 4). Fragmention is often intended in societies in which it is rational to have some land of each of a number of kinds, as in Alpine communities (Wolf, 1962; Burns, 1963; Cole, 1969) or, where there is an irrigation system, to have some land watered by one of each of the available canals (Berque, 1955: 225). (Beware, however, of assuming that irrigation from rivers inevitably justifies or explains fragmentation: see Hart, 1954.) It may also apply to communities in which the local economy is diversified but not in a way that gives security to those who take up occupations outside agriculture (J. Schneider, 1969; Davis, 1976b).

In most mediterranean communities where peasants own land, peasants are also tenants with a variety of contracts from landlords. The main exception is Valdemora (Freeman, 1970). But the reader may care to include in the category of exceptions those communities in which peasants with insufficient land get more, under one kind of contract or another, formally or informally, from other peasants – often kinsmen at a state in the cycle of their domestic group at which they have less need of land. So Vasilika (Friedl, 1963a) and Sakaltutan (Stirling, 1965: 54) might be added. The most detailed account of such contracts between peasants refers to Pisticci (Davis, 1973: 119-45) – but Pisticci also has a significant number of landlords and in that respect is not an exception. The variety of such contracts is the most striking feature: Lison-Tolosana remarks that there are as many kinds of contracts as there are tenants, and lists four kinds of sharecropping in which the share of the cultivator varies between a tenth and four-fifths depending on the division of the costs of production and the fertility of the soil (Lison-Tolosana, 1966: 23). The detailed evidence is assembled in Appendix 2 to this chapter.

Sharecropping exists in a variety of contexts. In some cases it is a way in which the old and infirm may get their land farmed with a return in kind or cash – not, in other words, a manifestation of peasant-landlord relations. This is the case in Turkey (Stirling, 1965: 54), in mainland southern Italy (e.g. Davis, 1973; 126-8, 137-9), and in Belmonte de los Caballeros (Lison-Tolosana, 1966: 23). A sharecropping contract may be a special reward to a favoured labourer, as appears to be the case in Tell Toquaan (Sweet, 1960: 65-6). In central

Italy the farms which were sharecropped included a homestead and outbuildings (that is, they were in *métayage* rather than in simple sharecropping), with multiple economic and political obligations reinforcing a relationship between landlord and tenant which might be heritable (Silverman, 1970b). In Sicily the sharecropping contract was not with a landlord but with a *gabelloto,* a tenant paying a fixed rent and at liberty to make sharecropping contracts with the peasantry. Mediterranean anthropologists are indebted to Blok for his description of this particular manifestion of sharecropping (1974: 43-4, 55-7, 64-5). He classifies it rent capitalism: it is characterised by fragmentation of tasks – so that some work is done not by the sharecropper but by the *gabelloto*'s employees; and further by short-term contracts; by a policy of helping the sharecropper to incur debts with the *gabelloto,* on which high rates of interest are charged; and by an extremely low rate of investment in agriculture. The Sicilian system described by Blok was generally recognised to be oppressive; that it survived at all he ascribes to the lack of government control at the periphery, and to the ability of the *gabelloti* to use violence to intimidate peasants. The chameleon characteristics of the sharecropping contract are apparent again in a case cited by Cutileiro (1971: 57-8): a wealthy landowner found that he could no longer farm his land profitably if he employed labourers but his sharecropped land returned a secure income. Cutileiro suggests that the land could be profitable to the owner only if the cultivator was persuaded to absorb the losses. How far that is true of sharecropping in other communities is hard to say: it is probably not true of central Italy.

Sharecropping is not an institution which is the same wherever it is found; it derives significance from the economic terms and political context in which it appears. The landlord may be a person of the same social category as his tenant; the terms may be more or less favourable; the landowner may invest in his land or neglect it entirely. So far as the sharecropper is concerned it is important to know whether he has land of his own or not: that may have consequences for his power *vis-à-vis* the landowner; it may also have consequences for the economic performance of agricultural enterprises. It would be true to say, in broad terms, that where sharecroppers are also smallholders the landowner's estate is effectively fragmented into parcels for exploitation which are scarcely bigger than a peasant-holding. In this case much that is said about the rationality of peasant smallholdings can be said too of peasant renting tenancies: they are often scattered and small, inconvenient if there should be any possibility of modernisation or intensification of labour input. Mere existence of large estates, in other words, does not guarantee that the structure of exploitation is much different from that which obtains when there is diffuse ownership by peasants.

The landlords of renting or of sharecropping tenants alike may be other peasants, or large landowners. The terms may be more or less oppressive; the tenancy may be for a longer or shorter period. But much less is known about rent even than about sharecropping contracts. The risk and opportunities are greater for the tenant; there is a much lower probability that investments will be made by either party. The one study is provided by the excellent Blok. It is an historical account of the Baronessa estate in Genuardo and amply confirms what has been said earlier about the mixed, heterogeneous nature of mediterranean agricultural enterprise. The chief tenant of the absentee landowner was a *gabelloto* who employed an overseer and five armed horsemen in managerial roles. There were thirty-two permanent employees, one-third of whom were shepherds, and about a hundred sharecroppers. Part of the work of preparing the land for the tenants might be done by employees, and the terms varied accordingly. Sixty day-labourers were employed for the harvest on the *gabelloto*'s home farm – all this on an estate of 1,500 hectares (Blok, 1969d). Sylos-Labini's remark that 'the structure of employment . . . is not less but more complex than that of an advanced country' (1964, cited Blok ibid.) is a mild understatement. (For a study of a village where estates are farmed by employees see Appendix 3.)

In any mediterranean peasant community people are likely to gain access to land in a variety of ways, and on terms which vary considerably between and within communities. As will become clear in the next three chapters the relationships between people which are given formal or informal expression through the arrangements they make about land – these relationships are often fraught with difficulties, giving rise to tensions and conflicts. This appears to be true whether landless labourers, tenants or share-croppers agitate against a landowner, or brothers dispute the division of an inheritance. The multiplicity of relationships is related to historical, technical and economic factors. Historical factors here means processes and events in the past which have determined such things as the present distribution of property in a given community: there is no significant rural proletariat unless there is a concentration of property in relatively few hands, a state of affairs which is not god-given and natural, but one which is created as a result of previous power relations, government decisions, movements in national and international markets, investments, and so on. Where there is a concentration of property, and men get access to land through a landowner or his agent, the relations between labourers are affected: labourers do not exchange labour among themselves and those friendly associations by which men and women help out or do favours and are helped out in return, seem to require a largish category of owner or tenant cultivators; and that kind of distribution of land is created not by the ineluctable fragmentation of dead men's property but by quite wilful and intelligent response to particular circumstances, themselves the product of an historical process.

These are all face-to-face communities, and men and women have various kinds of relationships with each other. To some extent this may account for the variety of means of access: land ownership is a common currency of relationship, and people use their rights in an expressive way – so that kinship and friendship may appropriately be given a content in land. It is also the case, however, that a variety of means of access may indicate significant characteristics of local economies: it is often associated with industrialisation and diversification of local economies in a way which does not demand full-time participation in either agriculture or manufacturing. So, too, the variety of rights may indicate a flexibility in the distribution of access to resources which permits members of the local community to adapt rapidly to particular exigencies of households which are at a particular point in their cycle of need. But the cost – from the point of view of an Anglo-Saxon anthropologist – is that such fragmented holdings, with their associated centralised settlement pattern, make it difficult to utilise women's labour and to produce those labour-intensive crops which might substanially increase rural incomes. Finally, it should be noted that the social evaluation of individuals or of families is often related to the way in which they get access to land. That is not ultimately separable from the question of how much land they get access to, but, generally speaking, people value independence of landlords and employers; and tenants and sharecroppers who can be seen to work for themselves to some

extent, are more esteemed than men who do a significant amount
of labouring.

V   On markets and merchants

Peasants buy some of the factors of production and some consumption goods, and sell some of their product. They may do each
of these things with locally resident merchants and shopkeepers;
with merchants who travel to regular markets in local market-
places; with pedlars, and with government agencies. It is difficult,
in the present state of knowledge, to make any firm generalisations
about the social and economic consequences of any combination
of buying or selling with the various kinds of seller and buyer.
Nevertheless it may be helpful to indicate some of the more
suggestive evidence.

First of all, then, locally resident merchants and shopkeepers.
These include artisans, café owners and providers of services –
men such as barbers and tailors – as well as corn chandlers,
bakers, grocers, ironmongers. Various points can usefully be made.
Shopkeepers and artisans rarely get all their income from their
trades: they are often engaged in agriculture as well. The Sicilian
term, adopted by J. Schneider, usefully conveys this fragmentation
of income: men try to make *combinazioni* of different resources to
achieve a competence. So Stirling says that in Elbaşi there were
four permanent shops and half a dozen intermittent ones run by
men who borrow some money, acquire a stock, sell it spending the
profit, and then close down (1965: 62). In Pisticci men also keep
their land when beginning a commerical venture, as a line of
retreat in the face of insuccess (Davis, 1969b). When they are
successful they sometimes keep their land, using government
funds to invest in new houses on it (Davis, 1973: 135-6). Peters
remarks that the shopkeepers in the Lebanese village he studied
got peasants to do the heavy work on their land – which implies
not only a combination, in Schneider's usuage, but a credit
relationship discharged by labour. (Incidentally it is worth
remarking that Peters, by failing to mention the name of the
village he worked in, has ensured that his own name has to be
mentioned whenever any one else wishes to refer to it.) On Nisos
(Kenna, 1971: 122-6) and in Milocca (Gower Chapman, 1973:
142) some of the shopkeepers were men of local importance,

holding office, for example, in the local administration. On the whole it is rare for even very successful merchants to abandon their land: they are, with the expansion of local economies in the last century or so, men whose fathers or grandfathers were peasants and who now still retain a source of their own food, 'home-grown' – always better, they said in Pisticci, than the stuff you can buy in shops (cf. Colclough, 1971).

Such diverse economic interest is not common among shopkeepers who constitute a discrete ethnic group. In Al-Karak (Jordan) in 1948 the *suq* had about 50 shops carrying no more than 10-20 lines, and the retailers marked up the goods between 100 and 200 per cent. In the succeeding two decades a large number of immigrant shopkeepers moved into the *suq* from Gaza and Hebron in Israel. The mark-up is now rarely higher than 25 per cent; most shops carry 'hundreds' of lines, and the first six months' credit is usually free: formerly it was charged with 10 per cent per month. In spite of these advantages to the purchaser the merchants, for reasons combined of their foreignness and their lack of land – 'a brigand is less crafty than a shop-keeper' – are not admired. The walthiest Hebroni, with the largest construction company, cigarette concessions, a bus company, petrol station, and rock-crushing plant, has never quite reached the pinnacles of power achieved by lesser but native-born landowners (Gubser, 1973: 37-8, 67, 70, 156-7). And so it is, down the scale, with his not-so-successful fellow Hebronis and Gazanis and Damascenes.

When shopkeepers and artisans come from outside they may not achieve the power which a local man can get, but they are not ex-pected to be kind to their customers and can thus, it seems probable, pursue purely commercial aims more straightforwardly than their native competitors. In Al-Karak interest rates and mark-ups fell sharply when the strangers arrived: it may be a sign of the intrusion of landless, kinless men with no political loyalties at stake. In part the fall in prices is explained by strategies which newcomers must adopt to gain a clientele, but it is not simply a matter of the introduction of market competition. Native shopkeepers, long established in a com-munity, have to bear costs which strangers do not. The straitjacket of *Gemeinschaft* is noted by several ethnographers, although Cutileiro (1971: 235-7) is the only one who compares the greater success of outsider shopkeepers with the lesser success of the native ones. One reason for this is that shopkeepers have to provide credit. A Vila Velhan, for example, went bankrupt in 1964, and was owed £15 by some thirty poor customers. In Mina, Lineton calculated, some £2,000 of debts were outstanding in 1967. The need to allow extensive credit (allowing for differences in scale from, say, Portugal to Greece) is partly the result of the quite surprisingly large number of shops. In Greece, in particular, coffee shops, which also sell other goods, have attracted notice. An ethnographically austere and theoretically over-luxuriant article by Photiadis provides some interesting information (1965). Lineton (1971: 27) and Campbell (1964: 232-3, 284) provides graphic accounts of comportment in public places, including coffee shops: Kenna (1971: 96-105) gives discrete information on the political associations of coffee shops, and in her 1974 report says that a café in Athens is the haunt of Nisiot building workers looking for jobs. Vasilika, with a population of 216, had two combined coffee-shops-cum grocers selling matches, tinned foods, salt and penicillin (Friedl, 1963a: 11-2). Elbaşi, with a population of 1,200, had four permanent shops as well as the temporary ventures already noted. On Nisos two grocers and four cafés served a population of 394 people (Kenna, 1971: ch. 1). In Vergadi, with a population of 750, there were no less than five cafés – two of them also selling groceries, and a third doubling as a fishmonger (Bialor, 1968). In Hal Farrug, there were eight shopkeepers to serve 1,290 people (Boissevain, 1969a: 11). The proportions do not seem wildly different even in larger towns. It is possible to calculate that in Pisticci there were about 370 shopkeepers, serving a population of 15,000 (Davis, 1973: 136, n. 3). The sheer number of shops explains in part the willingness of shopkeepers to accept debts. Willingness to do favours, to tolerate high levels of debt, is also associated with the political involvement of the shopkeepers. Here the mediterranean epitome is the Nisiot grocer: when he retired from formal political activity he closed down his shop (Kenna, 1971: 125). The two things go together – running a shop on debts and being an important man. In Milocca merchants and artisans (there were twenty-nine artisans; Gower Chapman gives no information on the number of shopkeepers) had an established clientele, drawn from the two factions: the supporters of the Angelillas and of the Cipollas had two different sets of tradesmen (1973: 142). A. Cohen says that in Bint el-Huḍūd 'each *hamula* [roughly, lineage – see pp. 111-12] has in its quarters a shop where everything from the monthly food ration to poultry, bread, vegetables and shoes are sold. Often there is a radio . . .' (1965: 116). Where there are numbers of shops and indebtedness is a way of securing customers it may also be used to acquire a political following. However the connection of politics with commerce and usury should not be over-emphasised. Peters remarks that he has never yet met a man who was both usurer and leader (1972: 183), and although there are some grocers-cum-usurers-cum-politicians on record, they are not many. Most likely – for there is not much information – shopkeepers may occupy an intermediate position in political affairs, known to favour supporters of one man rather than those of another, as perhaps in Milocca.

The poorer the community the more likely the shops are to be the outlet for the peasant's surpluses. Indeed, Lineton stratifies Maniots by the distance over which they were able to sell their oil: a man who sold in the city got more money (and took higher risks) than one who bought on credit and then paid off his debts with oil (1971: ch. 3, s.3, s.5): rank depended on contact with the city. Stirling's pun is apposite: 'Much of the business is done for grain' (1965: 62). This was the case in Genuardo in the nineteenth century (Blok, 1974: 24); it was still the case in Pisticci in the 1960s for some kinds of goods and services: a man might pay his tailor, or baker, or subscribe to a barber, with grain (Davis, 1973). Gower Chapman, writing of Sicily in the 1920s, says that women used eggs to purchase goods from local shops and ped-lars, while men used grain or almonds (1973: 38). It must be said that a shopkeeper who accepts eggs, which are in more or less constant supply, probably gets less benefit from the transaction than one who takes grain after harvest, when prices are low. Cozzi records that merchants in Shkoder (Scutari) would take repayment of debts (on which they charged 15-20 per cent) in kind at less than the market price: but in this case the tribesman from the mountains was put up and entertained in the merchant's house whenever he came to town (1910b). In other cases, too, although it is never remarked on in the ethnographies, it seems likely that cash is the usual measure of value, and that a debt is accumulated in cash accounts, until it is repaid in low-priced grain. A shopkeeper who can wait until prices rise receives a handsome increment.

In summary it seems useful to call attention to the variable de-pendence of shopkeepers on their commercial activities: the range is from Stirling's intermittent short-lived retailers to the specialist foreigners of Al-Karak. The latter may also be more or less excluded from political activity: certainly, they are not so deeply involved in factionalist loyalties as were the shopkeepers of Milocca in the late 1920s. Where there is a political involvement shopkeepers are likely to run credit accounts, not always unprofitably, and a high ratio of shopkeepers to customers is often related to the possibility of utilising sectional loyalty, as well as credit, to maintain a political and commercial clientele.

Most of these men and women operate on a fairly small scale. Some communities have local dealers who engage in quite extensive trading and deal in substantial quantities of goods. Lineton distinguishes between small men who have little contact with the cities, and bigger men with developed metropolitan outlets for the oil they accumulate locally (1971: ch. 3, s.5). They too may be men with local political ambitions, and this can affect their pricing policies (Davis, 1969b). They are in any case able to offer better prices to peasants than can the shopkeepers (who probably deal with merchants in their turn). In this respect they are similar to the merchants in regional centres, who again offer rather better prices for staples. So Gubser says that peasants have discovered that it is to their financial advantage to hire a truck to transport goods to Amman rather than to sell locally, and that this has had an effect on the local middlemen (1973: 37-8). It is rarely clear from the ethnographies, but it seems probable that millers (particularly in Alcalá where most grain is milled illicitly – Pitt-Rivers, 1961: 20-21) and oil-press owners are also middlemen, sometimes of some standing. That is particularly likely since it is common for them to take payment in kind – a percentage of the goods processed.

Italy, Spain and Morocco are countries where rural populations are served by circulating markets. A number of vendors travel from place to place on a regular schedule, setting up stalls in a market-place which is more or less deserted at other times. Domestic hardware and consumption goods seem to be those most commonly for sale although some farm implements and animals are also marketed. The periodicity of the market also varies: as in many sub-Saharan countries the market-places in Morocco are activated once a week, at least: but in Italy it may be no more than once a month. Studies of this kind of market are on the whole patchy and disappointing. Such evidence as there is concerns Moroccan markets, and it is mostly about organisation: it is hard to discover, for example, what proportion of the transactions were in cash, what in kind, although Benet intriguingly notes that cash was never used in transactions within Kabyle villages (1957: 199). On Morocco the most prolific source is Fogg (1938, 1939, 1940a, 1940b, 1941, 1942). Hart gives additional information on

Rifian markets (1954, 1957) and there is a more general survey by Mikesell, a geographer (1958). Some information about Jewish participation in Moroccan commerce is provided by Rosen (1968), Chouraqui (1950) and Willner and Kohls (1962). In general it is clear that Moroccan market-places were open-air, near a shrine and near water. They were held on fixed days of the week – so Mikesell describes how the market bus announces its destination by displaying the name of the day – and they were associated with the tribal groupings. Each local market served an area of 10-12 miles radius, and a tribe might thus have one market, or a whole week of markets within its territory. The Aith Waryāghil for example had six markets so located that any tribesman could visit any market and return home in the same day. Trade was in local produce, craft and leather goods; blacksmiths and vendors of European goods were itinerant from market to market. In addition to these, six markets were held each week and attended exclusively by women (Hart, 1954: 78-83). It must be said that anywhere else in the world exclusive women's markets would have attracted detailed attention and a cloud of theory: they have not excited mediterranean anthropologists. Very little is known about the commercial transactions which go on in Moroccan market-places. Much more is known about the other kinds of activity: Fogg gives considerable detail about the officers and their powers – about the Sheikh who tries men for giving false measure in, or copulating near, the market (1938), about the serried ranks of arbitrators, auctioneers, and viscera washers (1942) as well as about the various adjustments made by the Spanish – dispensaries, tax collectors, and the *Interventor* (district commissioner) with his troops (1938, 1942).

Both Mikesell and Benet record that in Spanish Morocco and Kabylia people were under some obligation to attend their markets. Mikesell recounts a tale of a woman who got a divorce on the grounds that her husband forbade her to attend (1958), and Benet remarks that 'Kabyle laws fine those who, under pretext of having nothing to buy or sell, do not attend the market' (1957: 193). They both, too, record the distiction between small markets associated with tribal sections and the larger inter-tribal markets 'at crossroads or strategic locations or . . . at the foot of mountains, on the borderline between ecological regions' (Benet, 1957: 197). Each kind is associated with a shrine; each kind enables people to acquire goods which they do not produce. But in the latter kind regional products such as mountain maize, squashes, cannabis or timber are exchanged aginst wheat and barley, fruit and oil from the plains: some thousands of people may attend and the volume of imported goods (tea, sugar, kerosene, soap) is considerably greater: these are brought from the cities by specialist tradesmen (Benet, 1957).

It is the itinerant nature of trade which is most striking in the accounts of Moroccan markets: traders move from shrine to shrine, from market-place to market-place, from border to border, and all cash transactions are done there. If a villager buys or sells land with a fellow villager he may make the terms in the village: but they go outside, to the nearest market-place with its specialist assessors and arbitrators and its judges, to make the conveyance. If disputes arise between a labourer and his landlord they go from the village to the market for a settlement (Fogg, 1942). In a society where the polity is maintained by a balance of intersecting oppositions (see below, ch. 3), markets located on peripheries guaranteed by shrines, are places where commerce occurs. Benet makes the point that the conventional peace of the market, in such a society, entails xenophobia: strangers are not encouraged to attend because they can escape the full consequences of any misdeeds they might perform – they have no part in the system of segmentary oppositions. A dispute in a border market, at least in theory, could be followed by maximal segmentary mobilisation. Travellers must travel under the protection of a local notable, who is presumably responsible for their behaviour.

Benet seems inclined to argue that various rules prevented the growth of an intermarket economy (1957: 207). He cites the rule that all debts greater than one *real* must be settled before the end of the market; and to this might perhaps be added the rule that any man travelling with merchandise may be stopped by anyone, and compelled to sell his wares. Such rules, if they existed simultaneously and in the same area, might indeed prevent the growth of credit-based speculation on varying prices between markets, but it is by no means clear that these conditions were met; still less, that that was the intention behind them. In any case the rules should not be taken to mean that the trade was insulated from the cities – the cities which are the source of many of the goods sold in the markets. The travelling merchants described by Mikesell are a particularly organised and commercial kind of traveller, with access to sophisticated markets for imported goods (see also Appendix 4).

Consider, finally, Waterbury's biography of Hadj Brahim, a Soussi

Economic anthropology of mediterranean societies

grocer (1972). It has already been cited for the evidence it gives of target migration to cities by tribesmen competing for supremacy in their homelands (above, section III); here, in default of other comparable material, the description which Waterbury gives of organising principles, of business methods, and of the effects of government control, can be proposed almost as a general model of trading in North Africa and the Middle East. It is, in fact, extremely unlikely that most trade is similar to that of the Swasa (pl. of Soussi). Although migrants from the Mzab control the textile and grocery trade in Algeria and Tunisia, not enough is known to be able to compare them with the Swasa (Alport, 1973, especially 149-50). Traders in Suhné did not use trade to compete for prestige; rather some lineages provided executives, others provided operatives (de Boucheman, 1937). If the Swasa grocers are used here, it is because most is known about them, and perhaps future researchers may note, and possibly explain, variations.

The first point to note is the use of traditional loyalties – friendship, kinship – to provide a framework for the management of business problems. The Swasa enter business, get access to opportunities, through the support of their close kinsmen. When they are in the cities they work in partnership with a brother or half-brother. The typical pattern was for two brothers to rent a shop, to share the initial investment and to contribute equally to the running fund. The running fund was used to meet the cost of stock and the partners took turns, usually of six months each, to manage the shop. At the end of his semester the outgoing brother had to replenish the stock to its agreed value and to restore the running fund to its former level: any profit was his. When he relinquished the shop he might go back to the Sous, or work as a manager for another Soussi. The same procedure was followed, but profits were split equally between them.

The Soussi enterprise is not more than a hundred years old, indeed it was not until the turn of this century that the first traders set up in Tangier – although by the 1930s 'practically all' Tangier grocers were Swasa (ibid.: 40, n.4). The use of traditional loyalties is therefore of particular interest. The rapid success of the Swasa is directly attributable to their segmentary organisation. On the one hand they are inspired by the desire to excel in the Sous at the expense of other Swasa. On the other hand, in the cities, Swasa exhibit maximum solidarity. They do not try to do each other out of business; no Soussi has ever been declared bankrupt for, although some fail, other Swasa cover their debts. Waterbury argues that this is not because Swasa trust one another more than others: rather, 'what the Soussi seeks is that situation in which *sanctions* can be most easily and quickly brought to bear upon the careless' (ibid.: 113-5). 'Careless' Swasa are sanctioned at home in the Sous by loss of reputation, of honour – which is what they originally go to the city for.

Until the Second World War most Swasa grocers were engaged mainly in retail trade, making small profits on a multitude of trans-actions: 'never let a customer go'; 'make small profits, but many of them' – the aim was to sell as cheaply and as rapidly as possible. For this reason Swasa were favoured by the wholesalers, who were mainly Jewish importers; from the 1950s Swasa were able to move into wholesaling because they were favoured by government measures designed to control speculation in tea and sugar. By 1969 the tea trade in Morocco was controlled by ten Swasa moguls; and since tea is the basis of all grocery trade in Morocco (because if a grocer has got no tea he gets no customers for his other stock) these men and their imme-diate supporters became patrons: they could dominate and control by regulating the supply of tea and they could be successful without segmentary support, if need be. They became townsmen, detached from their tribal rivalries, and rarely returned to the Sous. The con-sequence of government intervention has thus been to stratify Swasa as they were not stratified before.

Waterbury's exquisite book teaches future ethnographers to look carefully at the principles on which enterprises are based – at the loyalties and rivalries which permeate the risks of commerce; and at the consequences of government intervention in trade for the social organisation of traders.

The effect of government in the provision of factors of production, of credit and of purchasing agencies is noted by some writers. Most often governments take on these tasks as part of a programme to develop peasant agriculture. In Israel, for example, a ration of staples was provided cheaply through government-licensed shops with the expectation that it would be cheaper to buy staple foods than to grow them: therefore the farming population would switch to cash crops (A. Cohen, 1965: 131; Marx, 1967: 41-2). In Italy cheap credit, seed, fertilisers and insecticides are supplied partly through the Agrarian Reform agencies (Silverman, 1965), partly through consortia estab-lished in the 1920s and 1930s and re-vamped, not altogether happily (Rossi-Doria, 1963; Rossi, 1965), to suit the changed political style of the 1950s. The effects of government cheap-credit schemes on the Sarakatsani have already been noted (above, p. 23). Peasants use government buying agencies in two circumstances: when the prices are favourable, or where there are no other outlets. For example, Pitt-Rivers reckons more than half the grain harvested in Alcalà found its way into black market (1961: 20-21, cf. Colclough, 1971). When the government licenses producers to grow a crop and then buys it compulsorily there may be sufficient control of prices to make cultivation worthwhile; this is usually the case with tobacco. Otherwise it is by no means clear that government agencies are flexible: they may cushion producers against sharp falls in prices but they are usually unable to take advantage of sharp or short-lived rises – and that is what producers notice and remember.

VI On development and reform

Development schemes – and there is no mediterranean country without several – are another manifestation of relations between urban centres and rural periphery. In the most obvious sense, schemes to increase production or to alter the regime of production are a consequence of centralisation, of integration of local communities into national states, for they come with policing, schooling and health services. These latter are generally partial interventions: the integrating powers provide only some education or sickness benefit, but do it everywhere in their territories; development schemes are usually selective, affecting only part of the population. Socialist redistributions are the exception to this, but there is no thoroughgoing study of them. Halpern describes changes in local agriculture (1958: 264-74). Orašac was not much affected by the expropriation of holdings above 25-35 hectares since most holdings were smaller than that. Compulsory delivery quotas of main products were assessed, and farmers who did not meet them were imprisoned (ibid.: 211). Halpern thinks that the result of taxation policies and government levies has been to increase home consumption; the producers' co-operatives, established voluntarily under the incentive of tax concessions, never gathered more than a few Orašac households, and most of these were poor ones: by 1953 the co-operative movement had ceased to be the mainspring of government policy and it was abandoned, to be replaced by a new law which limited holdings to 10 hectares. About 7 per cent of Orašac households lost some land. Various later government and international projects to improve the quality of rural life have not been outstandingly successful. All in all the picture drawn by Halpern is of a community little touched by government, and in which social relations were not radically altered by revolution. But it should be remembered that before the Second World War Orašac was an area of peasant holdings, not of rent capitalism.

Barić, offering a more general picture, asks the question 'Why is there so little private investment in agriculture,and why is it so unproductive?', and points to various factors: investment and productivity will be lower, she says, the older the population, the greater the opportunity for young people to take up industrial employment, and the greater the uncertainty about administrative intervention and the courses it might take. There would have to be really rather high incentives to persuade people that private agriculture is adequately rewarded, compared with the incomes from industrial or mixed industrial-agricultural jobs. It is a fairly unremarkable conclusion (1967b).

So far as other revolutionary governments are concerned there is little information: Dalton's study of Libya (1970) is pre-revolution, though even then the effects of oil had been to reduce the number of pastoralists and to increase vastly the number of people employed by the state. There is no study of the controls and opportunities provided by the governments of Egypt, Syria, Greece, Tunisia and Algeria. Spain, too, is not well served in this respect; and only Cutileiro on Portugal offers any detailed information. In northern Morocco the general effect of independence from colonial rule and the establishment of a patrimonial state was to increase the inequalities between the various sectors of the population (Seddon, 1974). Government intervention has broken down the agnatic ties which had maintained some kind of solidarity between poor and rich members of the same lineage or alliance. Moreover, the government irrigation scheme segregated one sector of the population administratively (so that, for example, they might not divide land among their kin) and also created a need for technical marketing skills – a need which the irrigating farmers could not meet and which was readily supplied by entrepreneurs from nearby cities.

Finally, three anthropologists have written short accounts of the Italian Land Reform. Silverman, who studied a Reform Agency village called Policoro (1968a), concludes that the reform did not do what it was intended to. The re-settled farmers did not constitute a community of prosperous farmers, conducting an efficient agricultural enterprise. Rather, they added reform farms to the range of opportunities (to get access to land or to earn an income) which Basilicata peasants traditionally exploited. There were various reasons for this: the agency failed to pursue technical long-term ends when confronted by urgent short-term political ones; at first they invested very little in outlets for the increased production; the Agency's planners did not foresee such things as disastrous flooding or the exodus of labour to the factories of north Europe after 1957, and the start of the irrigation scheme – confided to another re-vamped agency surviving from an earlier period (above, p. 63) – was seriously delayed. All these factors, variously combined, aided the settlers in their not incomprehensible efforts to assimilate the reform farms to the stock of resources available to the community at large, and to manage them in a similar style. Blok considers why the Reform in Genuardo had such scanty results, and says that the landowners, forewarned of the expropriation laws, were able to rearrange the ownership of their estates so that only poor-quality land was lost; the settlers had to supplement their Reform incomes by sharecropping, and found it was easier to do that when living in the town rather than in the new houses on the Reform plots. The Agency's regulations were not strict enough, not strictly enough applied, to prevent this. Silverman indeed emphasises the legal rules of tenure which were designed to encourage the farmers to devote themselves single-mindedly to farming integrated plots: the farmers were forbidden to sell, lease, divide or to cultivate by employed labour. The Agency selected farmers with large families so that they would have enough hands to do the work, but this very rapidly led to problems: the rules made no allowance for fluctuations in the labour force due to the ordinary progress of the domestic cycle. Moreover, it is customary in that region for children of farming families to be given land when they marry: if that is not possible, children take up other occupations in order to earn a living and to support their new households, with a consequent loss of manpower on the farm. When settlers die there are no means under the Reform rules for all the children to inherit. As Silverman remarks, 'each major juncture in the domestic cycle presents requirements that confront the fixity of the farm,' and she might have added that the requirements are the more urgent the larger the family is. The local solution to these problems is evasion: the settlers do lease their land, they do reduce the labour requirement by reintroducing traditional extensive crops; they do *de facto* divide their land; and, in order to endow their out-marrying children, they divert savings from farm investment. The Reform officials turned eye to irregularities of this kind. What else could they do? They could scarcely expel the settlers, given the political aspects of the Reform. Some of the officials came from the local towns where the settlers were recruited, and relations of protection in their official capacity redounded to their credit in the politics of those towns. The Reform created new opportunities for the clerical and professional categories – janitors, social workers, co-operative officials and veterinaries – as well as for the peasants. Pisticci, which supplied both settlers and officials to the Policoro area studied by Silverman, was profoundly affected by the land reform programme. Moreover the new farms, connected by roads, with decent housing and outbuildings, a basic equipment of tools and carts, with irrigation promised – were new resources of an undreamt-of quality. The demand for them far exceeded the supply: there were 322 Reform farms in Pisticci and 1,500 applicants. Indeed, while the Reform was intended to benefit landless labourers in the first instance, it is quite clear that the farms were so good that quite a few land-owning peasants, small artisans and even clerks thought they would be better off with a Reform plot than with their existing resources (Davis, 1973: 146-8).

The same phenomena – of oversubscription, and of subscription by people who were not legally qualified – recurred ten years later in Pisticci when a state-owned factory was opened in the valley below the town: farmers, artisans, shopkeepers applied for work in the factory in their thousands. The competition for the jobs was intense, and took place in the arena of town politics, reinforcing the position of people who might claim to control the policies of a state corporation (ibid.: 148-55). The consequences for the local stratification system noted by Seddon were reproduced in Pisticci: local patrons or would-be patrons had their hand strengthened, and at the same time the existing hierarchy of occupations is turned topsy-turvy (Davis, 1973: 156):

> the introduction of a new modern resource makes all other opportunities appear worthless by comparison. It is not simply a question of creating 2 or 12 or 20 per cent more jobs to mop up 2 or 12 or 20 per cent unemployment. The Pisticcesi were forced to re-evaluate their occupational structure as a whole.

The factory in Pisticci employed women in skilled jobs, and it might be predicted that this too has consequences for the local stratification system: certainly events in Megara and Bishmizzeen suggest this is likely. 'The factory', Lambiri says of Megara, 'became . . . a vehicle for the acquisition of non-traditional values and for emancipation in the wider sense of the word.' Although at first the women attracted contumely the considerable financial benefits got with factory employment proved attractive to men: Lambiri suggests that they were able to command a better class of husband than they otherwise would. That is an example of the effects of factory employment on the rank of individual members of the category. Also, however, 'the role of the woman (in general) became less restrictive', and that was the result of the example set by the women employed in the factory as well as of an increasing openness in Megaran society (Lambiri, 1968). That may be read as a statement that women had greater freedom, and that the power relations between the sexes had been modified in consequence. Such a phenomenon is often reported, and it is another example of the way in which integration into a national society alters local hierarchies.

In Bishmizzeen, privately owned factories producing silk were financed by local money from sales of land (Tannous, 1941). In the early nineteenth century a local man began buying up silkworm cocoons, processing them into thread which he sold in Beirut. His example was imitated and the success of the Bishmizzeen entrepreneurs 'led to the creation of a new form of prestige in the village, the prestige attached to . . . cash . . . .' From 1875 or so five factories for processing the cocoons were set up by groups of kin in the village and they sold land in order to provide the initial capital. At this stage all work was done by men, but the expansion of the factories put strains upon the supply of male labour. The discovery that Bishmizzeen women were better at some tasks than the local men, and that they would work for less money, encouraged the factory owners to employ women and 'within five to eight years' the task of unwinding the threads was entirely done by women. In consequence the women employees got more freedom than they had had before. 'However [their families] had to put up with it, for the girl's work at the factory meant cash for the family and cash had already become a highly significant value.' In time the distinction between the employing kin-groups (who sent their daughters to schools) and the employee kin-groups became an essential division in the community; but all the inhabitants of Bishmizzeen began to look down on the neighbouring villages, where fewer girls went to school, and Tannous's informants did not lead him to think that there was class conflict at this time. The Bishmizzeen silk industry declined after 1925 and was in collapse by 1928 as a result of the invention of synthetic fibres: the factories closed down, the majority of workers left for overseas or for Tripoli. The village could not return to its former state: on the one hand, cash did not become less important just because there was less of it. On the other, land had been sold to provide funds for investment, and some of it had been bought by outsiders. The balance of traditional farming was upset and, when Tannous visited the village, men looked to commerce and to emigration for a living, not to agriculture.

VII Coda

That sad tale must introduce the coda to this chapter. For while the local economies of the mediterranean do indeed exhibit ancient idiosyncracies – at least, they did recently enough for them to have been observed by anthropologists – they are now absorbed into markets on a national, even international, scale and are dependent on them. Local economies, like local communities, are often shown as isolated and nearly autarkic. In fact there is scattered evidence of interdependence, of the repercussions of international market movements within local communities. In Vila Velha the decline of home-produced grain in the face of international competition forced down the prices for wheat land, and altered the political structure of the community (Cutileiro, 1971: 38; and below, p. 91). In Colpied truffles normally sell well but when the market conditions are bad people use them for kindling (Reiter, 1972). The effects of the Suez canal on Moroccan trade – and consequently on the livelihood of tribes such as the Ait Ndhir who protected travellers on behalf of the Sultan – are noted by Vinogradoff (1974b: 25). Berque, too, records the consequences of the sharp falls in commodity prices during the years 1920-4: in an Egyptian village wheat fell to 13 per cent of its 1920 price, rice to 1 per cent. 'The humble village economy . . . reflects the variability of prices in the greater world of crises' (1957: ch. V). Villages and tribes cannot make quick responses to such movements: there was no move in Bishmizzeen to create a synthetic fibre industry, or to capture a specialist market for high-quality silk – but their lives are altered sometimes even for the better (as they would see it), by external forces of government and market. Reiter has made the essential point: the consequence of modernisation and development, of integration, is always to remove control from local communities and to re-locate it at some higher echelon in an administrative hierarchy or economic system; there is a loss of 'diversity of structure' too, so that the range of choices and opportunities available locally becomes standardised (1972). This must be regarded with great sadness by any urban liberal with a romantic affection for other people's poverty, who observes, for example, how the people of Bishmizzeen were led by a desire for money to supply the silk market and were then left in the lurch. If the truth is told it must be that mediterranean poverty and backward idiosyncracy do not diminish or inhibit the desire for wealth, and wealth is pursued when the opportunity is offered. Friedl has two anecdotes which illustrate this point. Metropolitan visitors to Vasilika listened to local farmers complaining that they got too little money for their cotton. As the farmers explained their calculations the disbelieving visitors grew indignant because the farmers included their own labour as a cost in the accounting: no question that a peasant's life is to work the land, and if that is his life how can he count it a cost? The farmers thought different. Friedl also cites the example of a farmer who wished to know whether tractors were any use for growing cotton or not, and therefore cultivated half his cotton field by hand, half mechanically. When he saw the results he switched to tractors. This rational scepticism (the farmer had to see for himself) was common in a community in which, Friedl says, all investment and quite a lot of current consumption were financed by loans from the Agricultural Bank, and savings were used to provide dowries, house sites in Athens, and education of sons (1963a: 21-8). She concludes: 'the uniformity of acceptance of change has been possible in Vasilika ... because all the villagers ... work for the same goal: the enhancement of the honour and prestige of the family' (ibid.: 37). The same lesson might be drawn from Waterbury's study of Swasa grocers whose great wealth has been accumulated by an extremely flexible invasion of national marketing systems. Or from Lison-Tolosana's discussion of economic growth in Belmonte de los Caballeros (1969): there the word *chandro* is an insult which compels the person qualified by it to fight. Applied to a labourer or share-cropper it means that he is lazy; applied to a member of the upper strata it implies 'backwardness in the [application] of modern farming techniques' (ibid.: 328). Lison-Tolosana's article describes the increase in agricultural productivity resulting from acquisition of new land and from technical innovation in terms of the relations between generations: he thinks that a combination of experience at the front in the Civil War and a relaxation of controls on credit led the men who moved into positions of control in the 1940s and 1950s to reject the experience and attitudes of their fathers (see pp. 247-50). The value placed on hard work and innovation, however, were the prime movers in a process which had, in a century and a half, led Belmonte farmers to increase fivefold the amount of land they cultivated.

Whether the integration of village economies comes about by the desire and initiative of local men or by the decision of a central government, or by changes in international labour markets, there seem always to be particular consequences for local stratification systems. In one sense, that implied by Reiter, the whole community is absorbed into a national hierarchy at a low level: marginal communities, as most of those studied by anthropologists are, do not have much power or significance: 'we are all equal here' seems to be the universal greeting of mountain villagers to anthropologists, and what they mean is, *vis-à-vis* the rest we are equally excluded (see below, p. 80). This is so even when the villagers are thought to embody virtues and to exemplify a way of life which city dwellers think of as truly the national ones: 'There is a vogue for peasant handicrafts but not for peasant attitudes' is an aphorism which has greater application than Lee, writing only of Greece, has given it (1953: 59). The flow of goods and persons from the marginal rural communities to the centre is another aspect of such a national ranking: the strong centre attracts wealth and women and men from the weak periphery, creating a movement which, it seems generally agreed, is not offset by the flow of remittances to the rural post offices. Remittances, however, do affect the *placement* of individual families in local hierarchies, and may affect the nature of the hierarchy as well. This is suggested by Lopreato and Stirling. When communities are integrated into national markets the prices which villagers pay for goods are invariably higher than those paid by townsmen; and the prices they receive for their product are invariably lower than they could get in towns. The industrialisation and increased diversification of local economies which follows in some cases from integration also affects local stratification systems: in Pisticci the traditional hierarchy of occupations was turned upside down twice in a decade, forcing the population to realise that their resources were not enough, their landholdings

71

'too small' to enable them to live decent lives which require, now, increased expenditure on industrially produced goods.

When the evidence is so nearly unanimous why should anthropologists not simply 'assume' the economy, leave it to the common sense of their readers to recognise that integration has these consequences? There are two reasons. One is that the unanimity which the reader may perceive is in some sense a constructed one: the emphasis on stratification which has pervaded this chapter is a reflection perhaps of the preoccupations of contemporaries – it is certainly the only thread on which it has been possible to string the information in the monographs. But stratification itself, as will be clear from the next chapter, is not a uniform mediterranean phenomemon: rather it is a theme of rich variation and subtlety. That is sufficient reason for paying more attention to the variation of type and kind which underlies the assumed construct of 'the peasant economy'. The other reason is more theoretical: it is known that idiosyncratic institutions – lotteries, rotating hospitality, exchange of labour, even archaic forms of trade – co-exist with labour migration and state buying agencies. To record these as curiosities or survivals in a modern age misses an important point – how these local systems are articulated with the modern businesses; how men who carry clay on a donkey from village to village, making pots to order, can survive alongside factories producing cheap modern pottery (Casson, 1938) is a question of relevance to the theory of economic anthropology. It is also likely to be of considerable practical importance, for some rural communities in the mediterranean seem destined to become increasingly marginal.

Appendices to chapter 2

1   *On exceptions to the generalisation that most mediterranean economic anthropology is about rustics (see p. 20)*

Notable exceptions to the lack of accounts of industrial and craft activities are Prins (1965) on technological changes in the Syrian sea-going trade and Bernard (1967) on sponge-diving. Kenna has information on fishing (1971). Khalaf has a good article on industrial relations in the Lebanon (1965). Otherwise, writings are often nervous and evasive on the issues: Casson (1938); R. Price (1967) on Spanish barbers who are also dentists – the list could be lengthened, but the sum of trivialities is a triviality. Accounts of 'the effects of industrialisation on local structures' (e.g. Davis, 1973, ch. 9) are scarcely adequate substitutes for thoroughgoing accounts of the relations of the work place, and the consonance between those and other features of a particular society.

2   *On variations in the terms of sharecropping contracts (see p. 51)*

The variety of mediterranean sharecropping contracts affords the opportunity for a study of comparative economic subtlety, and indeed of economic
classificatory systems, but that is too detailed and speculative a topic to be
undertaken here. The following list, then, is not an indication of arbitrariness,
for each variation must be taken to indicate a variation in the quality of land,
in the contribution made by the sharecropping tenant and the landlord, and
in their bargaining strength. So no apologies are offered for attaching to the
necessary references figures to show the *fraction of the harvest retained by the
sharecropping tenant*. Hart (1954): gardens – one-quarter; one-third if
the tenant has repaired terracing; arable – one-fifth; animals – all milk and
butter, half progeny, half profit, half wool of sheep. Sweet (1960: 65-6): grain
and cotton – one-half, one-quarter when the landlord's input is uncustom-
arily large; gardens and melons – one-third. Pitt-Rivers (1961: 38-9, 43) –
one-half; contracts are for three years, a complete cycle of rotation.
Stirling (1965: 54-6) – one-half. Antoun (1965: 4) – a jellāh is either a landowner or a sharecropper receiving one-half the crop; a harrāth receives
one-quarter. Williams and Williams (1965) – a half. Wylie (1964: 22) – one-
half. Marx (1967: 43) – one-third; at p. 75 he cites a 1908 source for one-
quarter. Hansen (1969): vines – two-thirds, on contracts of twenty-five years;
wheat – four-fifths; garlic – ten-elevenths. Silverman (1970b) – one-half,
increased by government regulation to fifty-three hundredths, on long-term
contracts. These are homestead sharecroppers. Broegger (1971: 38):
vines – one-half; grain – two-thirds; olives – one-third. This is one case only,
apparently a long-term contract. Cutileiro (1971: 55) grain – from three-
quarters to two-fifths, on a two-year contract (see text above, p.52). Gubser
(1973: 29): from one-third to two-thirds. Blok (1974: 64-5; cf. 1966): grain
grown on fallow or pasture – one-quarter; on stubble – one-half. But Blok
reckons that when other payments (e.g. for protection) are taken into account
the tenant rarely got more than one-fifth.

3   *On the only study of a mediterranean community in which most of the land is
held in large estates and farmed by employees (see p. 53)*

It is by Maraspini (1968): unfortunately it is the second worst book on
mediterranean anthropology and, in ethnographic terms, admits no rivals in
error and omission. No figures for the distribution of land are provided, and
the figures for landowners are garbled from the official census. The book is
fatally flawed by an ignorance of the geography and administrative structure
of Italy which only an Italian would dare display. The Lucanian mountains
are said to be impassable (ibid.: 30); municipal employees are said to be
appointed by the state (ibid.: 110) while the mayor controls the *carabinieri*
(ibid.: 130) – and so on. The book includes a ludicrous and vulgar discussion
of women who wear trousers (ibid.: 175-6), attributes *Cristo si è fermato a
Eboli* to Silone (ibid.: 257), offers statistics on empty houses as a guide to rates
of emigration (ibid.: 68) and says that *campanilismo* is caused by a lack of
interest and by isolation (ibid.: 50-5).

4 On pedlars (see p. 52)

Pedlars are frequently noted in the ethnographies, but there is not enough information for them to merit more than a brief note here. In North Africa they were sometimes wandering Jews carrying cannabis derivatives, leather goods or spices. Some were itinerant artisans – cobblers and gunsmiths (Fogg, 1939). But Benet (1957: 207-8) records that in the late nineteenth century 6,000 native Kabyles took out licences to peddle cosmetics, ribbons and charms, and accepted local produce, even rags, in exchange. Gellner, in conversation, recalls a date pedlar in the Atlas: customers returned the date stones which were stuck back into the donkey's fermenting load – the further from source the more stone, the less meat; if the price remained constant it was a solace to Sahlins' soul. On the northern littoral, fish seems important (e.g. Friedl, 1963a: 10) as well as clothing and hardware. Very casual all these references are and little is known how such trading articulates with other kinds. Benet makes the point that only pedlars traded inside North African villages.

3

Stratification

I The three main idioms of stratification and their relation to modes of political representation

The societies of the mediterranean, without exception, exhibit crude differences in wealth. There is none in which wealth is in fact evenly distributed throughout the male adult population. In all of the societies there are socially recognised situations in which these crude material differences are deemed irrelevant: most mediterranean communities studied by social anthropologists are small, fairly close-knit, and their members meet and co-operate at times when equality is conventionally emphasised. But in some of these societies the social destruction of crude material differences is associated with political activity - not just when football is discussed, say (Lison-Tolosana, 1966: 91), but when the members are concerned with decisions and actions which affect them all. These societies are described in the final substantive section of this chapter (see section VI).

However, for the most part crude material differences are convert-ed into systems of stratification. A system of stratification is a socially construed embodiment of the realities of material differentiation which converts them into guidelines for social action. It is because there is substantial agreement within these communities about the ways in which greater or lesser wealth may manifest itself in greater or lesser power, that these societies, in contrast perhaps to those which have achieved systems of equality, do not rely on brute strength to maintain social order: a system of stratification permits the physically weak - the aged and the self-indulgent - to be powerful. But agreement is agreement: and although all the systems of stratification described do reinforce the position of the powerful - people not only use them to describe the differentiated allocation of resources but also to allocate resources differentially – they nevertheless limit and control the exercise of power: it is channelled through accepted institutions and thereby limited, made predictable and to some extent unarbitary. The account which follows is a static more or less functionalist one. That is a pity. While reading the materials carefully, idealistic visions open themselves up, of accounts of mediterranean stratification in which the interplay of ideology and wealth is traced through history, and is shown to produce the current and various relations of these which are found in the mediterranean. The reader should be warned that to take contemporary material differences as given, without discovering the sources of them in the allocative functions of earlier systems of stratification, is to tell only half the story. Peters (1972) points the moral: an election and consequent change in office holders transformed power relations in the Lebanese village he studied, compelling him to revise radically his earlier (1963) account of it. He remains unique.

There are three main forms of stratification which have been observed in the mediterranean: bureaucracy, class and honour. Each of them is related to the distribution of wealth, more or less directly. They are, for the purpose of analysis, ideal types, distinct elementary forms which, in substantive politics, are intertwined, mixed in varying degrees, variously important. Each is associated with an appropriate mode of political representation – again, ideal types, elementary forms , which in the hugger-mugger of actual political activity have variable importance. These are: insistence on citizen's rights; class struggle; patronage.

Such distinctions justify themselves by their aptness for the comparative task of sorting out the main variables and trying to give them weight. If the differences between the political life of different communities are to be explained in any systematic way it will not be found useful to present wide-angled portraits of 'the stratification system' of the community *x* or *y*. Excellent men and women have done precisely this: the qualities admired and respected by Stirling's Turkish villagers were piety (in its proper context), reliability, helpfulness, wealth, age, a good family history and so on: the villagers used many scales, mostly consonant with each other, but above all else contextual – some qualities are more admired than others in certain situations (1953). Other writers follow his example: Silverman (1966) and Bailey (1971c) have – in their different ways – produced conceptual analyses of respect and rank. The people of Genuardo have no single criterion of rank, but assess men on many scales (Blok, 1969b) – and so on. In particular, writers now emphasise literacy and the way that provides opportunities for social mobility and exacting respect: in addition to the writers cited, Callier-Boisvert (1966) noted that literacy can cut across most previously established hierarchies; and Cutileiro's story of the man who was so intelligent he could write with both hands at once (1971: 197; see above, p. 34) fleetingly reveals the extent to which literacy may permit imposition. But composite portraits of this kind, subtle and complete as they may be, do not permit easy comparison. It may be that an attempt to break the pictures down into their components and to give even an impressionistic weighting will be more fruitful – that is what is attempted here. As the comparative task proceeds, so the distinctions may justify themselves. It may be as well, none the less, to discuss the elementary forms briefly at the outset.

Honour and class are related to individual control of resources. Honour is a moral attribute of groups or individuals; it is derived from the performance of certain roles, usually domestic ones, though in some communities other kinds of role may be assessed. Characteristically, location in a particular position implies an assertion of a particular moral worth and, equally characteristic, the process of location implies a judgment made by other people, usually neighbours. Successful performance of the roles is related to economic resources because feeding a family, looking after women, maintaining a following, can be done more easily when the family is not poor; but the judgment of relative success and failure is made by a collectivity. Perhaps it should be said at the outset that honour is not primarily to do with sexual intercourse, with copulation, but with the performance of sexual roles: to be good of your kind is to have honour and that may include the ability to protect women from the sexual advances of other men and to attack other men through their women; but in reality sexual roles are chiefly economic and domestic. The sources are numerous and clear on this point, and it will suffice to cite only one – the anecdote disarmingly recounted by Alberoni of his research in Sardinia. His questionnaire included ' "Do you think it is right to kill for honour's sake?". The answers I got were rather puzzling . . . . One day . . . I tried asking what they meant by honour . . . I was astonished to find that [sex] was the last thing my informants were concerned about' – they spoke of farming, herding, of domestic matters (1961: 74). It is characteristic of honour hierarchies that they tend to become absolute: an absolute hierarchy is one in which each ranked unit – a person, a family, a descent group – occupies, or potentially occupies, a unique position, superior or inferior to each other unit. Indeed, when two units occupy similar positions the ethnographer may expect them either to be in conflict, struggling to become unequal, or to be unknown to each other (not uncommon in some of the larger agglomerations in the mediterranean).

Honour is local: it cannot be measured or assessed, except very roughly, by an outside observer. Nor can unattached outsiders be assessed readily, for that implies a moral relationship (cf. Codd, 1971). Bureaucratic rank and class position are transferable from one community to another, but for a man to have honour he must live on his own land. It is important that readers from mass societies should realise the small scale of honour ranking systems: for although it does appear to be the case that moral behaviour, assessed to locate persons in the system, is more open, less of the closet in mediterranean societies, rank is based on thorough knowledge of an individual's family and life-history. There is a deadweight of history which makes upward social mobility in moral terms very difficult; moreover, because honour systems tend towards absoluteness, successful mobility displaces erstwhile superiors whose interest is to resist other people's claims to higher positions. As Hytten (1966) remarks, 'Non è un morale di achievement, di raggiungimento, ma al contrario di adattamento.' Therefore honour does not constitute a moral ladder of an ethical kind: a low-ranking man who attempts to better himself is a threat and those whom he displaces try to vilify him, to deprive him of honour in his own land, which is the only place he can have any.

In certain circumstances, which are more or less identifiable, it is clear that the crude material differences between members of communities are socially construed in a class idiom. People speak of differences in power not in terms implying acceptance, nor infinitely graded moral worth, but implying conflict and the common interests of people who in other circumstances may emphasise the absoluteness of the differences between them. A man perceives the dominant characteristic of individuals to be their possession of common interests similar or opposed to his own. It is characteristic of class hierarchies that people who perceive themselves to share a common interest may group together to pursue collective ends: in elections and in the more unregulated strikes, occupations of land, riots, revolutions. It is characteristic of mediterranean class hierarchies that they are not permanently salient: the perception of shared interest waxes and wanes; a magnate is not permanently a class oppressor, but may be a friend, a patron, a godfather. A client may be one of the best, a decent diligent man of his kind, who every now and then gets carried away by seditious hotheads, and has to be taught his place. To give only one source here: in Milocca, where men's hats indicated their class position, and a dead man was carried to the grave with his hat on his coffin, 'there seems to be no co-operation' within a social class, and Gower Chapman accords class no greater weight than age or sex in her description of the social hierarchy (1973: 64). It is one of the tasks of this chapter to indicate what may be the correlates of changing emphasis and fluctuating perception; it is another to show that the institutions of class organisation – parties, labour syndicates, co-operatives – may have the same shifting indeterminacy. In contrast to honour, class is not local: a man may take his class where he goes; and his position, his perception of his interest, may change rather more easily than his honour can.

Why is bureaucracy in this list of elementary forms? It is unlike both honour and class action because it springs not from local will, from the fluctuations in local circumstances, but from some centre removed from the ethnographer's focused vision. Of course class hierarchy seems to become dominant partly in response to national and even international factors; class institutions are usually integrated into a national organisation; a Spaniard or Turk who goes to Germany is a *Gastarbeiter,* but an *Arbeiter* wherever he goes, whose position and interest as a member of a class can be brought forth out of the noumenon, made dominant and active, wherever he may be. But bureaucracy? It is not of that kind, even, and appears to have no local roots. Bureaucracy is here in the list because it is a manifestation of power at the centre. The integration of local communities into nations is a statement of the power of the centre. It can be done in various ways, but the commonest way in the mediterranean now is by setting up an administration. This is partly because of the demands of civilised opinion: a mediterranean government which set up a feudal system nowadays would be regarded as odd by its neighbours. More seriously, it is a manifestation of the state's need to control the outflow of its own resources: taxation, policing – these do not require bureaucratic control as much as education, welfare, public works and development do: bureaucracy is more efficient than any other means of controlling the flow of resources from the centre. Its relevance to local communities is threefold. First, most of the ethnographers of mediterranean societies now have to take into account the power of the field officers who represent the state: if they are not in the community, indeed if they are not of the community, they nevertheless play an important part in nearly every mediterranean society. Second, the process of integration (of long standing, but now greatly accelerated) brings the local community as a whole into a national power system: the community is absorbed into a hierarchy of power, almost invariably at a position of utter weakness and insignificance. Hence, perhaps, the tendency of members of marginal communities to say to Bailey and his pupils what is manifestly false: 'We are all equal here.' *Vis-à-vis* outsiders, of course, they are all equals, all equally powerless (Bailey, 1971a, 1971b, *passim*). On Nisos people similarly would say 'We are all the same', and Kenna comments that 'only after listing the conditions shared by all will an informant admit to differences . . . in the amount of land held, the size and fittings of the house, the earning capacity of the household head. . .' (1971). Third, the act of will at the centre, the determination that this or that village or tribe shall be brought within the fold, creates a new mode of political representation within the village. People see themselves from time to time not simply as clients, not simply as a class with an interest to defend or vindicate, but as citizens with rights. The elementary form then has two aspects: people can use their awareness that administration is rule-bound against the administration itself – they can attempt to control the activities of the powerful centre by turning its rules around and against it. Or they can switch their idioms within the local context: they can attempt to control magnates by asserting their equal dignity as members of the same state; they can assert that what they want – a job, a passport, medical treatment – is theirs not by virtue of their personal loyalty to a particular magnate, not by virtue of their ability to vindicate their claim by mass action, but by right.

Perhaps it should be said clearly: to write of honour, class, bureaucracy as idioms of stratification does not imply that they are all of equal importance or are all the same in every community: the terms are middle-level generalisations, each assembling under one head a variety of phenomena – as it might be Ottoman and Italian administration under the heading bureaucracy – and together apparently covering most systems of stratification in mediterranean countries. Any community is likely to exhibit more than one of these modes of stratification, and they are variously important and appropriate bases for action. It is possible that is some areas in the mediterranean the ability of a labourer to expect sickness benefit or a pension reduces his dependence on magnates, but these are few. However, mention of the effectiveness of the claim is not really relevant to the discussion of bureaucracy as an elementary form of stratification and political representation: that is an analytical notion, necessary merely to explain particular polities, and to compare them.

II Crude material differences in wealth

To start at the beginning: what are the differences in wealth within these communities? How unequally in fact are resources distributed? And how does one community compare with another? Anthropologists have not always bothered to give precise accounts of the distribution of material resourses in the communities they have studied, even when they are primarily concerned with stratification. Some 45-50 books and articles may be identified as having one or another stratification system and its attendant form of political representation as its main theme. Of these, five give good information about material differences; fifteen give barely adequate information, and the rest give either no information or information unusable for comparison. It is invidious to give names – there are so many extenuating circumstances – but the reader might care to try to contemplate with equanimity the perversity of writers who invent indices which conceal all information which might make their work comparable. The Prices (1966a) are not unique except for the amount of ingenuity they have expended to make their data irrecoverable. The information is often neither available nor readily gathered as it is not usually for the societies of the Maghreb, and that may partly explain these disappointing results. In even the smaller communities of the northern shore the diversification of local economies may make it difficult to identify with any precision how much of what belongs to whom, and at what points in the scale of wealth various kinds of dependence begin to operate. Nevertheless, where there are measured or measurable forms of wealth, even if they are not the sole forms of it, it is reasonable to expect the details of its distribution to be stated clearly. Here are five examples.

A model of its kind is Cutileiro (1971). In a population of 1,600 some 491 are landowners. The 8,900 hectares of land are distributed as shown in Table 1. When further necessary information is added the

Table 1   Distribution of land in Vila Velha, ca. 1966

Categories of size (hectares)	Landowners (%)	Amount of land (%)
< 10	82.0	11
10 – 50	12.5	14
50 – 100	2.0	6
100 – 500	2.5	29
500 <	0.5	39
	——	——
	99.5	99
	(n = 491)	(ha = 8,900)

Source: Cutileiro, 1971: 41-2.

simplicity of the Table becomes comprehensible: the land is variable in quality – some of the larger estates are hilly pasture; some Vila Velhans own land outside the boundaries of the administrative unit; some landowners have larger families than other, and thus need more land to attain independence. Some have incomes from other sources than the land. When all these qualifications are taken into account 11 adult males may be called wealthy and they do not live in Vila Velha; 26 are independent of wages and salaries and tenancies; 454 are more or less dependent on others for access to resources. 'Ownership of land . . . still determines the main social groupings.'

In Belmonte (see Table 2) the varieties of land are greater than in Vila Velha: some good proportion of it is irrigated and a family of four could live decently, by local standards, on three hectares of the right kind of land. Sixty-eight per cent of the landowners do not have three hectares of any kind of land, and thus depend on other sources of income. Together with the 16 poor men with no land at all, some 256 adult males in a total population of 1,229 are labourers, either permanently or occasionally. Lison-Tolosana calls attention to the plight of those with between three and five hectares: they used to be independent but in the few years preceding his research they had become dependent on others for the use of machines. Their holdings are too small to justify ownership of machines, yet do not yield cheaply enough unless machines are used. Hence in Belmonte there are two kinds of dependent person: those who require jobs (256), and those who require machines (49). So, of the 368 adult males chiefly occupied in agriculture 305 are dependent in one way or the other. However, the economy of Belmonte appears to be more diversified than that of Vila Velha although land ownership is still a crucial element in stratification, so that for example no one who has less than five hectares has ever held any political office.

Table 2 Distribution of land in Belmonte de los Caballeros, ca. 1958

Categories of size (hectares)	Landowners (%)		Amount of land (%)	
< 1	33	94	5	37
1 – 3	35		10	
3 – 5	14		9	
5 – 10	12		13	
10 – 15	4		11	
15 <	2		47	
	100 (n = 352)		95 (ha = 2,182)	

Source: Lison-Tolosana, 1966: 20.
Note: Lison-Tolosana at no point gives details of the amount of land held in each category of size of holding. The third column is therefore derived in a rough-and-ready way from inadequate information provided at p. 20. That is why it does not add up properly.

Anton Blok has provided some information about Genuardo, in Sicily: it is exhaustive about amounts of land owned, less so about land users: nevertheless, Table 3 may be extracted from his work.

Blok at no time says how many people in Genuardo's population of 2,556 are landless or insufficiently landed: it is the majority, and they are dependent on the category of managers (*gabelloti*) who exercise local dominance on behalf of absentee landowners. Characteristically his position as land agent enables a *gabelloto* to exercise power in

matters not directly connected with agriculture. Tenancies are of
crucial importance – but Blok is not able to provide sufficient information about them.

Table 3   Distribution of land in Genuardo, 1966

Categories of size (hectares)	Properties (%)	Amount of land (%)
< 2	49 } 89	6 } 40
2 – 10	40	34
10 – 50	10	34
50 <	1	24
	100 (n = 2,302)	98 (ha = 13,648)

Source: Blok, 1974: 251.

Table 4   Distribution of land in Pisticci, 1946

Categories of size (hectares)	Properties (%)	Amount of land (%)
< 2	73 } 93	9 } 23
2 – 5	15	9
5 – 10	5	5
10 – 100	5	23
100 – 1000 +	1	54
	99 (n = 4,058)	100 (ha = 22,216)

Source: Davis, 1973: 76.
Note: In 1952 some 9 per cent of holdings above about 100 hectares
were expropriated and redistributed in parcels of about 10 hectares to
308 families.

There are two points about Pisticci (Table 4) which require mention. The first is that the economy is more diversified than any of the other three appears to be: in effect all except the largest landowners are part-time farmers and have other sources of income – as labourers, teachers, skilled workers, lawyers, shopkeepers and so on. The second is that data for Pisticci show very clearly that formal taxable rights – which is what all these tables so far have been based on – are not always a good guide to *de facto* ownership, which may be acquired by informal cession or long-term lease (Davis, 1973: 118-45). Probably these two factors are associated: where land is less important informal cessions are likely to be common.

The difficulties involved in producing measures of wealth in pastoral societies are largely of a technical order: counting sheep or camels is not easy; the unit to be measured is hard to identify since there is a tendency for the size of flocks to vary from season to season. There is only one account, and that a partial one, of the distribution of ownership of sheep. Campbell managed to count and attribute the animals belonging to some Sarakatsani shepherds in their summer grazing area, Neochori, in 1955. One hundred and eight adult men owned 9,977 sheep and goats. In winter they were grouped into eighteen sheep management units – pooling their labour, herding their animals together – while in summer they re-grouped into twenty-six units. A management unit could contain one nuclear family, or several, or one or more extended families. So it would be possible to attribute the sheep to family units. But it might be misleading to compare the wealth of the nuclear family and that of a large fraternal joint family perhaps on the point of division: it might be more realistic to attribute sheep to adult males. The variability of the results obtained by attributing sheep to each of these kinds of unit is shown in Table 5. These figures seem to confirm Campbell's judgment that, among all Sarakatsani, some are clearly superior, some clearly inferior, while the vast majority – about four-fifths – struggle in the middle. (But the figures in column 1 of Table 5 suggest that the top and bottom categories are rather larger than Campbell states; it is interesting to observe that when Gini's coefficient – see below, p. 87 – is calculated for each of these three columns, the results are as follows: col. 1, 0.4240; col. 2, 0.3297; col 3, 0.2185. The nearer to zero the result is, the more equally the resources are distributed: the conclusion to be drawn, therefore, is that the consequence of grouping is to accentuate inequalities, not to eliminate them.) The greater

Table 5   Distribution of sheep by kinds of co-operating unit.
Some Sarakatsani, 1955

Size of flock	Sheep management units		Households		Adult males	
	%	% of sheep	%	% of sheep	%	% of sheep
0 – 40	5	1	17	3	12	4
41 – 100	17	3	17	8	62	53
101 – 200	17	6	36	35	24	36
201 – 300	10	6	13	18	1	3
301 – 400	—	—	11	20	1	4
401 – 600	28	32	6	16		
601 – 800	11	17				
801 – 1000	5	11				
1001 – 2000	5	23				

Source: Campbell, 1964: Appendix I.

spread down the categories of size of flocks when sheep are attributed to management units, rather than to any other kind of unit, is caused by that essential characteristic, that wealth attracts greater wealth, while poor men are ignored. The more prosperous a Sarakatsanos is the more he attracts associates to his company, and the leadership of a wealthy man is the focus for the aspirations of the middle sort of shepherd. Poor men do not associate with anyone. The multiplying attraction of the wealthy is a readily noted effect in pastoral societies, and has indeed been noted by others who do not provide such details as Campbell does (e.g. Abou-Zeid, 1965; cf. Chelhod, 1969a; and on Family Associations in towns, Khuri, 1976).

These are the five studies which provide the greatest detail of the crude material base of stratification systems. The calculation of these figures presents considerable difficulties, and they are in varying degrees partial. Sarakatsani do not have many resources other than sheep, but in Vila Velha there are some resources other than land; in Pisticci these seem to have considerable weight in the economy. Moreover land titles (on which the data are usually based) do not take account of variation in the value of land; nor do they cover the crucial area of rights, even formal legal ones such as tenancies, which may redress imbalances in some societies (Davis, 1973: 137). Finally, it is possible that the phenomenon noted for Pisticci (Davis, 1973: ch. 8) for Vasilika (Friedl, 1963a: 48-75) Elbaşi and Sakaltutan (Stirling, 1965: 134-40 q26), is found in other communities. That is, that some inequalities are functions of people's stage in the life cycle and are thus to be associated with the transient inequalities of age, rather than with the political inequalities of stratification.

Although any figures are therefore to be treated with great caution it is nevertheless interesting and instructive to use a statistical measure of the differences between communities: the data are often barely adequate – but the comparison is suggestive. The measure is Gini's coefficient, and it expresses the difference between absolutely equal distribution and the actual distribution of a given resource: the nearer to zero the coefficient is, the more equally the resource is distributed; the nearer to one, the more unequally. It is crude and limited, but is better than nothing (see Table 6). Remember the many ways in which these calculations are imperfect: the information on which they are based is variable in quality, to say the least; it is not always of the same order; it is usually information about the distribution of property among property owners who may be a variable proportion – and in some ethnographies an unknown one – of the total active population. In some cases what is counted is the property of landowners (individuals); in others, the number of properties (which may be held by more than one landowner; more than one of which may be held by an individual landowner). Moreover it is clear that some local economies are much more diversified than others: the distribution of land in a mostly agricultural community is of far greater significance than it is in one which has alternative sources of employment. So the calculation of the distribution of all wealth is clearly fraught with immense difficulties; the presentation of figures for the distribution of a single resource requires extraordinarily careful qualification if it is not to be misleading. When moreover the basic information is deficient it is positively malicious towards the reader to present crude, bogus misrepresentations of subtle and complex situations which each single ethnographer knows and understands, but cannot communicate and will not compare. That said, turn again to Table 6: it is crude – it is appalling – nevertheless it is suggestive. The range is roughly six and a half points from Alcalà to the Sarakatsani. Pitt-Rivers's data are weak

87

Table 6   Inequality in eight mediterranean communities

Community	Gini's coefficient
Alcala[1]	0.8653
Pisticci[2]	0.8094
Vila Velha[3]	0.7546
Belmonte[4]	0.2216
Genuardo[5]	0.6941
Al Karak[6]	0.5813
Orašac[7]	0.3160
Sarakatsani[8]	0.2185

Notes

1   Extremely poor data, Pitt-Rivers, 1961: 36. (See below, p. 93.) Gini calculated for 11,000 properties distributed among 604 households; what proportion of these households are landless is unknown – but 440 people were labourers.

2   Davis, 1973: 76. Gini calculated for size of 4,058 properties in 1946: some landowners have more than one property.

3   Cutileiro, 1971: 41-2. There were 491 owners in a population of 1,600. Calculation based on land within the boundaries of Vila Velha.

4   Lison-Tolosana, 1966: 20. There were 352 landowners, 16 landless 'owners' (p. 66) (presumably heads of households) in a population of 1,229. Calculation based on land within and without the boundaries – figures for the amount of land held crudely derived from Table at p. 20.

5   Blok (1974). Land within boundaries only; 2,302 properties, population 2,556 – of whom 500 were abroad. There were none the less large numbers of landless peasants – but Blok never states how many.

6   Gubser, 1973: 33. Figures for Governorate, 1953. In 1961 (Table 2, p. 30) 68 per cent of the 16,353 active population worked mainly in agriculture; of them 22.5 per cent worked mainly for employers – not for their families, that is.

7   Halpern, 1969. Laborious and crude reconstruction of data from Table 4, p. 73: includes both full- and part-time farmers who are, with their dependants, 93 per cent of the population.

8   Excellent data from Campbell, 1963, Appendix I.

– but is there really no difference in the distribution of resources in the two societies? The reader may note, wryly, that both the Alcaleños and the Sarakatsani are called 'egalitarian' by their ethnographers; and he may conclude that, on the face of it, the Alcaleños have to make a greater effort to achieve that blessed state of mind than the Sarakatsani do: the Alcaleños have more to ignore. The ethnographer who plans to work in the mediterranean may be advised to make some preliminary calculations of this kind – the data are often quite easily got, at least in peasant societies where there is a land tax, and the procedures are easily learned: qualification, hesitation, the peace of an understanding which cannot be communicated, these can all be acquired later. For it is the case that the stratification systems – and egalitarian systems, too – are social constructions derived from differences in wealth, and the full human ingeniousness of these systems cannot be explored unless it is known even in an indicative way what it is that is socially construed.

This section proves nothing except that social anthropologists have not often cared to record the data about distribution of resources. Although this failure is, utterly without shadow of doubt, the result of deep scruples about the value of crude data, nevertheless anthropologists should be prepared to collect it, even if it has to be qualified in words, and to present it in readily comparable form. Impressions, even the most sensitive and delicately argued ones, are not in themselves adequate for meticulous comparison on a broad canvas and they therefore need to be supplemented. It may be that in some cases the qualifications which scruple demands, undermine the comparative value of crude figures; but even in these cases it is important to encourage the comparative habit: to date *there is not a single study* which says 'resources are more equally distributed in this society than in that', still less one which draws out the consequences. Even if it is done inadequately it is important to have the intention of applying the principles of concomitant variation.

III Honour

Of the three ways in which material differences are socially construed the first and most important is honour. There is of course no society, anywhere, without prestige. But observers of the mediterranean often seem prepared to say that the rank which comes from the performance of roles judged by neighbours, friends, acquaintances, rivals, enemies, is a significant allocator of resources. Where this is so and where, furthermore, the roles which are judged include explicitly sexual ones, the word honour is conveniently used (Davis, 1969a: 69). Only central Italy has not produced reports of honour in this sense. Silverman (1966) speaks only of prestige and respect, but is perhaps too much inclined to produce a unified system of stratification. Wade (1971, 1973) does not use the term.

To say that honour is an allocator of resources is in apparent conflict with other statements about honour. Lison-Tolosana suggests that honour is an egalitarian principle, and that it has 'no connection with economic power' (1966: 108-9). Campbell emphasises the notions of true nobility which, when absent from the character and actions of a rich and powerful man, confine him to a 'prestige which is, at best, equivocal' (1964: 306). The conflict between these kinds of statement – the one moral and egalitarian, the other materialistic and hierarchical – is elevated to the position of a central explanatory ambiguity by Pitt-Rivers (1965): in his brilliant essay the ambiguity of a notion which combines status with virtue is the lynch-pin of a subtle analysis which shows how the shift from a description of the imputed moral excellences of the powerful to a prescription for the behaviour of the weak, can 'derive ought from is' (ibid.: 38, 73). Conversely, because the same word is used for both the status of the powerful and the virtue of the weak, the immorality of the powerful can be compared with the weakness of the virtuous, leading to the conclusion that there is no honour at court where, nevertheless, honours are most in evidence. This is the ethical move which is called 'egalitarian'; but it might more properly be called deflatory, for it pricks the pretentious, takes them down a peg or two – it does not assert the equality of all men's honour: it asserts that some men are not so much more honourable than the rest as they claim to be. Moreover, it is not certain that the deflatory use of ethical judgment is an important characteristic of honour: Pitt-Rivers is surely right when he places as much emphasis on status as on virtue. Moreover, it could be argued to the same effect that assertions of wickedness are common to all systems of stratification and are not confined to systems of honour. The weak and poverty-stricken consistently allege that honesty is associated with poverty, not with power; and it is irrelevant whether the rich man who cannot get to heaven is a capitalist who exploits them or a patron who, by rejecting their attempts to become his clients, refuses to exploit them. In Pisticci the patron and the capitalist may be the same person, discussed in different idioms at different times (Davis, 1969a: 77-8). Deflatory moralising is common to all systems of stratification and cannot therefore be isolated as the peculiar characteristic of honour: if it were, honour would be startlingly unique among systems of stratification for it would be the only one which has 'no connection with economic power'.

The best procedure at this point is to refer to the ethnographic evidence, and to relate this somewhat theoretical dispute to the realities which, perhaps surprisingly, seem to resolve it. The honour of Vila Velhans and of Pisticcesi is described in a way which is clearly 'materialist' (Cutileiro, 1971; Davis, 1969a, 1973); Lison-Tolosana (1966), Campbell (1964) and Pitt-Rivers (1961, 1965) supply evidence which, in spite of their intentions, can be used to support a materialist argument – and there is a host of lesser sources. An account is materialist when it supports the argument that honour is chiefly related to wealth – is an idiom in which differences in wealth are expressed. From these differences are derived differences in honour: poor people have less honour than richer ones and may therefore be insulted, treated as dishonourable, without damage to the honour of their superiors. In particular, the women of honour inferiors can be seduced with impunity. The materialist account of honour also asserts that disputes about honour are generally related to claims of equality (because honour-ranking has a tendency to absoluteness) or to instances of upward mobility (because, being a system of stratification rather than of moral precepts, and tending to absoluteness, honour mobility threatens to exclude erstwhile superiors from access to resources). In these cases of dispute 'honour is cleansed with blood' or, as the Albanian saying has it, 'the strong man's soap is gunpowder' (Cozzi, 1910a: 663-4) – whereas when honour differences are recognised, no soap is used.

Consider, then, Cutileiro's account of Vila Velha (1971). With a population of 1,600 in 1965, mostly dependent on agriculture, rather more than half the land was owned by eleven absentee latifundists. There were 480 resident landowners most of whom (95 per cent) had insufficient land to be independent of employment or sharecropping or tenancy contracts (ibid.: 45-68). It is clear from Cutileiro's description that the dependent farmers were losing strength, relative to the landowners and employees: wheat, the main produce of the area, was ceasing to be profitable, and indeed, the latifundists' accounts showed that *any* crop cultivated by hired labourers resulted in a loss, whereas net profits accrued if the land was sharecropped – a striking illustration, of the principle that profits can be made in any circumstances if only someone is sufficiently poor to have to contract to make the losses on his own account. The sharecroppers were thus losing rank, and had begun to marry their sons to labourers' daughters.

Honourable behaviour is maintained in two ways: patrons insist on it in their inferiors, as a condition of granting favours (ibid.: 238-45); and neighbourhood gossip is effective among equals (ibid.: 140), who note departures from the proper standards of domestic behaviour – including sexual behaviour. The gossip of inferiors is not considered to be damaging, except when servants discuss their employers' affairs, acting *pro vice* the mistress of their house (ibid.: 139). The proper standards are that a man should provide for his family, and his wife and daughters should be chaste. Failure in one sphere leads to suspicion of failure in another: Vila Velhans will ask a wastrel's wife if he shows signs of being jealous of her (ibid.: 40-1, n. 3). When it became known that a woman had been adulterous, Vila Velhans expressed no surprise: she was a spendthrift, and they expected no better of her (ibid.: 142). It is in fact the case that in Vila Velha some 95 per cent of the adult males were not able to provide adequately for their families; and among the labourers it had been accepted until about 1960 that their women would copulate with their honour superiors – with employers and rich shopkeepers – without detracting further from their honour. Such politic intercourse, Cutileiro says, was 'institutionalised as a means of securing patronage benefits' and 'a priority of family needs could be established, according to which adultery might be justified' (ibid.: 146). Among the poor Cutileiro noted 'an attitude of cynical resignation . . . [which] is associated with the material impossibility of living up to ideal standards of behaviour' (ibid.: 75). Vila Velha certainly conforms to the materialist account of honour, and exemplifies both the association of virtue with wealth, and the inferential judgment that a poor man's wife is unchaste (cf. Willems, 1962).

Pisticcesi seem to commit adultery rather less than Vila Velhans (Davis, 1969a), and they appear to talk rather more about honour. Most Pisticessi say that they would kill others who offended their honour, but in fact they do not often do so: in most cases when they cannot force a marriage they accept cash compensation, or a job. 'She does it to feed her family' is an accepted explanation of poor women's adultery with richer men than their husbands, just as men explain their actions by their need to provide for their dependents. Honour, which in Pisticci is associated mostly with a man's economic independence and with his ability to provide for his family without recourse to his wife's labour power in agriculture, is the prerogative of the relatively wealthy and, again as in Vila Velha, it establishes a hierarchy such that superiors may insult their inferiors more or less with impunity. Thus, when equals are involved in cases of seduction, homicide does follow; and a prudent amorist pursues the women of his social inferiors. The consonance of honour stratification with differences in wealth is clear; the occurrence of disputes chiefly between equals is extremely probable.

In Pitt-Rivers's work, dedicated to an explication of the conceptual intricacies of ambiguous notions, these features of honour are not immediately apparent. Indeed, his work is singularly lacking in the kind of data which would permit any analysis of the crude material base of Alcalà. Some information is given at 1961: 35; it is in a tangle such as only a pioneer's licence could justify, and any later writer is ill-advised if he imitates it. It seems likely that roughly 800 properties (the majority of properties; nothing is known about proprietors) occupy no more than 3.5 per cent of the land. It is possible that the owners of these plots, together with an unknown number of landless men, are the poor of Alcalà: a few have non-agricultural incomes; the rest are farm labourers, tenants and sharecroppers (ibid. 43-4). Pitt-Rivers says that occupational distinctions are not socially significant (ibid.: 48); nor is poverty significant within the pueblo *unless* it is 'translatable into moral inferiority' (ibid.: 60). *If* a man is unable to engage in ordinary reciprocities he loses honour, and is associated with those who commit offences of other kinds. It is difficult to know quite what to make of such conditionals: on the one hand, Pitt-Rivers often seems to suggest that moral respect should and normally does attach equally to all Alcaleños: 'the ideal of equality in honour reigns' (1965: 55); 'the status of respected elder in a community of conceptual equals is as high as any member can aspire' (ibid.: 53). So it seems that Alcalà is an ideally equal society in which some members fail occasionally to meet the required standards which would entitle them to equal treatment. Yet on the other hand, quite apart from the fact that people do dishonour themselves, and may be dishonoured even by the behaviour of their kin (– and why should dishonour spread to innocents, where an ideal of equality reigns?), it is quite clear that people both strive to gain more honour than others, and get deference when they are successful. Señoritos, of course, are recognised as honour superiors, but they are ambiguously members of the pueblo. Also, however, 'there are . . . degrees of deference paid according to their relative status even in the . . . pueblo' (ibid.: 54). The 'honourable status of the members of the community is a matter of continual comment. Reputation is not only a matter of pride, but also of practical utility . . .' (ibid.: 39). Perhaps part of the problem is that Pitt-Rivers was not particularly concerned with honour when he wrote his book (1961), which is concerned with politics, the ideologies of sexual differentiation, and family life, and it is not until he writes under Peristiany's editorship (1965) that his analysis of honour becomes fully developed.

Honour is contentious between equals because it 'derives from the domination of persons' (1965: 60); 'respect and precedence are paid to those who claim it and are sufficiently powerful to enforce their claim' (ibid.: 24). It seems that whatever the ideals of honour may be, it involves recognition of different ranks, of hierarchy: that is why there is continual comment about people's honour. Disputes about honour occur when someone claims more honour than he had before (ibid.: 4, 5); actions which would offend equals do not do so 'if there is . . . a difference in social status between the two parties' (ibid.: 58). Pitt-Rivers's account gives examples to demonstrate this last point which are all of challenges from an inferior to a superior (ibid.: 31, 57, etc.): could a high-honour Alcaleño dominate his inferiors, as a Pisticcese can? He does not say. Most of his instances are from aristocratic codes of duelling; but his analysis is so close to that of Cutileiro, the honour behaviour of the Alcaleños so similar to that of the Pisticcesi in principle, that there are reasonable grounds for assuming that the 'materialist' account of honour is applicable to Alcalá, in spite of their noted egalitarian ideals.

Much the same kind of argument must be applied to Campbell's material: he is another writer of absolute subtlety who denies the relation of honour to wealth and power, and who none the less provides evidence which suggests very strongly that they are associated. The 600 or so families of Sarakatsani shepherds are crudely ranked: 'There are those who are first, and those who are last . . .' (1964: 267). Most (see above, p. 85-6 and Table 5) are in between, and there is no consensus about their relative standing. 'It is precisely among these families of equivalent prestige that rivalry is greatest . . . pride and their common interest against further differentiation prevent any of their number from moving in an upward direction' (1964: ibid.). It is, incidentally, curious to note how often anthropologists who do not subscribe to the materialist account of honour, nevertheless let slip statements about relations between 'equals' (usually the undifferentiated middle ranges) which seem to betray their noble intention. So, Stirling: '. . . *namussuz*, without honour, or *ayip*, shameful . . . are in constant use, mainly for reproving children or for critical gossip. Except in jest, they are not said lightly by an adult to a social equal.' (1965: 231). Campbell states that ranking is 'prestige', not honour. Prestige is to do with wealth – with numbers of men, numbers of sheep. Honour is to do with integrity, nobility of spirit and body: a man is honourable when he meets certain exacting standards of manliness and is untainted by successful attacks on himself or his women (1964: 268-74). However wealthy a man is, however powerful, his prestige is 'equivocal' unless he is honoured as well. On this evidence, the distinction is as clear as clear could be. But there is further evidence which shrouds it again in doubt. Families with very high prestige can do things which, if they had less, would be dishonourable: they can, for example, contract incestuous marriages, and no harm done (ibid.: 267). Families with exceedingly little prestige have no honour however noble they may in fact be: you could copulate with his daughter, they say of a poor man, and he would hold your coat – a man needs wealth and numbers in order to assert his honour (ibid.: 273). When families in the middle range lose honour because their members fail to conform to the distinctive honour norms, they lose prestige as well: they suffer 'withdrawal of full recognition or response' (ibid.: 273). In an earlier article indeed, the distinction of honour from prestige is fairly muted: 'Men care passionately about their prestige, the prestige of their families and of their kinsmen . . . Whenever there is some incident . . . [people will] analyse minutely what a man is reported to have said and done and they will debate . . . whether he displayed manliness . . . in defending his honour' (1963: 78). The conclusion must be that prestige (wealth-derived) coincides or at least overlaps substantially with honour at the top and bottom of the scale; and in the indiscriminate middle they coincide to the extent that loss of one entails loss of the other. It is perhaps when a man in the middle range tries to claim increased honour, as it were to match an increase in his wealth, that the distinction is most forcibly expressed. That is the area where rivalry is greatest, and where all men conspire to 'prevent any of their number from moving in an upward direction'.

It is difficult to escape the conclusion that honour is, in spite of Campbell's assertions to the contrary, intimately related to wealth. Turn for a moment to two accounts of North African societies. When Bourdieu writes that '. . . honour is fundamentally opposed to a universal and formal morality which affirms the equality in honour of all men' (1965: 228) he means to make a point about the variable range of moral rules, of a kind which Ginsberg or von Fürer Haimendorf might make. But in spite of his insistence on the game-like, ceremonial nature of honour (cf. Davis, 1969a: 69) his article is redolent of rank and competitiveness, and Kabyle failure to recognise the equality in honour of all men must be read in a hierarchical as well as in a lateral sense (cf. ibid.: 213, on *tawsa* (*taoussa*)). Similarly Abou-Zeid: he does not discuss honour in materialistic terms but nevertheless describes the firm material base: 'a man feels proud of the size of his kingroup in the same way that he feels proud of the size of his flock. . . . His prestige and his social standing, which are constituent parts of his personal honour, are actually determined by the size of his herd' (1965: 249). Abou-Zeid indeed makes a distinction between honour and prestige (and social standing) but it is difficult not to feel that this is another society in which conflict is between near-equals struggling for an edge over their rivals, and in which (as among Sarakatsani) manpower, wealth, and the ability to flout rules which struggling men observe, go together (cf. P. Schneider, 1969: 153; J. Schneider, 1971a: 2).

The third writer in the list is Lison-Tolosana. He says that the people of Belmonte de los Caballeros could be divided into six categories according to their wealth. The three lowest categories were certainly dependent on the others, although the fourth lowest, affected by technological changes in agriculture, was also becoming dependent for machines which, necessary to get a decent living from the land, they could not afford to own.[1] These six categories are fundamental determinants of power, so that in the two hundred years up to 1960 no one in the three lowest categories had ever held public office. The strata were endogamous; members of higher strata expected members of lower ones to be good of their kind – to be good labourers, good peasants, industrious, frugal, deferential – and they all expected to associate only with members of their own strata (1966: 80-93). The strata are also differentiated by 'style of living, amusements and ways of spending money, of looking after the home, and of manners and speech' (ibid.: 94-118). When the people of Belmonte assess an individual, therefore, they consider first of all his position, what stratum he belongs to, and then his standing among fellow-members of the stratum, shown by his style of living and so on. Each of these is related to his command over production, to his economic resources.

Lison-Tolosana then argues that honour (*honradez*) has no connection with economic resources (ibid.: 108-9). It is, he says, moral integrity, which has nothing to do with membership of strata (see Appendix 1). That is as may be. The reader can be sure that Lison-Tolosana, like all other anthropologists of the Mediterranean, met poor and despised men of the greatest personal integrity and honesty, which may even be recognised by their social superiors. But the assertion that there is *no* connection of wealth and honour in Belmonte is puzzling, for people there do make moral judgments which coincide with crude material differences. In fact they do have higher expectations of people who have high position, expecting them to behave handsomely (ibid.: 106-7), and 'the behaviour of the lower groups is of less importance unless it takes on obviously scandalous features'. And in fact, 'Drunkenness, theft, premarital pregnancies . . . are . . . more prevalent among the lower groups.' This of course is said to be common to all systems of stratification; but Lison-Tolosana quite explicitly says that in Belmonte the greater prevalence of dishonourable behaviour among the poor is explained by saying that those people have a less developed sense of shame (ibid.: 108). *No* connection?

Who is *honrado*? It is the man who embodies civic and domestic virtues and has enough money and shame to keep up to standard (ibid.: 313-48). The work of *braceros* is normally degrading because it never leads to a life of leisure (ibid.: 319). Medium farmers (*proprietarios*) fail financially and consider themselves dishonoured. To accept orders from another is an assault on integrity and is therefore degrading (ibid.: 329). *No* connection? It may be that in Belmonte people say that every man is born with his honour and sense of shame intact: but from the moment of birth it is undoubtedly whittled away for those who are born into the lower groups – about three-quarters of the population. They are *in fact* ranked, in moral terms, whatever the ideology may be. 'The upper strata impose . . . their own tastes and ideas; the system of crucial values in the life of the community is theirs' (ibid.: 106). If Lison-Tolosana is right, he has made an astounding discovery: he has uncovered a ruling group, secure, which has 'imposed' an 'egalitarian principle' (ibid.: 108) on a population almost entirely within its control; moreover – as if that were not astounding enough – he has discovered a subject population which, offered moral integrity on an equal footing, continues to behave dishonourably.

The essential characteristics of honour are first that it is a system of stratification: it describes the distribution of wealth in a social idiom, and prescribes appropriate behaviour for people at the various points in the hierarchy; it entails acceptance of superordination and subordination. Second, it is an absolute system: when honour is used to allocate resources, when men try to gain access to jobs, land, influence, they try to discriminate absolutely between themselves so that each competitor occupies a unique position in the hierarchy. One of the weapons in such discrimination is the distinction between honour-virtue and honour-status. The weapon is used by rivals so that 'people are often willing to concede integrity to their superiors which they deny to their equals' (Boissevain, 1965: 50). To put this another way: honour stratification invites equals to quarrel, and asserts the co-operative dependence of those who have less honour on those who have more. Third, it does seem to be characteristic of honour that it is associated with integrity: the whole man is contemplated. What a whole man is, though, varies from society to society.

There is no space in this short book to present an analysis of variation in notions of 'the whole man', of integrity. Sarakatsani males are expected to be chaste except within marriage; in Belmonte de los Caballeros an amorist should conquer but not invade; in most other mediterranean societies there is a double standard: women should be chaste, men should not. Although there are some reports of mediterranean societies where women are not chaste, it often turns out that they are women who cannot afford chastity, as in Vila Velha. Both Vinogradoff (1974a, 1974b) and Maher (1975) write of the prostitution of Berber women in the intervals between marriages, and Vinogradoff relates this to the effects of colonialism on Moroccan society (1974a). Otherwise female unchastity may be related to the impotence or infertility of husbands. (See e.g. Filipović, 1958: in such cases 'one ought to "change the cock" (as one does with hens)'.) Nevertheless in all these societies honour is not primarily a matter of sexual behaviour. True, honour can be lost more easily through sexual failings than by any other means; but more women lose honour than fornicate, and the subtle discrimination between families requires more diacritics than copulation alone can provide. Most people discriminate between men by their performance of everyday roles as strugglers to survive, between women by their performance of their roles as makers of the best of a bad job (cf. Adams, 1971: 169; Blaxter, 1971: 121). It is important to remember that practical criticism of honour, the consequential assessment of behaviour, occurs chiefly in the indeterminate middle section of the communities, where rank is not certain. Most men do earn some sort of livelihood, but not securely; most women do put on some sort of show of keeping a family fed and clean and decent, but the veneer may crack without warning. So while an anthropologist may write resonantly of honour and of the sense of shame which preserves it and the reader's heart may swell as big as a Grandee's in response, nevertheless most concern with punctilio, for the greater part of the mediterranean populations, is pettifogging, concerned with the minutiae of day-to-day domesticity.

There remain two points to make on this topic. The first is that most of the behaviour described by Bailey as 'competing to remain equal' (1971a: 19) is in fact honour-oriented behaviour, even though the word honour is rarely used in that book. Bailey indeed cites Bourdieu (1963) and discusses 'reputation' as Pitt-Rivers might discuss honour (1971a: 14-5, 19-22); Blaxter's discussion of *mauvaise langue* (1971: 123), Adams's of the connections between denigration and struggle (1971: 171) – all these may lead the reader to think that the virtual absence of the word *honour* is casual: certainly the book includes no account of why it might be inappropriate, and the 'obsession with equality', which is so frequently reported of these mountain peoples, can perhaps be attributed to the creditable idealism of the writers all of whom, with one exception, were then young. In short, given the relative lack of ethnographic detail, it is an open question whether or not the obsession with equality is a secondary phenomenon: thwarted in their attempts to gain dominance, men settle for the next best – 'we are all equal': at least they can resist others' assertions of dominance (cf. Antoun, 1968: 169; and Silverman's severe critique of Bailey and his pupils, 1974). For it often seems that Bailey is unduly teleological: people do compete and they do, none the less, remain roughly equal. Equality, such as it is, is often the consequence, but by no means the purpose, of endemic competitiveness. Of course, in some instances people do quite consciously 'think away' their inequalities and take steps to make them irrelevant to co-operative endeavour. But they usually do this by lottery, or by circulation of office – institutions discussed in the last section of this chapter – not by competition.

The final point is to raise the question – why does honour exist? It is sufficiently established that honour is *sui generis,* is a mode of stratification in its own right, and cannot be assimilated to class or organisational rank in a kind of composite system of stratification. If it were not so, then there would be as many composites as there are communities. Rather, there are only three kinds of stratification easily discernible in the mediterranean; and local variation is the result of the particular weight with which each is present in any given community. For 'a kind of stratification' is identified not by examining the particularities of power in local communities (*that* examination results in the identification of kinds of communities) but by examining the consequences of talking about power in one way rather than another. And so the question arises naturally to the inquiring mind – why honour?

It must be frankly admitted that only the excellent Jane Schneider has asked and attempted to answer that question in print (1971a). She has argued that honour is an ideology of defence: it is associated with the defence of patrimony in states without government. The honour of a group is the gravity which attracts otherwise centrifugal persons to the defence of a viable common patrimony. Where pastoralist lineages disperse, where agricultural nuclear families fragment, but where territory has to be defended, the honour of the group is a countervailing ideology, and also an aggressive one – mustering sufficient loyalty, recruiting sufficient force, to conduct raids and encroachments. Where women are things, moreover, they become part of the patrimony whose integrity has to be maintained, and with which men identify their own integrity (ibid.: 21):

> The economic autonomy of nuclear families demands an inheritance system that undermines the position of the father in relation to his sons, and militates against a co-operating association of sons. Father and sons . . . could become unmerciful competitors at great cost to social order, were it not for their abiding interest in the comportment of the daughters of the family.

There is no doubt of the attractions of such a wide-reaching discussion, which manages to relate honour and shame to the organisational problems of pastoralists and agriculturalists in the mediterranean – to problems experienced over a period to be counted in centuries. True, there are some immediate difficulties: honour is not, was not, a speciality of shepherds nor of farmers with bilateral inheritance: how does honour move from those pastoral milieux to the cities, to those aristocratic codes so often used to illustrate the essence of honour? If honour is an adaptive response to organisational problems, why does it exist also where those problems do not exist? Balkan societies in general seem to have honour but not the organisational problems of fragmenting families; and the same is true of what is known of Turkey (Stirling, 1965: 230-3 especially. Professor Stirling has been kind enough to communicate that the limited account of *namus* and *ayip* in his book is a reflection of earlier fashions: honour was not one of the ideas which a man went into the field determined to investigate, in the 1950s (idem., 1969)). It is worth noting that land shortage was not a problem in Stirling's Turkish villages until the twentieth century. So, while Jane Schneider's emphasis is on functions of honour in defence of patrimonies, Stirling provides examples of communities with honour but without the threat of encroachment on resources.

In spite of these difficulties the Schneider thesis remains attractive. She invites and deserves discussion. If this present account of honour makes a contribution to such a discussion it is perhaps that she has underemphasised the struggle for honour: honour is a system of stratification, and people struggle for honour because they can, when successful, gain access to resources. The kinds of society in which honour stratification is important seem to share the characteristic of having relatively undiversified economies: it is difficult to speak, with the sort of conviction a sociologist of England or Germany has, of occupational hierarchies when describing Vila Velha or Pisticci or the Sarakatsani: there are too many people left undifferentiated. It does appear to be the case that disputes about honour occur most frequently in the undifferentiated ('equal') middle ranges of communities. Third, they are communities in which access to resources is of crucial significance, either because resources are really few, or because standards of decent living are rising. These are all characteristics of honour which have to be taken into account when trying to explain why honour should be an important form of stratification.

IV Bureaucracy

It is necessary to begin this section with an apology: anthropologists have, indeed, paid more attention to bureaucracy than they have to the distribution of resources; but what they have written is still inadequate to support any sustained effort at comparison. The most general consequences of state administration have been noted already: integration of local communities seems usually to entail incorporation at a very low level – a loss of autonomy (above, p. 71), while at the same time individuals are given access to resources which in theory are independent of the control of local magnates, and may to some extent actually be independent. However, the more common effect, whether because states appoint local magnates to representative positions, or because citizens elect them, is that internal differentiation is increased.

So much can be extracted from the ethnographies with only a little synthesising imagination. But anthropologists have not sought to make many sharper distinctions. Pizzorno has remarked that a fundamental distinction exists between Roman-law based administrative systems and Anglo-Saxon ones: he characterises the former as designed to protect the power and property of the state against the depredations of the citizenry, the latter to erogate in just measure where right demands (1960). Argyriades suggests that the nature of the Greek state after liberation from Ottoman rule was such that no 'civil service tradition' developed: moreover, Argyriades says, contemporary Greek indifference to the state was caused in part at least as 'the legacy of Turkish rule' (1968: 342). It is easy to perceive the truth of this intuitively, more difficult to work out how such a statement might be given any status which would allow it to be compared, as a fact about Greek society, with yet-to-be-established facts about other societies. Although the sources thus reflect what must surely be the expectation of common sense, that bureaucracies and administrations vary from society to society in their intentions and forms, the present conclusion must be that not enough work has yet been done by anthropologists to show how these variations could affect local communities: Turkish (Stirling: 1957, 1958), Italian (Boissevain, 1966a, 1966b, 1969b; Davis, 1973), Portuguese (Cutileiro, 1971: 162-72) and Moroccan (Seddon, 1973a, 1974) officials and regulations appear undifferentiated in the villages which anthropologists have studied.

All of the European and most of the Maghreb and Middle Eastern communities are in contact with men who are representatives of national authority – policemen, development officers, mayors, district officers and the like. Officials do not travel with transhumants, and the Sarakatsani and Bedouin herders are thus the only mediterranean peoples who do not have resident officials: all sedentary communities have some kind of administrator present. This has not always been the case: the Maghreb was loosely administered, if at all, before the colonial era. The Ait Ndhir, for example, protected travellers through their territory, but sometimes they did so with the authority of the Sultan, sometimes without it: they were variously *makhzen* policemen or *siba* brigands, but their activity – the extraction of tolls from travellers – remained the same (Vinogradoff, 1974b; cf. Waterbury, 1972; Hart, 1958; Brown, 1973). In Albania the Ottoman administration was remote and extractive: decrees ordering that feuds should be settled were issued from time to time but 'the first to excite Albanian propensities [to feud] . . . were precisely Turkish functionaries who, deprived of the fines payable for killings, found that peace merely damaged their incomes' (Cozzi, 1910a: 655). Administrators are broadly speaking of two kinds: those who are not natives of the community they administer, and those who are. Of the former, it must be said that they are usually at the bottom rung of their ministry's hierarchy, and that for them to be posted to be field officers in the sort of village anthropologists choose to study is the culminating accolade of failure. These men none the less represent authority, have access to state resources and are consequently political personages even if – in the larger towns such as Pisticci or Vila Velha – some local men may wield greater influence over their superiors than they themselves possess. Anthropologists should attempt to give some idea of the range of their authority and power, and of the people within the local community over whom it is effective: in both Spain (Pitt-Rivers, 1961) and Portugal (Cutileiro, 1971) the authority of police, for example, varies with the standing of the natives in the local community and national society.

Local officials drawn from the community may be elected or appointed: postmen and policemen are obviously appointed but so are mayors and councillors in some of the corporate states. In Spain, for example, mayors are elected in communities with more than 10,000 members (though no anthropologist has studied one so big), otherwise they are appointed. In Alcalá two councillors were elected by heads of households, two by the syndicates and a further two were chosen by the elected ones from a list supplied by the governor (Pitt-Rivers, 1961: 122). Gower Chapman's study of Milocca dates from

1928-9 and thus portrays a *podestà* appointed by government, but mayors and councillors alike are now elected throughout Italy. Whether a mayor is elected or not he has the status of a Janus: expected to speak for his community in the province, he must publish the decrees of government in the parish: his office can be uncomfortable in both corporate and other states. His duties vary considerably: in Vasilika (Friedl, 1963a) and Valdemora (Freeman, 1970) he organises communal labour; in Vasilika he is partly responsible for assessing liability to tax. In Italy, where the office is won by a party, the mayor and his supporters can have considerable funds to distribute through public works and other relief programmes (Davis, 1973; Boissevain, 1966a, 1966b, 1969b). These and similar tasks in addition to the more ordinary ones of holding meetings, signing declarations, drawing up budgets and negotiating for public works. The best accounts of local government in southern Europe come from the mountainous regions (Bailey, 1971e, 1973d) where development for winter sports offers decaying villages a way out of their impasse, and creates considerable local political controversy.

Recruitment to office of this kind varies: in Belmonte de los Caballeros no person of the lower orders has ever held office (Lison-Tolosana, 1966; see above, p. 96); but where communities are large and office is elective poor men may come to positions of authority. In some cases restricted recruitment is related to the attitude towards office within the local community: in Vila Velha there are considerable personal advantages to be got from office, and access is restricted. In Elbaşi and Sakaltutan, where elections are held by government order, young men are in effect appointed to office to save the really important men the troubles of dealings with the administration (Stirling, 1965: 256). The possibility of getting personal advantage is clearly related not only to the resources which office gives access to, but also to the moral ideas which attach to office: in Vila Velha, for example, an outgoing chairman of the Junta was reproved by his successor not indeed for having utilised publicly owned tools for his private purposes during his period of office, but for failing to return them when it ended. Such moral expectations may attach to appointed posts as well as to representative office: the man in charge of Vila Velha's local post office, determined to retire, merely nailed the postbox to the house of the man he himself chose as his successor (Cutileiro, 1971: 173). When an old woman complained to a local policeman that a shopkeeper had maliciously killed her cat he picked up his own: 'Take this one!' Anecdotes of this kind complicate an issue which is often posed simply in terms of 'corruption' – the use of office to pursue personal advantage, or the use of kinship or other ties to persuade an official to grant favours officiously. Anecdotes about this latter kind of activity abound: the sheikh of Mediouna rented land from Tangerine speculators and sub-leased it to villagers beholden to him; he was also the only man with a gun, as he had to countersign all applications for gun licences (Schorger, 1969). The Barhams in Bint el-Huḍūd supplied the local officials as well as the local school teachers: campaigns against truancy were seen by other villagers to be self-interested (A. Cohen, 1965: 98-9). It would be tedious to rehearse the details when the general point has been well made by Stirling (1968; his analysis is to be preferred to Galt's distinction between the 'official' and the 'real' system (1974)): personal morality extends over and envelops office of all kinds where the Weberian ideal typical bureaucracy (which Anglo-Saxon ethnographers sometimes seem to assume is the reality of their own countries) demands impartiality. What is needed now is an account of the varying intentions and forms of administration in which such anecdotes may find a setting: Waterbury's account of patrimonialism in Morocco (1973b), for example, puts the sheikh of Mediouna's behaviour in a context – a context which is quite different from that in which superficially quite similar anecdotes of Italian or Portuguese officials are properly set.

This book must occasionally set out the notes and queries which are unanswered by ethnographers and which seem important if full accounts are to be given of particular institutions in particular communities in a way which will allow them to be compared. By way of summary of this section it may be helpful to do that. One form of power in most mediterranean communities is derived from central government and is vested in its representatives. In the first place it is important to attempt some characterisation of the formal organisations of government, remembering that not all administrations aspire to Weberian ideal-typical status: variations in this sphere will surely affect the use of power by local officials. In the second place it is important to collect as much information as possible about local officials and their relation to the communities in which they have power. How many officials are there? How are they recruited? Do they work in their native communities? What are their spheres of action, and what are the limits to their power? How are they regarded by other inhabitants (cf. Kenny, 1968)? How do they regard other officials? Other inhabitants? How do they behave when there is a conflict between their official duties and the values of the communities in which they work? How do they represent the inhabitants' interests to their superiors? Do they act in the same way towards all local people? If not, what are the correlates of differentiation? Is such differentiation in conflict with local values? With the values of the administration? Finally, note that an office is a kind of status and should be compared and contrasted with other statuses which exist within the community – for example: teacher, friend, father, kinsman, employee, employer.

V Class

The percipient reader of this chapter will expect the difficulties which now arise when it becomes necessary to discuss class formations in the mediterranean. For many writers have been content to use the word *class* wherever there is unequal distribution of crude material resources, and to use it whether or not local people consciously use a class model when devising forms of action. But to do so here would reduce honour and bureaucracy, painfully established as *sui generis* forms of stratification in the preceding pages, to dependent variables or epiphenomena of the more general phenomenon *class*. On the contrary, the position adopted here is to treat of class, honour, bureaucracy as separate construed versions of the distribution of material resources. The reasons for doing so are partly theoretical, partly empirical. Theoretically, it seems important to establish that honour, say, is in fact a conscious idiom of stratification, related to the materials of life, rather than an elaborate epiphenomenal metaphysic or an intricately false consciousness: but that cannot be done if class captures the field of true stratification. Theoretically it is more sensible in the first instance to use concepts which are directly related to those used by people, rather than to use concepts such as class which seem to subsume all human experience of stratification, and which then must be qualified and distinguished in ways which, more often than not, bear little relation to human experience, expression and endeavour. For, empirically, it seems clear that, for example, relations of honour can give rise to struggle just as much as relations of class do; and, empirically, it seems clear that men, armed with a variety of idioms of stratification, may chop and change, manoeuvre to find that which best suits their current interests. Moreover, anthropologists who make enveloping use of class are usually those chiefly concerned with societies on the northern littoral. It is pardonable to think the word would not trip so slippery from their pens if they watched the southern shore: for there their colleagues happily speak of honour and rank without mentioning class, or do no more than expect class in the near future. If class can be absent, about to arrive, then surely it must be able to co-exist – with honour, with bureaucracy? But to adopt such a usage abandons *class* in its form of a useful observer's shorthand. It must cease to be a piece of reality which natives may or may not be conscious of; the usage in this book requires that men be conscious of class before the observer can attach that label to the phenomenon. The reader must consider the possibilities, and judge for himself. On the one hand, he may choose to speak only of class and to see it embodied in the distribution of material resources. Honour, bureaucracy, then become manifestations of class, more or less blatantly oppressive, more or less salient, more or less false. The advantage of doing so is in the direct line of connection to modes of analysis which have been well tried elsewhere, and in the interesting and important questions which that context of analysis suggests. There is a danger that that context may supply answers too readily, but it is not a severe danger. The disadvantages lie more in the loss of empirical subtlety, for a method which remains (in the first instance) close to what men say and do puts the burden of subtlety on them, rather than on the abstractions of theoreticians: it is they, after all, who create and use these complex shared worlds in order to live day to day and to achieve long-term security.

Consciousness is thus a prerequisite: observers must have evidence that men speak of material differences in a way which implies class formations and action before they themselves may use it. 'Consciousness' and 'implies' are not precise words – rather, ones which must be used by ethnographers after an exercise of sympathy and judgment. An old man, wishing to characterise a Pisticcese politician of the 1920s so an outsider might understand better what he was like, compared him to Masaniedd di Roma. But who was Masaniedd? Without any doubt he was a Neapolitan (not Roman) fishmonger who led a revolt against the Spanish in Naples *in 1647* and got a European reputation as a heroic leader of the oppressed, so that medals were struck with his head on one side, Oliver Cromwell's on the other (Davis, 1974a: 45-6). In this case it would perhaps be correct to speak of class, even though the continuity of revolutionary tradition was largely unconscious – the old man did not know about Cromwell or Spinoza; nevertheless his account of the Pisticcese politician was brought into a context of European proportions, stretching over four centuries. Although Pisticci had had some form of class organisation since at least the 1910s, it would still be appropriate to speak of class, in an extremely qualified way, if the mention of Masaniedd were a unique incident. To ignore it would deprive the analysis of a historical and European dimension which must in some sense underlie most political activity on the northern shore of the Mediterranean – just as there is a more recent tradition of anti-colonial struggle which underlies much Maghrebi local politics. Another example, this time from Portugal. Vila Velha is in the Alentejo region which in the late 1960s had the political reputation of leftism (Cutileiro, 1971: 23); but it is almost true to say that since the foundation of the new state in 1926 the political struggling muscles of the population have atrophied – a strike of harvesters in 1962 (ibid.: 87), a grumble in a road gang during the lunch break (ibid.: 221), an indiscreet vet, quickly put down (ibid.: 221) – that was about the sum of opposition in the *freguesia*. Yet there was in the mid-1960s a continual awareness of the possibility of revolution – a knowledge (which Cutileiro thinks mistaken) that there was a clandestine revolutionary propaganda apparatus, feeding people with hope, making them aware of injustice. The movement, the struggle, was latent. In both these cases it is appropriate to speak of class, even though the formation is weak, even though (as Cutileiro says, ibid.: 48) it was the rich new latifundists who spoke most of communism and of revolution. Indeed, Cutileiro's work discusses social categories whose members, given opportunities which they lacked in the 1960s, *could* have united in pursuit or defence of common interests; and the covert, discreet, inquiry underlying his book is precisely the question why they did not do so (cf. Colclough, 1971; Alberoni, 1961; Boissevain, 1966b).

Similarly, and in another dimension, it is possible for the observer to note and describe proto-class formations: if class symbolism can be present in an apparently classless society without any significant class action, so too there can be class action without central organisation or continuity: sporadic and shortlived manifestations of solidarity among people of similar socio-economic interests. The major analyst of such movements is of course Hobsbawm (1959). He calls 'primitive' those 'pre-political' movements without a specific language in which people can express their aspirations about the world (ibid.: 2). Although Hobsbawm has been sharply criticised (e.g. Blok, 1972; cf. Hobsbawm, 1972), his work remains the keystone of any comparative study. His classification revolves around the question of organisation and rationality of purpose: peasant movements seem to need organisation from outside; without it, peasants are easily defeated or defeat themselves, having little fixity of purpose. In Italy, certainly, the movements to occupy land have more often than not begun (as the law required) as grand schemes of universal co-operation, only to collapse within a couple of years into individual peasant holdings, some abandoned, the rest picked off one by one by the landowners. Rossi-Doria makes it quite clear that the south Italian occupations of land in the period 1945-7 were extremely local. By the end of 1946 he calculates that about 250,000 hectares had been occupied or legally assigned to co-operatives. A year later about 100,000 hectares had been abandoned (1956: 346-9). When the peasant movement, localised, attracts interest at the centre, the metropolitan supporters as often as not have a self-interest incomprehensible to the peasants, and incompatible with their aims. The problems of relations between the city and the countryside are not confined to capitalistic oppression.

It is nevertheless characteristic of such movements, however latent and however primitive, that people may be organised; and that organisation can extend beyond the boundaries of the community in a way in which honour does not: participation in a movement, membership of an organisation, gives a man a political identity which will travel. The spread of organisations for working men, however feeble they are, however impractical the ideas, is always a cause for alarm among rulers (see e.g. Davis, 1975). However, it is also the case that at the village level even the most efficient and centralised organisations are permeated with personal and particularistic tendencies (see below, ch. 4).

In these senses then class formations are latent throughout the European mediterranean. It is not clear that in the Maghreb there is the same conscious or unconscious tradition. Clearly Libya, Tunisia and Algeria are socialist states; and there are more or less clandestine socialists in Morocco. What is not clear is that there is a tendency to class formation as a mode of political representation – that the language of political discourse is a class one. The only anthropological writing on the Maghreb which appears to discuss this in any detail is John Waterbury's *Commander of the Faithful* (1970) and his articles on patrimonialism (1973b) and the coup of 1971 (1973a); there, the emergence of a class movement is predicted – it is still in the future. In his account of Hadj Brahim (1972) the involvement of tribal groups in commerce and politics on a national scale is clearly revealed, but without much attempt to put it in a wider context of theory.

In short, the treatment of class in the mediterranean *by anthropologists* vacillates between two extremes: on the one hand, some have called all social inequality a manifestation of class; others have not mentioned or discussed class at all. The exceptions are Waterbury, A. Cohen (1965; see below, ch. 4), and Colclough (1971).

VI Egalitarian systems

It is appropriate to preface a section on egalitarian systems with a note of explanation. For on the one hand a considerable part of this chapter has been devoted to demonstrating that systems of honour are wrongly called egalitarian by their ethnographers. On the other it is quite clear that the societies to be discussed in this section are not ones in which all human creatures are in fact equal: it is necessary to tread a wary path through the data, and to do this a short excursus may be helpful. In fact a variety of characteristic institutions justifies the use of the term egalitarian.

First, it is proper to announce that none of the egalitarian institutions about to be discussed provides for the equality of children or of women. To use the word egalitarian therefore will undoubtedly be offensive to many women and to younger readers.

The word 'egalitarian' should be applied to institutions, not to whole societies: it is necessary to look at particular aspects of a society (cf. Pitt-Rivers, 1963). For example, Dunn (1973: 94-5) describes the population of Tafilalt, south-east of the Atlas: with several thousand *shurfa* and *mrabtin,* groups of independent cultivators, of haratin and slaves, as well as about 6000 Jews, it was clearly not an equal *society,* yet possessed *institutions* (complementary and rotating elections, hagiarchy – discussed below) which must be qualified 'egalitarian'. Tafilalt in fact appears the most stratified of the areas in which such characteristic institutions are found and is a limiting case; even so, the reader should remember that egalitarian does not mean 'equal' but rather 'creating equality in specific situations'.

The institutions reviewed here are specifically political, occasionally economic. It may mollify critics somewhat if they are told that utterly different results would emerge if what was reviewed were domestic or religious institutions: that is admitted. What is of interest are those institutions in mediterranean societies by which differences in crude material wealth are excluded from consideration when important political decisions are made: by which the reality of differentiation is socially destroyed instead of being construed to create a stratification.

These institutions are of various kinds, which must be carefully distinguished. It seems sensible to identify first of all those institutional arrangements in which, in theory at any rate, equality is automatic, mechanical. Segmentary lineages are said to be of this kind: the principle that political groups maintain their independence by massing with closer allies against more distant allies necessarily entails that any two groups in a state of conflict over a long period of time should be fairly equally balanced. A balance of terror only secures the peace if it is in fact a balance. The corollary of this is that when groups are not balanced something has to be done about the weaker one. What happens most commonly is that groups which are less equal than others are absorbed by the stronger ones, or expelled (Gellner, 1969: 28). What is important is that such groups, individuals, *are not subjugated,* are not converted into a lower class of people who failed to be equal. This process of absorption or exclusion may remind the reader that there is a distinction between egalitarianism and welfareism: the former is not necessarily gentle, the latter not egalitarian (cf. Hart. 1958: 189, n. 20). The kind of egalitarian tendency which is embodied in a segmentary system is almost certainly not willed: it appears automatic, without conscious intention, mechanical. Moreover it concerns groups, not individuals: the groups contain leaders, wealthy men and men of influence. Gellner is right to emphasise Bourdieu's remark that this is *democratie vécue,* experiential 'democracy', for it is structural not ideological and not individual; the same point is made by Favret in her critique of Durkheim's analysis of Kabyle segmentary systems in chapter 5 of his *De la division du travail social*: the master never asks whether equality is 'un principe ou une situation de fait' (1968).

Segmentary lineage systems are reported from all tribal areas on the southern and eastern shores of the Mediterranean, but they are very often incorporated within an active state organisation. For this reason some anthropologists, notably A. Cohen (1965: 2, n.1, but cf. the usage of Rosenfeld, e.g. 1968), have preferred to use vernacular terms – Cohen uses the Arabic *hamula* throughout, for example. Although the village of Bint el-Ḥudūd contained *hamula* not all the villagers belonged to one; and although members of the *hamula* were collectively liable for wrongs done by any one of them, lived in the same quarter of the village, preferred to marry within the *hamula,* and expressed these common interests 'in the idiom of patrilineal descent', nevertheless there was no alliance of *hamula* on agnatic lines, and the groups were incorporated as a village into the administrative political and economic organisation of the Israli state. In these circumstances A. Cohen is right not to use 'lineage'; on the other hand the way in which the villagers rejected the opportunities offered by the state to become class-stratified citizens, and reasserted the political grouping of *hamula* (see below, p. 152) indicates an egalitarian tendency, a resistance to stratification.

In the Maghreb the lineage system is frequently associated with a cross-cutting system of alliance called *leff* (also *soff* and, by Hart and Waterbury, *liff*). The first man to analyse the *leff* system was Montagne (1930); his views held sway until criticised by Berque (1955: 424-32) and Gellner (1969: 64-8; but Gellner's critique was already formulated eleven years before – see Hart, 1958: 204, n. 44). Hart gives two main accounts of the *leff* system in the Rif (1958, 1970; the account in 1954 is not mature) and has produced a fine comparative essay exploring the differences between transhumant and nomadic groups of the middle Atlas and Rifians (1966a). The crux of the *leff* system in Montagne's scheme is that it is an alliance which divides descent groups, and places the members of a descent group in opposition to each other. So while the members of a descent group were obliged to support each other in war and arguments against members of other descent groups, in true segmentary style, they might also be obliged to attack each other in *leff* alliance with members of descent groups to whom they were in segmentary terms opposed. *Leff* alliances could also sometimes transcend tribal boundaries, so that each minimal section of a tribe could expect support from two kinds of ally: from its segmentary allies; and from half its segmentary allies, plus half its segmentary enemies, plus – in some cases – half the members of neighbouring sections of other tribes. These groups constituted the *leff*.

That is the formal pattern of a *leff* system and a segmentary system combined. It was said by Montagne to be a device for limiting warfare and feuding and he thought that if he knew enough he would have been able to show that all tribal Morocco was divided into two such alliance groups – 'moieties' – and that *leff* alliance was infinitely transitive, to use Gellner's word (1969: 66). Montagne's insights are now universally praised, but his scheme is usually criticised. Hart (1970 – note that this article was written before Hart, 1966a (q.v. at p. 77, n. 23)) has emphasised the fundamental instability of the *leff* system. Favret (1968) neatly rehearses the arguments against the use of the term moiety. The *leff* system was not in fact a Morocco-wide one: it is simply not the case that all tribal Morocco was or could be divided into 'moities'. A series of exclusion clauses applies: *leff* alliances were most developed among sedentary tribes where territory predominated over agnation as a focus of solidarity, and transhumant and nomadic groups, where agnation was thought to be more than a metaphor, had decidedly weaker manifestations of *leff*ism (Hart: 1966a). Gellner found no trace of *ilfuf* (pl. of *leff*) in the Central High Atlas, and attributes that to hagiarchy – 'rule' by saints; on that count he wishes to exclude, on grounds of probability, all hagiarchic societies (cf. Vinogradoff, 1974b: 51-4).

There were thus some groups which did not have *leff* alliances or which had them in a 'weak' form; and they could not, therefore, have participated in the chequerboard Morocco-wide system suggested by Montagne. It is clear from Hart's work that even where tribes did have *leff* they did not always have extensive inter-tribal alliances. So the alliance between contiguous sections of the tribes Bani Bu Frah and Bani Gmil in the Rif, recorded by Blanco Izaga, did not involve all the members of each tribe but only those which faced each other across the border (Hart, 1958: 203). Similarly among the Aith Waryaghar of the Rif internal alliance groups were unbalanced and the weaker alliance drew support from more outsiders than the stronger one did (1954: 63). Even so, Hart says, the stronger alliance usually won the intra-tribal wars (1970). The Rifian tribes each had their own internal *ilfuf,* and in some cases the alliances crossed boundaries between tribes: not a big chequerboard but rather a series of little ones, with the possibility that some were partially connected.

Gellner raises a theoretical objection to Montagne's account of *ilfuf*: 'The two moieties can only maintain order with respect to conflicts at the level of segmentation at which the . . . alliance happens to be found' (1969: 66-7). Two significant points arise: the first is healthy scepticism about the peace-maintaining functions of *leff* systems. Do *ilfuf* really contribute to peace? The second is more technical and more answerable: how did *leff* divisions work when they did *not* bisect a particular segmentary section of a tribe? Imagine a tribe with a standard genealogicial segmentary system; suppose, now, that this segmentary system is bisected at the level of secondary sections by *leff* alliances, so that each secondary section belongs to one or other *leff*; Gellner's question is: what happens at other levels? Are there no ways of achieving peace there? 'If conflicts are contained at the levels other than those at which the *leff* is drawn up, then the *leff* is not essential at the one level where it does exist' (ibid.: 67). The evidence for the Rif, to which Gellner does not refer, suggests that there is no single answer to the logical problems which he perceives. In his article on Blanco Izaga, Hart includes a long footnote describing the several ways in which tribes were in fact divided (1958: 203, n. 44). (It should be remembered that Hart later repudiated part of this note – that part which is based on an assumption of equilibrium (1970: 42; see above, p. 113)). So in tribes with five primary sections *leff* alliance might divide them into 'three against two' (as the Igzimayen were divided); or into two against two, with the fifth primary section split in half (Waryaghar and Thimsaman); or each primary section might be split (Asht Tuzin), apparently at each level of segmentation. Tafarsith had only two primary sections and two *leff*s: each primary section was divided into two halves, each half allied with a half of the other primary section, and they were allied with *ilfuf* of neighbouring tribes. In the few tribes with four primary sections it seems that the *leff* system acted as a super-segmentary level (Hart, 1958: 203, n. 44). The range thus appears to be from the super-segment, in the case just cited, where *leff* alliance creates a level of segmentation higher than the genealogical charter allows for, to the case of the Asht Tuzin where every segment is split by the alliance of its members with one or other part of a corresponding opposed segment. In this case the *leff* alliances superimposed on a segmentary system constitute a counter-segmentary principle: in theory a man could turn either to his agnates for support, or to his *leff* allies at any level of segmentation.

That is an empirical answer to Gellner's 'theoretical' doubt: different groups had different arrangements. Vinogradoff's study of the Ait Ndhir (1974b) permits some elaboration of this complex picture: the Ait Ndhir, she says, were vague and flexible about their *leff* 'system'. How many clans were there? she asked; 'from above', they said, there were five; from below, it looked like ten. The ten clans each had one partner, usually occupying a different kind of territory, and bound to mutual assistance. The pairs were further grouped into 'halves' (each half being called Ait Omnasf – the 'people of the half') which corresponded very roughly to further territorial discrimination. These pairings were effective in intra-tribal warfare but were ignored when the conflict spread beyond the tribe. 'The Ait Ndhir', Vinogradoff remarks, 'seem to have operated in terms of the two models, segmentary and alliance . . . without suffering the strain and stress of the ethnologist who tends to view these systems as contradictory and incompatible' (ibid.: 54, 68-72). 'The "order" of this society . . . is riddled with contradictions, general amorphousness and overlapping units' (ibid.: 78): the Ait Ndhir were concerned to win when they were involved in conflicts, and used what institutional means lay to hand to gain allies. A somewhat similar point is made by Seddon (1973a: 121) who uses the theory of factions to present data on 'action-specific' and relatively impermanent alliances (see also Favret's reconstruction and fine analysis of Kabyle alliances (1968)).

It may be helpful to broaden the discussion slightly and to introduce here material presented by Peters (1960, 1967) which is discussed in greater detail in a later chapter (see pp.214-18). Peters describes the segmentary organisation of Bedouin in south-west Cyrenaica who, like the Waryaghar, occupy territory which is ecologically very diverse. The argument put forward by Peters is that the Sa'adi Bedouin are theoretically allies of their immediate neighbours: every injunction of agnation is to the effect that they owe greatest loyalty to the nearest groups. But because it is precisely their desert neighbours with whom they compete most for scarce resources the Sa'adi establish marriage alliances (i.e. repeated cross-cousin marriage between groups) with more remote agnates occupying ecological niches with rather different conditions. The Sa'adi in fact use these alliances not only for refuge in times of scarcity but also to conduct selective raids and attacks on their closer agnates. Peters's emphasis on the way in which sharing an ecological niche stimulates conflict, setting up a counter tendency to agnatic solidarity and demanding solidarity and alliance elsewhere, has proved extremely suggestive (e.g. Favret, 1968). It could explain the variability of the *leff* system and the range of forms which it takes; and it could also relate the two kinds of solidarity, *leff* and agnatic, in a way which has not yet been done.

So much for *democratie vecué*: segmentary systems and *leff* systems singly or together contain egalitarian tendencies which are not willed but which none the less militate against the creation of permanent political authorities. Gellner heads his discussion of segmentary systems with the epigram 'Divide that ye need not be ruled' (1969: 41); and Waterbury, discussing *leff* alliances, adds the necessary extension: '. . . systems of overlapping alliances . . . stifle or restrain actual conflict. . . . As E. A. Ross has remarked, such a society is "sewn together by its inner conflicts" '.

Consider now those institutions which do limit the establishment of permanent political officers, and which seem to be manifestly designed (as segmentation does not) to restrict the import of crude material differentiation on the exercise of power. It is necessary once again to emphasise that 'egalitarian' does not mean that men (and women and children) are in fact treated equally; but that there are institutions which limit the chances of any man or group becoming permanently dominant. Indeed, as Hart has stated (1958: 187):

> [Rifian headmen] also tend to be the wealthiest men in their communities, from a material standpoint, as well as being those most able to draw on the largest reservoir of manpower to support them in an argument or in a fight. . . . Thus, in the Rif as elsewhere, political organisation and the structure of power are inextricably intermeshed.

But it must be added that the terms on which a powerful and wealthy man can occupy a position of authority are extremely restrictive. So what are these institutions? They are rotation, complementarity, *initia,* hagiarchy and lotteries, and they are found singly and together, and may be combined with segmentary organisation.

Complementarity and rotation are concerned with the election of headmen or chiefs. They are best shown with the aid of an example (see Figure 1). The Ait 'Atta number about 150,000 people whose overall segmentary organisation can be described using no more than seven levels. This is quite standard, except for the existence of five primary segments above the level of tribe, and should be immediately recognised by any anthropologist. What is unusual is that some levels of segmentation (I, IV, VII) are represented by chiefs: the points of conjunction are offices. Complementarity and rotation refer to the method by which men are appointed to these offices. For example, the chief at level I is elected by men representing the five primary sections at level II; and right to the office rotates annually between these five sections, in a five-year cycle: so in year one the Ait Wahlim are elig-

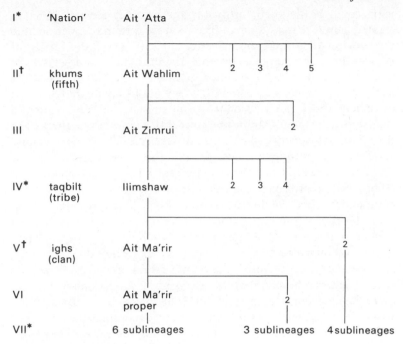

I*	'Nation'	Ait 'Atta
II†	khums (fifth)	Ait Wahlim	2 3 4 5
III		Ait Zimrui	2
IV*	taqbilt (tribe)	Ilimshaw	2 3 4
V†	ighs (clan)	Ait Ma'rir	2
VI		Ait Ma'rir proper	2
VII*		6 sublineages	3 sublineages 4 sublineages

*Chiefs hold office at this level
†Electors represent groupings at this level

Figure 1   To illustrate segmentation and election of chiefs of Ait'Atta, after D. M. Hart (1966a; 86-7)

ible, in year two, the members of the second fifth, and so on. This is rotation. Complementarity (discovered by Gellner) refers to the rule that when the Ait Wahlim are eligible they do not elect, and as eligibility rotates so does disbarment from voting. The principles of rotation and complementarity apply at all levels of segmentation at which elections are held. 'The mode of election is such as . . . to prevent the emergence of permanently dominant individuals or sub-groups' (Gellner, 1969: 82). The chiefs so elected tended to be 'lame ducks', in Gellner's phrase, because they were elected by their enemies, or at any rate not by their supporters, and the man they chose to rule over them would have, ideally, no more than the *minimum* requirements for carrying out his duties (cf. Berque, 1955: 107). A chief who was no good could be deposed forthwith, and another elected. What is created therefore is a system of provision for essential governmental services, on an annual and insecure basis, in which the functions become fewer and the power becomes less the higher the chief is in the hierarchy, even though the men appointed to the higher offices are likely to be personally egregious. It goes without saying that this is an extremely abbreviated account of the simplest of the systems of chiefship in the monographic literature. For example, the question of the relationship between chiefs at different levels is complex and variable: some informants have said that the higher chief ratifies the election of lower-level chiefs; some that he appoints them. Hart (1966a: 89) records one case where the top chief was elected in the manner described; he then appointed chiefs, his representatives, at every level of segmentation below him. That seems to indicate a greater concentration of power than is allowed for here, where lower-level men elect a chief to do things they cannot do themselves, and *thereby* create the higher level of segmentation. Hart may be optimistic when he says that the Ait 'Abdi of Koucer have 'far and away the most complex' system (1958: 88, n. 34. See Gellner, 1969: 100-4). Both Gellner and Hart remark that the complex formalities of such a system were not always realised. Vinogradoff, with her characteristic realism and good sense, provides ethnographic detail. The Ait Ndhir in theory had a council (*jmaa*) for the whole tribe, and in theory they elected a chief (*amghar*). But they often failed to complete the formalities and might then be taken short. So, in the 1930s some Ait Ndhir, fighting with the French, found themselves continually under attack from other Ait Ndhir. 'We got tired of this and all of us got together . . . and chose Hajj Alilou Boubimani to be our *amghar*. This then meant that all the other qaids [sub-chiefs] . . . became as if they were the [appointees] of the newly chosen *amghar*' (1974b: 66).

The principles of segmentation and of annual rotating complementary elections may be overlain by another: that of hagiarchy, by which authority is vested not in ordinary men but in marginal groups of saints. Hagiarchy is a fully Gellnerian locution: beware of assuming that the saints are unambiguously rulers. The root RBT, giving *mrabtin*, in Arabic connotes tiedness, obligation. So Peters (1968) can distinguish *mrabtin bi 'l baraka* (holy *mrabtin*) and *mrabtin as-saḍgān* ('*clients* of the fee' – tied to nobles), not to mention *mrabtin az zibal* (clients of the manure). It is not clear that the Berber *igurramen*, used of saints, could be used in analogous ways; but there is an inherent

118

ambiguity in the notions of patron and client, by which one is always liable to shade into the other (see below, p. 139, and also Mohsen, 1967: 222). Holy men of one kind or another (*shurfa* and marabouts) exist throughout the Maghreb; in some areas they perform the tasks of guaranteeing agreements and supervising elections and judicial processes. The fundamental point is that the saints perform essential governmental services and that they are outside the normal segmentary structure of the lay tribes. When segmentary laymen are unwilling to allow government to be held by one of their kind, it is an ingenious solution to get the tasks done nevertheless, but by marginal men.

There are thus three essential characteristics of saints: they should be set apart; they should have sanctions; they should be territorially interstitial – they should be on the spot where disputes between groups occur. *Igurramen* are said to be set apart by their possession of *baraka*, divine blessing, which is manifest in pious behaviour and is acquired, in the case of the Ihansalen studied by Gellner, by descent from Sidi Said Ahansal – that is to say, by inheritance. In fact Gellner argues that the two go together: a man who is so descended is latently an *agurram* (singular of *igurramen*), and if he so chooses may behave piously; the line of a man who behaves piously will in time acquire the appropriate genealogical links with Sidi Said Ahansal (below, pp. 202-5). Pious behaviour chiefly consists in generosity and pacifism: a saint is a man who gives blessings and who receives offerings in exchange, and therefore is able to be generous; he is also a man whose holiness is respected, so that men do not attack him, and therefore he can be a pacifist. A man who has both these qualities and who performs governmental tasks for important lay tribes is likely also to be known to perform miracles. What does a saint do? Gellner lists six overtly political tasks: the supervision of the election of chiefs (1969: 85-8); mediation of conflicts between groups; arbitration of disputes where a layman's decision proves unacceptable to one party (ibid.: 128-36); supervision of trials by collective oath (ibid.: 104-25; 1958, cf. Cozzi, 1910a: 673 for an Albanian case); the provision of sanctuary (ibid.: 136-7); and the re-location of persons displaced by conflicts within the tribal structure (ibid.: 62-3). To these he adds a number of latent functions: where occupation of lay office is so transitory, the saints provide continuity and guarantee trade and so on. Saints are able to do these things because they are set apart from local segmentary conflicts. They also have sanctions: the Ait 'Atta are the 'secular arm' of the Zawiya Ahansal saints and in the past could be called upon to be enforcers; the lay tribes, in short, might do for the saints what they were forbidden to do themselves, and which their spiritual sanctions alone might not achieve. The ability to invoke lay support reveals the ambiguity of the saints' relation to the lay tribes. On the one hand they were guarantors, supervisors, providers of sanctuary; on the other, they were protected men, who in theory received land from the lay tribes in return for their services. For this reason saints were established by their protector-clients on boundaries between groups where conflicts were most likely to occur: this is true not only of the main settlement of Ihansalen whose saints mediate between sedentary and transhumant sections of the Ait 'Atta, but of the 20-30 subsidiary lodges set up, by invitation, during the diaspora of saints. Indeed the Ait Haddidu, who 'employed' a small group of saints living 'in their midst' for internal purposes, also recognised and used other saintly lodges for their disputes with non-Haddidu groups (Gellner, 1969: 93). With this partial exception the power and continuity of Berber society in the Central High Atlas were located at the boundaries, vested in interstitial men of ambiguous status, pacifist and holy. So the lay Berber tribes of this region maintained egalitarian tendencies in three main ways: by segmentation, producing 'automatic' or mechanical tendencies towards egalitarianism, a *democratie vécue*; by complementary and rotating elections to chiefships as a result of which less and less authority was vested in each higher level of hierarchy; and by 'employing' or 'paying tribute' to saintly mediators who were disbarred from fighting. They thus created a state 'in which it is the subjects who have the monopoly of legitimate violence, and the rulers were *ex officio* excluded from employing force' (ibid.: 65).

This does not exhaust the list of egalitarian institutions described in the Maghreb. There remain two: the *initium* and the lottery. Berque's account of the Seksawa in the Western Atlas (1955) provides examples of both; and Freeman's account of Valdemora in Spain is the only European example of an institution which was once more widespread. The Seksawa in the Western Atlas were studied by Berque without benefit of Gellner and so far as the present topic is concerned (the elimination of inequality by rotation and complementarity) it must be admitted that his work presents details which are more tantalising than conclusive. Nevertheless, the Seksawa – a group of about 12,000 people of diverse origins (ibid.: 63; cf. Gellner, 1969: 40,

120

ñ. 2) – have a saintly shrine at Lalla Aziza, which is controlled by members of three lineages who perceive the revenues and offer sanctuary for the settlement of disputes by collective oath, negotiations between Seksawa and other groups, and perhaps for elections. In most villages what Berque calls the *initium* is vested, for different purposes and in different ways, in individuals and groups: *initium* is the right to initiate certain activities – irrigation, pasturing, warfare, cultivation, harvest. In one village (Targa Ufella) lots are drawn for the *initium* of irrigation; in others they are vested in a family of the descendants of the earliest occupants, and in still others in a descent group. In Agadir, the Ait Naçr initiate cultivation, the Ait Hammo initiate irrigation, and the Ait Naçr close the cycle by initiating harvest. In Wanz'id three groups divide the *initia* for cultivation, harvest and warfare. And in one other village with no *initia,* one group 'ensured success on military expeditions' (*'dispensaient le bon augure en matière d'expeditions militaires').* Berque says – and in the absence of detailed accounts of observation it is as difficult to agree as to disagree – that *initia* are usually vested in groups which have been longest established rather than in groups which are most powerful. The importance of *initia* also varies: they can involve whole populations in days of economic and ritual preparation; they can be almost cursory – almost, but not quite, for they are never simply an *'amusette folklorique'* (1955: 131-41). The Seksawa *initia,* with their ritual and organisational connotations, are related to the functions of chief (*imgharen*) in the Central Atlas: important directive tasks are vested in offices which are not necessarily or usually controlled by the most powerful groups but are distributed by lottery and by tradition. The chaotic variability of appointment reflects the diverse origins of the groups and their gradual conquest of the area over a period of ten or more generations, with oral traditions spanning up to six or seven centuries (e.g. Berque, 1955: 64).

The Seksawa groups are predominantly settled agriculturists spending some months each year on the high plateau to the east and south where they graze their animals. They grow mostly maize, barley, almonds, walnuts, fodder and – in the north – olives. These crops are grown both on dry fields and on irrigated land, terraced carefully in the valleys. Irrigated land is mostly owned by individuals who may possess up to fifteen or twenty scattered parcels of land of about 100-150 square metres each. Members of different descent groups often have adjoining land. Water, however, is often distributed by descent groupings, taking turns, and it is because it is difficult to match water rights with land, that there is such a 'flourishing, even excessive, virtuosity' (ibid.: 51) in the methods of distributing water.

It seems to be a prerequisite that irrigation should be done by turns: if there were enough water for all, there would probably be no need of irrigation. So, irrigation is done by time flow – so long here, so long there; and then back to the start again. The Seksawa have cycles of from seven to fifteen days depending on the size of the territory to be covered and the number of right-holding groups. There is, then, a given, technical, cycle of time which has to be matched against land and against social groupings which do not coincide with sub-divisions of land. Berque lists three main ways in which this matching is achieved (ibid.: 151-7). The first is what he calls *gentilice,* by descent group. Water is distributed in turn to all the land belonging to each *ikhs.* The individuals of the group have scattered land, so that this scheme 'ignores space' (ibid.: 153). It also ignores the variation in amount of land belonging to each group, and to individuals within it, for each groups gets its turn: on a twelve-day cycle at Tuz'urut, eleven days at Fensa, and so on. The order in which turns are made is settled by lottery. This method, in which 'topography counts for nothing' (ibid.: 155), Berque takes to be the oldest, and it is found only in the upper reaches of the valley. The second method is sluice-gate by sluice-gate: it ignores descent groupings, is considered 'decadent', and is explained by the abundance of water, or by referring to quarrels among descent groups in the past (cf. ibid.: 197-9). In the Ait Lh'sen area there are two sub-groups, Ait Mençur and Ait Dhaud, with intermingled holdings. They distribute water by descent group for the first three days of the week: one group gets water for thirty-six hours, then the other (and there is annual alternation of the first place in the order); and then sluice by sluice for the remaining four days. Finally, there is one group, the ait Abdella, where the irrigation controller (*ammazal*) decides which crops need water most, and distributes it accordingly. He comes always from a family said to be descended from the fourteenth-century 'kings' of Seksawa (ibid.: 157).

In Valdemora inequalities certainly exist (Freeman, 1970: 65-82, 147-74) but they are discounted whenever members of the village act together (xv):

Here is a Castilian hamlet where taking turns – or 'alternating' as it is called – is the order of the day, and where differences in class and wealth do not separate one family from another, where patronage plays no part in villagers' relations with each other, and relations between families are modelled on the ideal of relations between siblings.

Alternating is organised by the *adra,* here a house-order: irrigation turns succeed one another as the houses along the street; the duty to dig graves passes along the street (ibid.: 34); when only part of the men of the pueblo are required for communal labour they are selected by *adra* (ibid.: 36); the baker who fired the communal oven, the herdsmen who guarded the hamlet's animals, were sometimes selected by *adra* (ibid.: 38). When a job such as grave-digging has not been done for some time, and people have forgotten whose turn it is, then a lottery is held and a starting place determined: *adra* for different tasks rarely coincide. Communal office also rotates, but the order in which people are arranged is one of seniority of membership; the *alcade* (mayor), deputy mayor and the third councillor's post are held in practice by rotation (ibid.: 85). The fourth post, that of aide to the mayor (*alguacil*), is reserved for the youngest full member of Valdemora, and he holds it until he is displaced.

In the past, institutions of equality seem to have covered a wider area of activity: for example meat sharing was institutionalised, and even nowadays people who are members of the pueblo but not members of the same household do not eat together except when they *all* eat together (ibid.: 42, 46, 93). Although there are also other occasions when all members of particular sub-groups, such as young unmarried men, eat special foods together (ibid.: 94), these occasions are religious ones, so that there is a general association of common membership with religious celebration and commensality. These, too, are the days on which important business, such as repairs to communal property, checking the pasture accounts, organising the burial society, is done.

The sense of common, equal, membership is maintained partly because the community is small, partly because the boundaries are carefully maintained. Full membership of Valdemora is reserved to married adult farmers: when Freeman did her fieldwork in 1963 there were 10 of them, accounting with their households for 39 people. Another household head was a retired member and 6 others were children of members; finally, 10 were headed by people who though legally resident did not qualify for membership. The total population was 87 (ibid.: 30-1). The distinction between legal residents and full participants in the community is a local one, not a government one and it seems that it was accepted for the most part by excluded residents: they did not stand for office, for example, and seem not to have insisted on other rights which their legal status assured them and local custom denied them. Boundaries are carefully maintained in other ways: the members are usually scrupulous to avoid any communal action which would affect the management of family estates; and when moves were made to start co-operative communal ownership of farm machinery the feeling was such that no vote was ever put (ibid.: 159-61). So, the 'equality' of the participants in communal affairs is maintained by excluding from communal affairs the chief area of life in which the members are unequal – their farming. There are other, perhaps more symbolic ways, in which unity, community, is expressed: suitors for Valdemora girls are subjected to rough treatment, and they have to pay a fine if they marry one (ibid.: 59-60), even though the population was so small that virtually all Valdemorans, men and women, marry people from other villages. All members use the same public fountain for drinking-water and for washing: although there are privately owned sources they are not used (ibid.: 87-8). Valdemorans thus make a conscious effort to achieve political unity and equality: no member ever employs another; no member ever eats with another except on formal occasions at which the unity of the village is celebrated. Non-farmers are excluded from full membership although they may by grace enjoy some of the benefits (ibid.: 62). Offices, tasks, advantages are allocated by lottery or rota. Farming – from which differences in wealth are principally derived – is excluded from the arena of public business (cf. Freeman, 1968a: 478). Indeed, all relationships which could create stratification are made with people outside Valdemora: extra labour is brought in from other villages; networks of kinship and friendship, by which Valdemorans gain advantage, radiate from the village but apparently have no mesh there. The only person whom Freeman is prepared to call an intermediary is the station restaurant manager – a semi-outsider who uses his wide acquaintance among engine drivers to get parcels and messages passed along the line. Freeman is particularly struck by political equality in Valdemora, and by the way Valdemorans strive to eliminate the consequences of inequality in wealth: it is on that effort that she mostly concentrates. The book would perhaps be stronger if efforts to become less equal were given as much emphasis: if she did not describe Valdemora quite so much as an isolated community: 'Five kilometers between two European villages have been from the point of view of social anthropological comparison, longer than five kilometers in most other parts of the world' (Freeman, 1973: 745). The use of kinship and friendship outside Valdemora is merely hinted at; patterns of marriage, she says, cause surnames to move slowly across the countryside of the Sierra Ministra like shadows of clouds which take two centuries to pass: these are described in some detail, while the way affinity is used to recruit labour is but briefly mentioned. There is no account of the real differences in wealth among the villagers. So, while Freeman's admiration for the Valdemorans' achievement in eliminating inequality in political matters is undoubtedly contagious, her readers may find that their resistance would be even lower if fuller information were provided about the realities of inequality which are so pertinaciously excluded from pueblo life. That is the only account of a European community in which there are institutions of equality.

This review of egalitarian institutions appropriately ends a chapter on stratification. The unequal distribution of crude material resources is universal in the mediterranean; and access to power and influence is never evenly distributed throughout the populations. In most societies the material differences are socially legitimated, are recognised bases for political action, though the ways in which they are socially construed are themselves varied. In some societies there are institutions by which men have made attempts to eliminate them, to destroy them socially and to deny their legitimacy, and these are quite properly singled out with the epithet 'egalitarian'. It is absolutely true that wealthy men, able to command a following, have more power than the poor, the female and the infantile: as Hart remarks, any Ait 'Atta can become top chief in much the same way as Any American Can Become President (1966b: 85) – but he still calls the Ait 'Atta 'remarkably egalitarian'. The point is that there are institutional means of preventing any one person or group from acquiring permanent domination over others – segmentation, complementarity and rotating elections, hagiarchy, lottery, *initia* – all these tend to destroy crude material differences.

Stratification

Appendices to chapter 3

1   *On points of terminology: 'prestige' and 'honour' (see p. 97)*

The reader is warned that Campbell and Lison-Tolosana use the terms prestige and honour rather differently. For Campbell honour is the prime social virtue, giving mere prestige that extra something which makes it unequivocal. In Lison-Tolosana, prestige is the culminating social classifier, and is composed of honour, intellectual ability and age. The last two are not discussed here. P. Schneider (1969) considers this an empirical matter: his ability to distinguish social honour and personal integrity in Sicily allows him to make a contrast with Spain.

2   *On the critique of French ethnography in the Maghreb*

In recent years a number of scholars of whom the most notable is Burke (1973) have shown the coincidence of French interest and romanticism with the common ethnographic distinctions between Siba and Makhzen and between Arab and Berber. Burke's work seems chiefly concerned with the history of these ideas. The consequences which such a revision might have for ethnography are apparent in Vinogradoff (1974b: 5-13; 63-4, etc.).

4

Politics

I   The relation between modes of representation

The last chapter was concerned with forms of stratification. This
chapter is concerned with modes or forms of representation: for the
most part, given the preoccupations of the ethnographers, it is therefore concerned with patronage (the settlement of dispute and violence are treated in the appendices to this chapter).

It is of course, as remarked earlier, a violation of the realities of
other people's lives, to separate, as distinct entities, the ways in which
people subordinate others or dominate them, from the ways in which
they try to secure their own interests. For on the one hand any particular political decision-making system must create or modify a ranking system; while changes in an actual system of stratification must
eventually affect the way in which political decisions are made: there
is dynamic interaction between stratification and representation. On
the other hand, a person who lives his politics in a community does not
make the distinctions which analysts may make: to him, it is enough
to know that he is a citizen of Italy or Yugoslavia or Libya, and certain
consequences for action will follow. To be a member of this or that
social class is to have a course of action already planned and set out.
To be a man of greater or lesser honour than the others already defines
certain important aspects of the relations between them, and
identifies the ways in which one man may get his interests taken into
account by another. The analytical distinction of stratification from
action is thus false to their historical interdependence, and to the
experience of the men and women who manipulate the systems
anthropologists describe.

To use categories of analysis which do not coincide with categories of experience may be justified when it meets short-term needs. In the present case the need is to separate, first of all, the various institutional components of mediterranean political systems. That is partly for purposes of comparison (because it is easier to compare the workings of component parts than it is to compare the subtle and complex 'total pictures' which anthropologists have occasionally succeeded in producing); and it is partly for didactic purposes: some colleagues, for example, have spoken of patronage as if it were a sub-section of bureaucracy – as if all that would be said about patronage could be said under the heading 'corruption'. In southern Italy it was quite common to hear local politicians speak of patronage as if all that needed to be said about it could come under the heading 'blackleg' or 'false-consciousness'. In order to combat these misapprehensions, and to open the way for future ethnographers to create a status for patronage equal to that of class struggle, equal to civil service administration, fundamental distinctions were made in the last chapter. There, the argument was that differences in the distribution of crude material resources within a political community could be either destroyed or construed. Broadly speaking there are three ways in which mediterranean men have construed them; bureaucracy, class, honour. It is now argued that each of those idioms of stratification carries with it a mode of representation: vindication of rights, class struggle, patronage. Probably in all, certainly in the northern, communities these three modes of representation co-exist. Patronage is the dominant mode in many communities and, theoretically, there is no reason why the entire political life of a community should not be subsumed under patronage. Similarly with class – though it does not seem likely that any community's politics are ever completely organised in terms of class. Finally, the extent to which men can achieve representation of their interests by claiming a citizen's rights from a bureaucracy is always likely to be much less than it is through any other mode, but in some communities it is undoubtedly *one* way which is open to them.

There are two fundamental points, then: one is that the mix of these three modes is a variable; the other is that when two or more modes coexist, men in effect have two or more modes of representation open to them. To some extent they will use one or the other according to a social classification: it is recognised that (say) jobs are most likely got through patronage than through a labour exchange; while a pension can be extracted from a bureaucracy through patronage or by presenting a request in due form – but not by organising a strike or creating a party.

Finally, note that these three modes affect each other: it is quite clear that patronage in a corporate state exhibits characteristics which are quite different from those in a democratic or state capitalist one. It is quite clear that the dynamics of the relations between the modes varies according to the resources available to the state. For example, it is argued below that a state such as Italy is unlikely to become a class-dominated one – there is such great national wealth that nascent class modes can be averted by that mixture of bureaucracy and patronage which Weingrod and Silverman characterise as state patronage. In Morocco, on the other hand, Waterbury argues that the state is too poor to be able to maintain an effective patrimonial system, and that the monarchy will eventually be forced to come to terms with a strong class movement. The value of such arguments is not the predictions they can contain (the schema of analysis is always too simple) but in the practice of examining the component parts of a political system and their interrelations.

II Class action

The difficulties of speaking about class stratification in the mediterranean were sketched in the last chapter: quite apart from the usual lack of ethnographic evidence, the phenomenon itself is extremely variable: class symbols can occur in local communities almost without awareness of their metropolitan significance; class action can occur without any enduring class ideology. Turning to the use of class as a mode of representation it is clear that there is a similar range: it is possible to do no more than list and annotate the few sources.

Cutileiro describing two major class movements in Vila Velha: in 1910 some labourers united to try to get wage increases. They got promises which were not kept, and organised a strike: 'elderly people still remember that when it became known that the strike was on its way everyone in the village shut himself up at home because its exact nature was not understood'. The leaders were imprisoned. The next manifestation of class solidarity in Vila Velha occurred fifty-two years later, when strike action was taken against piecework in agriculture and to achieve an eight-hour day. The demands were at first rejected, then granted in 1963, after the solidarity of the magnates had collapsed. In both these instances there were similar movements outside

Vila Velha, and Cutileiro suggests that that explains why Vila Velhans took action in those years rather than any others. In neither case
was there any kind of organisation which survived the action itself; in
neither case were there demands for changes in the distribution of
property. 'Civil peace and order are . . . maintained, but do not result
from an historical evolution of mutual concessions made between
landowners and labourers' (1971: 86-90).

The only other writer to discuss class action at any length is Khalaf.
He did an analysis of 7,536 Lebanese labour disputes brought to
government conciliation panels. More than half were brought by
employers; about 7 per cent by *ad hoc* groups of workers; about 4 per
cent by labour unions. The rest were complaints by individual workers. It may be that such panels were not highly regarded by the
unions; but Khalaf also analysed 66 strikes in the twelve months from
July 1960. Not one strike was concerned with unionisation or with
bargaining procedures, and nearly one-third of them ended when an
agreement was reached to set up a committee to look at the issues in
more detail. Strikes, he concludes, are not a test of strength at the end
of long bargaining, for there is no bargaining; they are, rather, de-
monstrations of protest, which, since there is an over-supply of
labour, are not taken particularly seriously by employers.

The same indeterminacy of aims and of organisation is apparent in
the few detailed accounts of elections which ethnographers have
provided. In Bailey's description of a local election in Losa the main
political theme is the credentials of the candidates and their ability to
secure patronage benefits from the outside world (see pp. 153-7) – a
theme which is also apparent in some sketchier accounts of Italian
local elections and electoral behaviour (e.g. Boissevain, 1966b; Davis,
1973: ch. 9). To some extent the Moroccan election to an agricultural
management committee described by Rosen (1972) can also be seen
in this light: two candidates contested the election, one a local man,
the other also local but having support from the national cadres.
Rosen points out that the kinds of relationship invoked to secure votes
were extremely diffuse: economic indebtedness, kinship, neighbourhood, common membership of a religious brotherhood and – most
spectacularly – the act of submission made by one of the candidates
who sacrificed a sheep to his electorate, thereby compelling them on
pain of supernatural sanctions to give him what he wanted. The can-
didate with central support lost the election and at first the national
authorities comtemplated giving support to his attempt to have the

election declared invalid. What they eventually did, however, was to strip the office of its functions and to re-locate them within the appointed, non-elective, administration. Such a tactic does not seem possible in Italy – although it has been known for the state's discretionary relief funds to dry up when a local administration of the wrong colour is elected.

The relation of political action of a kind normally taken to express class interest (party organisation, voting by class interest, strikes, occupations of land) to other modes of political behaviour is generally cursorily treated by mediterranean ethnographers. In Boissevain's work, for example, it is possible to read interpretations of voting statistics which apparently assume that people vote for their class interest, but when they do not that is because they have been duped and led to a false consciousness by their masters. If there were more information it might be possible to argue rather differently, to the effect that men, even ignorant peasants in the most backward community, are more or less aware of what they do. Start with that assumption, and then see whether or not it is possible, empirically, to sustain it. Are people aware or not of the systematic nature of patronage? Do they distinguish it from electoral politics and political ideologies? Do they contrast bureaucracy and party politics with patronage in their ideal forms? What do they say these ideal forms are? How do they account for any discrepancy between the ideal forms and the actual ones? Have informants approached (say) the state bureaucracy through their patronage connections? Have they used their party membership to extract their 'rights' from the administration? How do they perceive any areas of overlap between these forms? All these questions could be asked, and will give rise to others: it will undoubtedly be possible to distinguish various levels of utopianism in men's accounts of the ideal forms of bureaucracy and party and it may be possible to suggest explanations for these. The ethnographer, too, may care to examine the validity of the reasons given for discrepancies between the ideal and the actual, and for the overlap and mutual penetration of these forms of representation; he may find that he needs to include other forms, or that he can exclude one or more of those sketched here. But at least he will begin to break down the seamless web of community politics, to locate his subtleties where they belong – in the reality of human experience – rather than in the rarefactions of analysis, and will begin to produce accounts of political activity which contain rather fewer assumptions, and which are comparable with others. That said, and with hope for empirically based analysis in the future, it is best to turn quickly to the one political subject on which ethnographers have produced plenty of material – patronage.

III Patronage

All political representation is concerned with the control and use of power, and the ways in which it is controlled and used depend necessarily on the ways in which the crude material bases of power are cloaked, softened, converted to moral agreement, transformed into social facts. When a weak man is confronted by a strong man he can ally with other weak men, and together they may overcome. When a strong man sets up an administration he allows what may be called legitimate representations to be made to him, while he also creates, through his local delegates, new sources of power – legitimate power – in local communities. It is to the third possibility that this section is devoted: confronted with a stronger man the weak may adopt a posture of deference, may give way, and then salvage what he can by exerting moral pressure – the pressures of acceptance, deference, friendliness, of godparenthood even – to try to control the prepotence of his acknowledged superior.[1] Patronage thus occurs whenever men adopt a posture of deference to those more powerful than they and gain access to resources as a result. It is associated with honour because honour is a moral code in which rich and poor are ranked and in which their interdependence is emphasised as in no other idiom of stratification; because the language of honour is that used by the weak to mitigate the consequences of their helplessness in this relationship; and because honour aids choice: it is at least potentially an absolute differentiator; and a patron, choosing among several would-be clients, chooses the more honourable. It is in this way that honour is an allocator of resources, and creates conflict among those 'equals' who struggle for a livelihood.

This use of patronage contrasts with that adopted by Peters. who has used the word in a much more restrictive sense: discussing the various kinds of status which he has excluded from his account of patronage in Cyrenaica Peters concludes (1968: 186):

> I will readily admit that the various statuses have common forms of relationships. Dependence is one form they have in common, and protection another. But dependence of one sort or another

occurs in practically all sets of social relationships, and therefore lacks all discriminatory usefulness . . . . To place many disparate statuses in one category leads to confusion and misses the sociological significance in them all.

What Peters selects to be the identifying characteristics is first that there should be genealogical differentiation of patrons from clients: the tied never have a free man in their genealogy, however far back they may trace it. Second, that patrons should be the legal representatives of their clients – clients should have no legal personality when they are tied to a patron: if a client kills a man in another section, it is his patrons who are liable to reprisals or to make composition.

This identification is derived from Fustel de Coulanges and adopts criteria thought by that writer to describe patronage in classical times (nd: 224-8). Peters does not include *all* Fustel's identifying characteristics: he leaves out, for example, the inability of clients to make sacrifices, in which Fustel saw the inferiority of clients most clearly expressed. It may be that the more recent exploration of the topic by Badian (1958) is now a better guide to a definition – if indeed a formal definition is to be derived from the ethnography of ancient societies. Badian's account of relations of corporate Rome and of individual Romans with Italian and other (African, Balkan, Spanish) corporate and individual clients could indeed serve as a model of the contemporary politics of community-nation relationships, most happily for Italian cases, but for other northern littoral countries too. True, patrons were possessed of an important resource – Roman citizenship. True, client status was successible (ibid: 4). But it would be mistaken to think of a Roman's clients in Sicily, say, as dominated by their client status: they were able to become clients because they were important men in their own land; and they might have more than one patron to represent their interests at the capital (ibid.: 155, n. 1.). Moreover, contractual clientage (ibid.: 2, 4-10) was not inconsistent with being or having a (Roman) *pater,* which Fustel de Coulanges takes as the main genealogical qualification of patrons. Finally, emancipation often followed the probationary period of corporate clientage of a defeated or annexed Latin town: the inhabitants then became citizens, voters able to hold office (ibid.: 18-9). The austere formalism of Peters's definition thus excludes some of the most important kinds of Roman patronage, although of course manumitted slaves, clients who succeeded to their status, and perhaps those who applied for client status from gratitude for benefits received in time of need (ibid.: 8-9), would fall within Peters's definition. Austerity and formality are admirable characteristics but should not be pursued at all costs: Peters would exclude perhaps half the ancient patronage on which he ostensibly bases his definition, and might find that Cyrenaican Bedouin alone provide a contemporary example. His point that dependence and protection are features of most social relationships is well taken; but if the only formal barrier he can erect to exclude (say) conjugal relationships from the category of patronage also excludes everything else except Sa'adi patrons, then he might be charged with placing too much faith in formalism, too little in common sense. This is not merely a verbal quibble: while it would be relatively easy to find another word for relationships of political and economic dependence in which clients retain their legal personality, any categorisation which separates into different kinds those various *political relationships in which inferiority is accepted and then defended by moral suasion* – any such categorisation does a disservice to the comparative study of mediterranean political systems.

So, it is argued here that patronage is a *sui generis* political form. Its essence is an acepted act of submission involving a superior and an inferior. Its purpose is usually to acquire access to resources. In the mediterranean it usually co-exists with other forms, and is influenced by them: that is to say that while the content of patronage varies, naturally enough, with the kinds of resources which are at stake, it varies, too, with the general political context in which it exists. It can be shown to be different in fascist states and in democratic ones. It is probably the case that whether the bureaucracy is Roman-law based or Islamic also affects the content of patronage.

Most patronage in the mediterranean involves individuals. There is one well-documented case in which patrons are a corporate group, and there are hints of others. There is no known case in which clients are a corporate group, but the possibility should not be excluded. On the northern shore, however, the pattern is usually one in which an individual client contracts with an individual patron. Moreover there is, with the absence of descent grouping, an absence of the ascription of status: there are no groups from which patrons are drawn exclusively, nor none of clients. Characteristically, men are clients to those above them, while at the same time they patronise their inferiors. Hence the phenomenon, which has drawn a lot of attention, of chains of patronage and of networks of influence.

Patronage is sometimes said to 'be' an extension of friendship or kinship or of some spiritual relation. It is none of these. Rather, it is the ways in which the autocracy of local magnates is controlled by the weak. The study of mediterranean patronage thus reveals a series of checks imposed by clients on their patrons' use of power: it may be friendship, or real or fictitious kinship, or spiritual kinship. In some communities all of these are available to clients; in others, some may be conventionally excluded; in a couple of cases (pp. 142, 146) no moral restraints are available to check the rapacity of the powerful. This is an expansion of Bailey's point: '. . . it is the supplicant who seeks to make the relationship diffuse: to make it a moral relationship . . . because it is in his interest to do so' (1966: 395).

This brief sketch is intended to guide the reader through the rather complex passages which follow. For it is distressing to have to reveal, again, that anthropologists have not been very thorough in their study of mediterranean patronage; nor have they been sufficiently imbued with comparative intent. Relationships of patronage are recognised to be extremely common and few books about the northern shore fail to mention the subject (these few include Cronin (1970) – where the term appears in the index but not in the text: it is not absolutely clear that the concept is discussed in the text – and Broegger (1971)). While the southern littoral has its documented examples, while there is a growing theoretical literature, none the less there is a dearth of detailed cases. Authors may say patronage is important, but are recusant in the face of their plain duty to record examples. Making due allowance for Weingrod's historical account of the development of state patronage in Sardinia (1967-8) and Blok's almost simultaneous (1969c) attempt to do the same thing on a wider, *welthistorische,* scale, nevertheless *no monograph exists,* not a single one, in which the author has said that the patrons and clients he studied differ in this or that way from those studied by someone else (but see Colclough, 1970). At best, and with the exception of Campbell (1968 – see below, p. 145), the reader is given cursory examples of little value (e.g. Boissevain, 1966a; Davis, 1969a) for making those distinctions which are essential for identifying the range of phenomena. The task is itself crucial.

The one well-documented example of a case where clients attach themselves to corporate groups is Peters's description of the Bedouin of south-west Cyrenaica (1968). All are sheep and camel herders, owning their herds; but one category, the Sa'adi noblemen, claim ownership of all land and water. The rest of the herding population is called generically *mrabtin as-saḍgān,* clients of the fee, and in theory they have access to land and water only when it is conceded to them by collective decision of a Sa'adi tribal section: the concession is annually renewed and may be revoked. In fact a large minority of *mrabtin as-saḍgān,* estimated in the 1920s at 40 per cent, have land and water which they control; and although they acknowledge client status they have a segmentary organisation like the Sa'adi, would defend their territory against them, and are *de facto* independent: Peters does not say so, but it is unlikely that they perform services for the Sa'adi. The rest of the mrabtin have no territory; they are dispersed in groups of from three to six tents which are attached by negotiation to Sa'adi tribal sections. When they are attached they are treated as creatures of their patrons: they may be involved in feuds, but only as agents, for it is the Sa'adi who are responsible for the mrabtin's actions. Clients are liable to make contributions to blood-wealth, to wedding and funeral expenses, and to occasional arbitary levies of grain and wool; but although these liabilities check clients' accumulation of movable wealth Peters argues that their exclusion from political activity depends rather from their lack of real estate – 'the core of the distinction is in property rights' (ibid.: 175). Sa'adi get their political strength from weight of numbers, among other things, and it is quicker to acquire a following by granting water rights than by the chancy venture of procreation. Moreover, water rights can be withdrawn, allowing the owners to match their numbers to the supply. Groups with no water rights cannot acquire clients; groups without clients cannot discard members when the rain fails to fall (ibid.: 185). Peters says little about the relations of the dispersed client families with the tribes of formal client status from which they have presumably been detached by water pressure. But he allows his readers to think that these segmentary groups are in process of becoming Sa'adi – a process, familiar from non-mediterranean literature, by which people who have acquired the 'secondary' characteristics of dominance (territory, water, segmentary organisation) gradually acquire the proper genealogical credentials (see also Gellner, 1969).

The decision to allow mrabtin access to water depends partly on what other needs a Sa'adi group may have to meet: for example matrilateral kinsmen have a prior claim. A Sa'adi group, too, may have no particular political ambitions, or may have sufficient strength to do without clients. The demographic characteristics of prospective clients are also considered: a Sa'adi group may require men rather than herds, or vice versa. Although the mrabtin may thus seem to be in a precarious position they are not obviously in an inferior one: Peters says that they lack precedence on formal occasions, but are otherwise indistinguishable from their patrons in daily life, and the association is less variable than the rainfall. A very few mrabtin – usually the most isolated individuals – marry women from their host groups and their descendants thus acquire matrilateral status. Peters mentions, but does not discuss, other kinds of dependence which he is unwilling to call patronage (1968: 168, 186, and see above, pp. 132-3). One of these is between Sa'adi and *mrabtin bi 'l baraka,* holy men granted resources for spiritual services. The somewhat similar acquisitions of land by Berber *igurramen* lineages in the High Central Atlas described by Gellner (1969) and discussed above (p. 119) do not create relationships which could reasonably be described as dependence. What Berque describes as *patronnage des Saints* (1955: 268-79) would perhaps no longer be called patronage. Maunier is resonantly inexplicit about the protection afforded by tribal groups to travelling traders in the Maghreb at an unspecified period (1937: 39-40). Lineton discusses the relationship of Niklian aristocratic clans to Achamnomeri immigrants in Mani before 1750, but has only scanty evidence to work with (1971: 186s, 231, 245ss), and that material is not mentioned by other writers on Mani (Andromedas, 1968; Mirambel, 1943). Eberhard (1953a, 1953b) describes the relationship between newly settled nomadic transhumant tribal leaders and their followers in South East Turkey as 'feudal' but does not explore the possibility that the dependent groups retained corporate identity. Gilsenan (1973a), on the other hand, does suggest corporate dependence, but is not concerned with patronage. Albanian material is usually of too early a date to consider the topic. In general it seems sensible to look for corporate patrons or (more rarely) corporate clients in those mediterranean societies with unilineal descent groups. In bilateral societies commercial and state corporations are sometimes said to exercise patronage but what is usually meant is that individuals within them may contract with individuals outside them – as indeed, individual Sa'adi may contract with individuals among their matrilateral kin, using corporately owned resources to establish relations of personal support and dependence (Peters, 1968: 176, 183).

Sa'adi patronage happily provides a general model, for it exhibits essential characteristics while lacking the more confusing complexities of the other examples from the mediterranean. The relationship is contractual. People agree and negotiate the relationship, perhaps more explicitly in Cyrenaica than in Portugal, Italy, Greece, where the assumption of client status is tacit. For example, Campbell describes the way in which important Sarakatsani can get credit from shopkeepers or cheese-merchants or can establish friendships with officials in their winter-pasture villages and can thus acquire help and influence (1964: ch. 9). But even when there is an explicit contract to sell milk there is no explicit contract to become a patron or client: the distinction between a would-be supplicant client and an actual one is shrouded in the ambiguity of a relationship gradually established by trial and error. The contract exists but there is no point at which a client is told, 'Tomorrow you make take up your rights and duties.'

The relationship is also dynamic. Sa'adi may give their daughters and sisters to *mrabtin as-saḍgān,* thus reducing the distance between the parties and making the tie more stable. This phenomenon is nearly universal in the mediterranean and appears to occur much more frequently on the northern shore than on the southern. A passage from patronage to friendship to some kind of kinship is reported by every student of the matter. Campbell is the only writer, however, to point out that some kinds of patron – those whose resource consists in market knowledge used on behalf of producer clients – are more reluctant than others to permit the closer intimacies (1968, especially). Once it is said, it is obvious that the distance-reducing dynamic is variable; but it is not a point which has been much studied.

The relationship is associated with the control of resources: of land and water, as in the case of the Sa'adi; of land which is rented, sharecropped, worked under management in Portugal, Spain, Italy. State resources controlled by elected politicians or by government officers are another source of patronage. Campbell adds market skills possessed by cheese-merchants in Zagori, by fruit and vegetable wholesalers in Athens, which may induce shepherds and market-gardeners to contract dependence (1968).

The common characteristic of patronage systems which the Sa'adi and *mrabtin as-saḍgān* do not exhibit is the free contract. In that part of Cyrenaica potential patrons and potential clients are identified by the status they occupy. True, any Sa'adi section can contract with any mrabtin family group but the mrabtin are always clients and the Sa'adi are always patrons. On the northern shore, however, any man may patronise any man who is prepared to accept client status: the status itself is contracted and clients may have lesser clients whom they patronise. The exhaustive classification of the population in Cyrenaica is obviously related to the existence of corporate descent groups, and to the genealogical or legal fiction that all crucial resources are owned by one category. Bailey (1971c) and Colclough (1971) describe communities in Italy in which the population is divided by a relatively impermeable boundary into gentry and others, and such social distinctions are found in other northern communities; but it is not the case that this distinction coincides with that between the property-owning and the propertyless, nor with that between patrons and clients. In most of the mediterranean, property is unevenly distributed more or less throughout the population. Moreover, what resources are crucial to any category of the population may vary with its economic position, with the consequence that all the way along the economic scale the poorer are dependent on the richer.

As Peters describes them the Sa'adi can never be clients nor can mrabtin ever be patrons. It seems likely that if mrabtin do acquire undisputed title to land and water, they will also acquire the requisite genealogical credentials. But where patron and client are not ascribed statuses, it is possible for a single individual to be a patron to one man, client to another. That possibility makes patronage systems more complex when there is a series of dependencies, as there is when the population is gradually stratified. So, there can be chains of patronage, linking a pure patron at one end, a pure client at the other, and with intervening men who are both patron and client. But, since patrons usually have more than one client (as the Sa'adi do not, all the clients of a particular tribal section come from the same family) the chain may be thought of as having several branching chains. Further, in diversified societies, with different kinds of scarce resource controlled by different individuals or officers a man may have several patrons: the chain becomes, in this case a network, with multiple interlinkages. This is clearly more complex than the Bedouin example, but it is not an essential difference.

Some idea of this complexity may be got from the examples of patronage at work given by Boissevain from his research in Sicily (1966a). More importantly, Boissevain's accounts give useful information which is a starting point for the comparative analysis of patronage. A student needing permission to get his thesis accepted after the closing date used intermediaries to obtain an introduction to the appropriate professor: he promised to help the professor's electoral campaign and in return his thesis was accepted and he passed his examination. This case involved an initial approach by the student to a lawyer who was indebted to the student, and who provided him with the first of a series of four introductions. (This example is also used in (1966b) and in (1969b) where further details are included, and where the whole is given a different theoretical framework. Boissevain's most recent use of this data is in 1974: 150-3). The second example is of an older man who wanted a job in his town's council offices. The appointment was approved by the town council but had to be confirmed by a provincial committee. In order to secure confirmation the man applied to his commanding officer from army days, and to a lawyer: these two applied 'pressure' (1966a: 27) to the members of the provincial committee, and the man got his job. In the third example a school teacher suspected his colleague of giving his son low marks: the son would thus fail to qualify for university entrance, and the school teacher's family's prestige would fall. He was able to discover that his colleague had applied pressure on 'an important decision-maker' to exclude the son from university, and was able to apply counter-pressure from a still more powerful source, leading the decision-maker to change his mind (ibid.: 28, and see also 1974: 159-60). All these examples involve chains or networks.

The empirical context in which Boissevain places them is composed as follows. The electoral system of proportional representation first, tends to create near-equality between parties at local and regional levels: 'small parties and factions began to play a role out of proportion to their numerical strength' because the larger parties needed support in their struggle to defeat each other (1966b: 228). Electoral support and voting support in councils thus acquire exceptional value and electors or men who can control electors are correspondingly important. Small parties and factions are similarly able to drive hard bargains by offering or threatening to switch their support. The argument is that the needs of politicians in a particular political system compel them to enter the arena of patronage. They are *able* to do this because of another ingredient of context, which Boissevain discusses under the heading 'maladministration' (ibid.: 231-3). This refers to the possibilities created by 'the lack of tight control over the town's government' (ibid.: 232): the argument is that were the checks on municipal administration stronger the politicians would not be able to do what they do do with it: between 1958 and 1963, twenty-one new posts were created to accommodate the clients of important patrons, increasing the establishment by 50 per cent. In the same period the debt of the municipality of Leone increased by 1,000 per cent, from 30m. Lire to 310m. Lire, and that was partly the consequence of the inability of a weak administration to collect taxes from a changeable electorate. The almost perfect equilibrium of this particular mixture of patronage, party and bureaucracy is illustrated by Boissevain's final discussion of the reasons politicians do not use their positions to secure development funds for their towns. Because bureaucracy is weak, decisions are made slowly as conflicting pressures are resolved. Because proportional representation creates weak coalitions no politician can be sure that he will be in power when funds eventually come through. But if he is replaced by an opponent or rival, that man will be able to use the funds to extend his clientele and to secure his electoral position. Because votes can be secured by patronage, therefore, no politician is prepared to use his position to provide the means of patronage to his rivals.

This example illustrates the interaction of particular kinds of party and bureaucracy, and to some extent makes the content of patronage relationships in Leone intelligible. In Portugal the state is of a different kind, there is only one party with any weight in the rural areas, and patronage, too, has a different aspect. Cutileiro (1971) describes Vila Velha, an administrative agglomeration of scattered settlements in the grain-growing 'mediterranean' area of Portugal: it had a population of just under 1,600 in 1966. Apart from forty men who work in a paper mill, the population is to all intents dependent on agriculture. The majority of inhabitants have also been dependent on landowners for supplements to their own resources. At the turn of the century magnates were in electoral competition with each other and to secure votes they used their resources lavishly: in addition to supplying land for sharecropping (which they still do) they paid indemnities to obtain their supporters' children's release from military service, they gave away houses and garden-plots (1971: 214-22). But the consolidation of the Portuguese corporate state after 1926 had assured the magnates' local domination by the 1960s at least, and Cutileiro's ethnography does not emphasise competition between magnates. In Milocca the period following the creation of a fascist state was one in which factions struggled to get control of local party organisation: the motherland was suddenly found to have only one teat, and her children fought over who should sell the milk (Gower

Chapman, 1973: 5-10). But in Vila Velha the magnates were able to prevent changes which might diminish the dependence of the peasantry: they resisted irrigation and emigration; they checked the spread of schools and prevented the establishment of factories (ibid.: 189-200). When estates changed hands the new owner could turn his predecessor's sharecroppers off the land without fear of the electoral consequences. Powerful men used their position to exact a moral conformity from their clients – constraining them to attend church, to abandon mistresses – and had little need of political support, except when large numbers of signatures were required in expressions of loyal gratitude to the state. Cutileiro makes the point that patronage usually implies that some bargaining power remains in the hands of the client: in Portugal this was not so – the patron is not concerned to gain anything from his clients. Before the 1926 revolution some groups of individuals had had some power: by the 1960s they had none (1971: 221-2).

To compare Vila Velha with Boissevain's Leone is to realise the importance of political and state context. It is probably the case that agricultural contracts in Leone are less clearly exploitive than they are in Vila Velha (see above, p. 52) for, although Boissevain gives no details, the sources of patronage in Leone seem to exist in greater number, which may give clients a greater power. In the corporative state patronage is unmixed with party politics, and with class representations. In Italy, where there is elected multi-party government at all levels of the administrative system from municipality to parliament, political support is an important good which can be exchanged within the patronage system. Often enough, in Italy, the services which a patron provides 'are citizenship rights to which the client is anyway entitled' (Colclough, 1970), but the distribution of social goods is much greater in Italy, even in Leone, than in Vila Velha: there are schools, dispensaries, public works, factories; the magnates of Vila Velha were able to deny these goods to their community.

Pitt-Rivers describes patronage in a one party state at a time when Andalusia had not been fully penetrated by the world market in grains (1961: 35). The land was unevenly distributed, and there was a variety of ways in which Alcaleños got their living from it. The distinctions which Alcaleños make between themselves are almost certainly associated with patronage by *señoritos,* with the attempt to extract favours from those in a position to grant them. Schooled, educated, generous, the *señoritos* hold themselves apart from the pueblo, accepting neither drinks nor considerable favours from people who rank lower than they. A *señorito* uses the familiar form of address to his inferiors and receives the formal one in return. He 'looks after his dependants and uses his influence to protect them. He willingly accepts to be patron to them' (ibid.: 75-6). In the old days tenants had no legal rights of continuity, and security of tenure was probably then a favour, as access to tenancy was in the 1950s. Even the casual labourers employed by small farmers from time to time probably tried to establish moral dependency (ibid.: 44-5).

What do patrons typically do? Pitt-Rivers is not exhaustive, and does not relate the social distinction of *señorito* to that of employer and employee, nor to the ways in which land is exploited. For example, there were some 500-odd labourers in Alcalà. A few of these were permanently employed by landowners; slightly more were employed for periods of a week or so; most worked from day to day, contracting with an employer the evening before they went out to work. This majority scrapes along 'working seven days a week when there is work in order to feed a large family, dreading the long weeks of rain when no wages are paid and bread must be begged from the baker on credit' (1961: 59). To these men the distinction between having a patron and not having one must have been very nearly a matter of life and death; but there is very little information on how they struggled to acquire the support of an employer. It is nevertheless clear that Alcalà was a community in which patronage was the major mode of political representation. For example, a major mill owner and patron in Alcalà was involved in a lengthy dispute over water rights against two main opponents (ibid.: 141-54). One of them, Curro, attacked his arbitrary proceedings openly, found his way blocked, and eventually lost. (The other, Juanito, negotiated secretly, got compensation and only at the eleventh hour went to court: the mill owner, out-manoeuvred, lost the case.) Pitt-Rivers's account is of a wealthy and powerful man who can fix things to his own advantage: municipal clerks reject applications for summonses; Curro's neighbours betray him, giving information to the patron so that he can anticipate Curro's next move. The powerful patron can use his clients to isolate his enemy and to cut them off from law, as well as from water. Now, although Pitt-Rivers tells his story in a chapter on authority, as an illustration of the way in which patronage mediates formal state authority, it is clear that the manipulations by patronage in this case were successful because they were based on a general

143

stratum, bedrock, of willing clientage: clients bear tales, farmers and millers need water, labourers need work. Where there is scarcity of resources, men can establish a moral dependence to get access to them – even, if need by, going to church (ibid.: 51).

Campbell (1964) describes the patronage relationships of Sarakatsani shepherds in Greece; and in a later article (1968) he contrasts some of these with the relationships of peasant market-gardeners and wholesalers in the Athens fruit and vegetable market. Sarakatsani shepherds are dependent on the Presidents of their winter villages for access to the ever-scarcer pastures, and on the Presidents of their home summer villages for various services, most notably the formal certificate of freedom from debt which they must secure before they move out for the winter, certificates for the Agricultural Bank, and other documents (1964: 224-9). They are also dependent on the lawyers who settle their disputes, on shopkeepers who give them credit, and on the cheese-merchants who grant credit against milk from their sheep. With all these people, Campbell says, they have no ties apart from common citizenship and shared humanity: 'in Greek society this is not an adequate basis for . . . social obligations' (ibid.: 246). With them, therefore, the Sarakatsani try to create ties through spiritual kinship (below, pp. 223-32), gift-giving and their own wary brand of friendship.

Friendship is initiated and maintained by a continuing exchange of favours and goods, which are carefully accounted. It is the Sarakatsani who initiate relionships of spiritual kinship and it is probably the Sarakatsani who initiate friendships with outsiders; probably most of their friendships are mostly with outsiders: they are normally hostile to unrelated Sarakatsani, and they do not need to be friendly with their kinsmen. The Sarakatsanos can offer only his vote in exchange for friendship, and make an unambiguous acknowledgment of dependence on the President. Some Presidents think they are independent of support from Šarakatsani voting power, and treat the shepherds roughly; others use Sarakatsani to swing an election where their local strength is uncertain. A President who needs Sarakatsani friends can assure himself of more votes by choosing them among those shepherds who themselves have followings. For the influential Sarakatsani documents and certificates arrive without delay; the better grazing land is allocated to them, there are favourable errors in the head-count of sheep when the shepherds' liability to rent is assessed. They drink publicly with the President and, although their inferiority to him is clearly marked, they gain in the eyes of other shepherds who see the outward sign of favour, and envy the advantages which flow (ibid.: 233).

Shepherds also make routine placatory gifts to Presidents, as well as special gifts when they are in a particular trouble. The gifts, Campbell says, must be presented with finesse: 'a man of honour is not to be crudely bought by social inferiors' (ibid.; 235). But even so, gifts are less effective means of getting favours than clientage is, especially perhaps because gifts are usually *ad hoc*.

Similar kinds of relationship are established by some Sarakatsani with veterinaries, teachers, town councillors, members of Parliament. The goods and services exchanged may vary slightly from case to case; the acceptance of subordination does not, nor does the demand for special treatment. With cheese-merchants the content of the relationship is much more specific: milk is supplied against credit – essential credit if the shepherd is to maintain good standing among other Sarakatsani. Of course, some cheese-merchants are important men with influence over Presidents and members of Parliament, so that the distinction between cheese-merchants and other patrons is not absolute. Nevertheless, credit is the basis and point of departure of the relation.

The shepherd's year has a number of constraining points which were described above (pp. 23-4). These are mainly the payment of debts to public funds, and the shepherds borrow the necessary cash from their cheese-merchants whose credits thus permit the Sarakatsani 'to live honourably in their traditional way of life', and each party clearly recognises this (1968: 150). The advantage to the merchants of having an assured supply of milk is such that they will borrow the money to advance to the shepherds at 10 per cent – an interest which is not passed on. The merchants may make other loans to the shepherds. In the winter, shepherds usually have a lean time and may try to extract supplementary advances from the merchants. These, when they are given, are in kind and the cost of the loan is passed on to the shepherd by charging flour, say, at a higher price than its quality warrants. These different conditions for supplementary loans mark out two aspects of the merchant-shepherd relationship: the merchants appear to recognise a traditional obligation to support Sarakatsani, to enable them to be Sarakatsani, but they temper this with a reluctance to become too closely tied to them: it is only wealthy Sarakatsani who succeed in getting merchants to accept the diffuse obligations of patronage (1964: 254-5).

Campbell's final example is of peasant producers who pay a commission to wholesalers for selling their fresh fruit and vegetables in the Athens market: about three-quarters of all fruit and vegetables there are sold by the producers in this way. It is well known that the wholesalers are fraudulent – their expenses are inflated and their bills of sale record lower prices than they received – but the producers have to get their perishable goods sold quickly; and they 'are afraid to take a strong line with their wholesale merchant because they fear that they will lose their market outlet' (1968: 151). The peasant's strategy in this case is to accept the fraudulent procedures of the wholesaler and to continue to sell through him, in the hope of eventually establishing a personal relationship and of consequently being defrauded less. Indeed, says Campbell, the wholesalers may sometimes be constrained by the need to ensure continuity of supplies, and thus 'exercise a small measure of self-restraint' in particular cases (ibid: 152).

In these two works Campbell presents fine analyses of what might be called failed approaches to patronage. True, some Sarakatsani may succeed in creating a solid and enduring relationship of subordination to their village Presidents or cheese-merchants, but most shepherds are uninfluential and have to approach resource-controlling outsiders through other Sarakatsani, through intermediaries; and the Athenian wholesalers appear to have no permanent ties with their clients. For the majority of the shepherds and peasants, the relationships they have are never secure enough.

From the wholesale market in Athens to the desert of Western Cyrenaica, to the plains of south-eastern Portugal, men take up postures of subordination in order to gain access to resources – to market expertise, to water, to dried milk from welfare agencies. Submission to a patron is commoner and more widespread in the mediterranean than bureaucracy, or fascism, communism, or any of the varieties of democracy: it can exist without any of them, and co-exists with all of them. It is an independent *sui generis* mode of political representation.

Some writers have written about patronage as if it were one particular manifestation of itself – as if say infiltration of the state by patronage in one particular local community were what mediterranean patronage is. But it should now be apparent that the hard core of patronage is a contractual act of submission which has chameleon characteristics, indeed taking shape as well as colouring from its surroundings. Moreover it affects more areas of life than formal politics or bureaucracy do: it is the bedrock of political life in most of those mediterranean communities which anthropologists have studied. To say, as so many have done, that patronage is one of its particular forms betrays a regrettable lack of comparative intent.

Another kind of narrow vision results in assertions that patronage is not itself at all, but, rather, kinship or friendship or spiritual kinship, or a mixture of these. So Pitt-Rivers speaks of 'lop-sided friendship' (1961: 140):

> It is a commonplace that you can get nothing done in Andalusia save through friendship . . . . The more friends a man can claim the greater his sphere of influence; the more influential his friends are the more influence he has . . . . So while friendship is in the first place a free association between equals, it becomes in a relationship of economic inequality the foundation of the system of patronage. The rich man employs, assists and protects the poor man, and in return the latter works for him, gives him esteem and prestige, and also protects his interests . . . . The relationship of *padrino* and *hombre de confianza* is a kind of lop-sided friendship from which the element of *simpatìa* is by no means excluded. . . .

The theme is taken up by Campbell. The Sarakatsani may have 'true friends' among their cousins (1964: 100-2), but friendship is characteristic of those useful relations of inequality which cross the boundaries of the shepherding community: village Presidents are friends.

> In assymetrical friendships, since it is assumed that the patron has more favours to offer than the client can return, or that reciprocal favours are so dissimilar in quality that accountancy is difficult, there is often greater stability than in friendships between equals, which are very frequently bedevilled by accusations of ingratitude (ibid.: 233).

Finally Wolf, in an important article (1966b), identified those political groupings which arise in communities peripheral to complex societies. He contrasts corporate groups with ego-centred coalitions – kinship networks, instrumental friendships, patronage. This last, he says, shares some characteristics of the other two: trust, affection, are necessary to maintain all of them; they are all many-stranded. Patronage is distinguished, however, because 'the two partners no longer[2] exchange equivalent goods and services': it is lop-sided friendship again. It would be hard to deny that there is some similarity between patronage and friendship. Equally, people have pointed out that patron is etymologically related to *pater,* father; and in private conversation they can be heard to say that systems of patronage are out-growths of kinship: a kind of extension which is crystallised in those communities where godparenthood is used in a political form. But etymologies do not make good bases for structural analysis and to concentrate on particular concatentions of notions does not help to solve problems of comparison. And if patronage is to be called kinship, of one kind or another, what about Campbell's distinction between kinship – which is intra-community – and friendship which (apart from 'true' friendship) always crosses community boundaries, and at the solicitation of the Sarakatsani themselves? (See Appendix 1 to this chapter). Friendship, kinship, spiritual kinship are secondary characteristics of patronage which is fundamentally no more than subordination and superordination by contract: the secondary accretions are a protective colouring imposed by the powerless to mitigate the consequences of their dependence. Such attempts at control are understandably derived from the common moral and religious categories of the communities and they vary in their mixture and kind so that the extent to which one or other is used is idiosyncratic, particular to villages, nations, religions. They vary, too, in their success: except in those cases where patronage is associated with democratic political systems it is normal for clients to solicit friendship – or whatever – from their patrons; it is very rare for patrons spontaneously to limit their power with moral or spiritual obligations. Campbell's examples of wholesalers and of cheese-merchants show clearly that it is clients who try to set the dynamic, distance-reducing forces in motion. It may be that the peculiarly weak position of political patrons in democratic systems is the reason they accept moral ties with their clients; why, too, state resources tend to be more widely distributed in these societies than in others.

Just as the essence of patronage is not caught by the terms nepotist and blackleg, so neither is it caught by kinship, friendship, godparenthood.

There remain three points about patronage which can be dealt with briefly. The first concerns the ideological basis for patronage. It is sometimes said that the communion of patron saints provides a spiritual justification for earthly corruption (e.g. Boissevain, 1966b). There are several objections to this. One is that it is vague because those elements of social organisation which the panoply justifies are not clearly specified: some patrons, the majority, are local dispensers of goods with no outside contacts, or negligible ones. They are not intermediaries as the members of the communion are. In other words, most mediterranean people's experience of patronage does not usually involve intermediaries; the argument that heavenly patrons are a reflection or a continuation of mundane ones thus has to obscure a discrepancy between the two systems; and perhaps that is why the argument is so often couched in terms of patronage being the way in which communities are linked to nations. The second vagueness is that eschatology is also variable: description of the panoply is never precise enough for the reader to understand how the variations in the heavenly worlds of the mediterranean are related to differences round the sea. This is only to be expected: if mediterranean anthropologists never write that the system of earthly patronage they have studied differs in this or that respect from the one someone else has studied, still less do they compare systems of heavenly patronage. Of course, it would be odd if an accepted cosmology did not correspond in important ways with the accepted ways of getting access to resources; but at the moment the fit between cosmology and practice has not been shown to be tight. Only recently has Boissevain shown that the decline of patronage as a political form in Malta has been accompanied by a corresponding decrease in emphasis on saintly intermediaries (1975a). Still, Greek Orthodoxy provides no contrast with Catholicism, even less with Islam. The festivals of patron saints in Valdemora (Freeman, 1970, ch. 4) celebrate the solidarity of a community which has no patronage. Finally, the postulate of cosmological continuity or reflection encourages vagueness in the analysis of political systems. Because it is very difficult for anthropologists to discover what does in fact go on in those echelons of party or bureau above the level of local community, they tend to treat, say, the higher cadres of the falange as analogous to saints – unknowable dispensers of goods; they tend to treat the Prefect as a *deus ex machina*, and the Minister as a version of virgin. This is unfortunate since the unknowability of god and his circle is of a different order from the unknowability of party functionaries, and to assimilate them is to relegate to the social construction of reality things which are not merely defined as real (Stirling, 1968). It is a fair charge that much more could have been known by now about the reality of what goes on beyond the hyphen of community-nation relationships if anthropologists had not been lulled into vagueness by the doctrine of cosmological continuity (Davis, 1975).

The second brief point is that those who attribute the origins or causes of patronage to the imperfect industrialisation of mediterranean communities, to their imperfect integration into national economies (J. Schneider, 1971b; Graziani, 1973), are wrong. At most, they could explain the particular forms which patronage takes at a particular time in a particular place: at best, by showing the adaptability of patronage they could explain its persistence. Patronage is autonomous and flexible: it existed before national economies seriously impinged on local communities, and was adapted to meet them as they grew in local significance. Patronage, as it is defined in this book, is a near-universal form of manipulation which cannot be explained by referring to its particular manifestations.

The same remarks apply to the explanations of patronage which rely on its functions in articulating community-nation relationships. These explanations are of two kinds: the earlier, originating with Pitt-Rivers, emphasises the functions of patronage within the community: 'Through the system of patronage the will of the state is adapted to the social structure of the pueblo' (1961: 155). The other, implicit in Wolf, is developed by Silverman (1965) and to some extent by Boissevain (1966b); it emphasises the role of patrons as intermediaries between the rusticity of the towns and villages, and the urbanity of the state: patrons are men who have the ear of provincial and national office holders, therefore they are important men. The theories seem to rest, in each case, on the recognition that local communities are imperfectly integrated into the nation-state, and that, in a hostile world, the peasantry needs someone to alleviate its harshness. Often not much is said about the harshnesses of the outside world in a way which would allow them to be compared. Those descriptions which exist (Boissevain, 1966b; Campbell, 1964) frequently rely on accounts of the perceptions of the peasantry, seldom attempt to escape beyond the construction of reality. There is, of course, no doubt that patronage does bend the will of the state, does aid villagers in their adventures in the outside world: but this function is pre-dated by others, and the examples given cannot explain more than the particular configuration of patronage at a particular time.

IV   Class, bureaucracy and honour applied to three cases

The three modes of representation discussed in this chapter are analytical isolates, and in mediterranean countries none is usually found
on its own: indeed, the apparently peculiar richness of small-scale
political activity in the mediterranean, its occasionally breathtaking
ingenuity, is probably a product precisely of the variety of options
open to a man who has an interest to defend or to further. Class,
assertion of rights, patronage – these are separated in order to aid
comparison. That process violates the seamless web of the often
scrupulously careful reconstructions of politics in this or that community which ethnographers have presented to their readers, and it is
owed to them to attempt to show that some benefit can be got from
such violation. This section, then, is an attempt to analyse some real
politics and to show the relation between the analytical concepts and
real-life political activity: it is scarcely possible or desirable to classify
all mediterranean political life in terms of the weighting to be given to
the three factors, under their various kinds; but it may serve to demonstrate a concern with the seamless web of the quality of life, as
well as the utility of the analysis, if one or two examples are now
presented to the reader.

   The first is taken from Cohen's study of Arab villages in Israel
(1965: 60-8): it is what he calls the case of the labour exchange office
and concerns the local branch of the Histadrut which is a syndicate of
labour unions which has acquired important para-state tasks and (in
1959) owned 30 per cent of all Israeli capital. A branch was opened in
Bint el-Huḍūd in 1959 and a local man, 'Uthman Barham, was
appointed secretary. He was a member of the leading patrilineage
(hamula) of the village and of one dominant family within it: his
father, for example, was *mukhtar,* headman, of Bint el-Huḍūd. Since
the office was new 'Uthman was able to make what he could of it – he
invented the role of Secretary, so far as the village was concerned
(ibid.: 61):

> Within a short time, 'Uthman managed to concentrate in his
> hands tremendous power, as he became the man who could
> virtually hire and fire hundreds of village labourers. As an
> employment officer, he received orders for labour from the
> regional labour exchange centres, or direct from employers, and he
> himself distributed the jobs. In due course he became the
> intermediary between the labourers and the local representatives

of the military governor of the area. His word decided whether
or not a man would get a military permit for working outside
the border area.

'Uthman excited resentment; he was said to favour members of
his *hamula* over others, and disappointed labourers complained to
their elders, who in turn brought the matter up with the *mukhtar*
at their formal meetings. The *mukhtar,* who was 'Uthman's father,
took little heed, and 'Uthman seemed secure enough in his
oppression. However, after a slight recession in the local labour
market 'Uthman had to sack a number of men and when it was
thought that here again he discriminated against members of other
hamula than his own he was beaten up by aggrieved labourers and
petitions were presented to the Histadrut head office. Some
hamula which had been closely allied to the Barham group for
some time now broke away and challenged Barham supremacy
within the village. The *mukhtar* and his son, they said, were Jewish.
stooges who betrayed the Arabs to enhance their private position.
Members of Israeli opposition parties fanned the flames: the
mukhtar and his son were supported by MAPAI (the liberal-
socialist governing party) they said, and that was a reason for
voting against MAPAI when the time came. MAPAI saw its
support dwindling, and curbed 'Uthman: a committee of
representatives of all the *hamula* in Bint el-Huḍūd was set up; they
received notification of the jobs available from 'Uthman, and
distributed them *pro rata* among the *hamula,* notifying 'Uthman
of their decisions: he then reported back to his superiors.

Cohen locates this incident in an elaborate context: the incorporation of the village into the national economy diminished the control of
leading families within the village. The general increase in prosperity
which resulted caused a decline in the importance of what Cohen calls
class, and an increase in egalitarianism: certainly, consumption patterns altered. The declining Barham family relied on state functions,
devolved through the Histadrut, to recapture their eroded dominance, but in doing so they made themselves a liability to MAPAI. At
the same time, overtures made by opposition parties led the elders of
the various *hamula* to realise that they could extract benefits if only
they could control votes; and the solution to the 'Uthman problem,
proposed by the elders and accepted by the Histadrut, in fact conso-
lidated the position of *hamula* elders. Together with other incidents,

the case of the labour exchange office was part of a general trend away from class towards a re-emergence of patrilineal organisation adopting administrative and electoral tasks. Rosenfeld has suggested that renewed emphasis on *hamula* organisations among Israeli Arabs in the 1950s was a general phenomenon which is related to their incorporation at the bottom of the Israeli social hierarchy (Rosenfeld, 1972: 69-71): it was a situation in which, had they been interviewed by Bailey's pupils, they might have said 'We are all equal here.'

Turn now to Bailey's account of the local elections in Losa in 1968 (1973b). There, a mayor *(sindaco)* had lost the support of those elected to the town council with him and, in the elections called by provincial authority to remedy the situation, he allied himself with the right wing in competition with his erstwhile supporters who drew themselves up with the left. Various notables – a bank manager, an ex-partisan international business executive – thus found themselves on the same side as local socialists. They denounced the rightists and their leader for corruption (fairly standard practice, this), proclaimed against the electoral symbol they had adopted (a cross with the motto 'our one hope of salvation'), and fairly justifiably claimed to have more contacts in the higher reaches of government than their opponents. The leftists made one false move which in Bailey's opinion lost them the election: they tried to insist that there should be public debate in the village square on the issues confronting the electorate and on the record in local government of the two groups. It was a false move because the rightists refused to have such a debate, and that provoked the leftists into unseemly behaviour in their attempts to force one on the speakers from the right. Indeed there were various episodes but Bailey thinks, and there is no reason to doubt his judgment, that the very proposal to have public debates was profoundly inconsistent with local ideas, and created a repugnance which the episodes merely confirmed. It was not the proposal in itself which was offensive, for there are public debates in provincial and national elections; nor was it the probability that debate would promote scurrility: for defamatory scandal circulated, as it always did, by word of mouth and on posters, signed and unsigned. Rather it was the combination of debate with local elections which was descrepant, innovatory and offensive. It was offensive because politics – in the restricted sense of electoral activity – was considered inconsistent with village harmony: politics is divisive, and is in any case associated with the outside world – with the powers seen to be responsible for the decline of a community *vis-à-vis* the nation as a whole. Losesi were collectively on the defensive against the political world, and here was a group of leftists (and fairly ambiguously left some were) who emphasised their contacts with provincial authority, who were associated with the (wide-horizoned) partisans, and who attempted to introduce practices which connoted outsiders, men sowing disruption. They voted, therefore, for the inarticulate, graceless, arrogant and bullying rightist, their ex-mayor, and for his neo-fascist associates.

The third and last case is that of the attempted coup by the military in Morocco in 1971. This is analysed in detail by Waterbury (1973b), and – although it took him by surprise – it fits in to his earlier analysis (1970) of Moroccan elite politics. Some guidance is also given by Gellner (1973c; cf. Favret, 1966), Coram (1973) and Marais (1973). True, Gellner is concerned with rural rebellion, and that in the period before the elite groups involved in the bloodshed at Skhirat were firmly established; but Waterbury's fine analysis of the factional organisation of Moroccan politics (1970, ch. 3) links Gellner's discussion of local segmentation to the processes of central government. Briefly, Waterbury first of all identifies 'primordial factions' – ones to which recruitment is by membership of territorial or descent groups or marriage alliance, and occasionally by membership of religious groups. The balance of power which more or less obtains in conditions of 'pure' *siba* is replicated at analytically higher levels of segmentation: 'mixed' factions are recruited chiefly by reference to objective interests – they are clientele groups borrowing personnel and ideology from primordial groups, but having material goals, and a high proportion of what Bailey would call followers, rather than core members. As Waterbury points out, such clientele groups may be thought of as the *makhzen* equivalent of *siba* primordial factions – although there is now no particular geographical distinction in the distribution of these two kinds. Finally, 'interest-oriented' factions, again controlled and recruited through clientele, are those which have the additional form of political parties, labour unions, chambers of commerce and the like, or of currents within them.

The subtlety of Waterbury's account of the coup is that the rebels are shown to have been acting on these three levels simultaneously. The conspirators were mostly Berbers, and they used cadet soldiers, not regular units, to carry out the massacre – which may or may not have been intended; 'the scene as described evokes images of the

traditional tribal *razzia*, the sweeps against decaying regimes so per-
ceptively analysed by Ibn Khaldun centuries ago' (Waterbury 1973a:
410). The chief conspirator appears to have been General Medbuh
who had recently returned from a fact-finding mission to the USA
where he had discovered that the civilian wing of the regime had been
involved in large-scale corruption to which the army had no access
and from which the king took no cut: although doubtless Waterbury
is correct when he says that disgust at endemic corruption was an
important motive of the conspirators (ibid.: 409), it seems important that this was unofficial corruption (endemic but not planned, in
Waterbury's terms); and that the civilians involved were treated
leniently (ibid.: 401). To a military elite which depended on stalemate
(as Waterbury calls Gellner's 'balance of power' when manifest at the
higher echelons of factional segmentation), this could only signify
that the balance of royal favour was being tipped against them and
that their position in the stalemate was being undermined. Moreover
the balance within the Berber military elite seems to have been unst-
able: regular units were not used in the coup, and there was a suspicion that Arab junior officers were themselves likely to revolt, putting
Berber generals at risk. Finally, it seems possible to imagine that some
of the generals' resentment was expressed in terms of the threat to the
professional status of the military. As Waterbury says, senior officers
may have accepted their frequent and transitory postings while they
were rewarded with the fruits of patronage; but French-trained professional soldiers, with their position in the patrimonial patronage
system apparently threatened, would surely have expressed their
fears in these terms (Coram, 1973b: 426, 427).

So, the coup-*razzia* occurred after the military exposure of private
civilian corruption and after the lenient treatment of the culprits
(Waterbury, 1973a: 401); in the name of purity the coup leaders
announced, prematurely, that they had destroyed a corrupt regime.
The ambivalence of the Berber cadets – were they against the king or
against the corruption which surrounded him? – had the consequence that they swung round in the middle of the coup in the palace
and 'betrayed' their officers. The coup relied heavily on primordial
Berber loyalty, and was seen by Moroccans as a Berber coup (Coram,
1973: 425-6; Marais, 1973), but it also displayed characteristic forms
of loyalty derived from Waterbury's second and third types of factionalism: some Berber senior officers, pre-empting an expected coup
by Arab junior officers, attacked the king to destroy a civilian rival

elite group in an incident which clearly got out of hand, turning into a *razzia.*

These three case histories are each unique examples of political activity in unique settings: an ethnic minority on a troubled frontier; a declining mountain village in the Italian alps; a political elite group – a rejection of the pretensions of a powerful family to control a labour exchange; an election; a failed *coup d'état:* what could be more different? Each incident has its own flavour, its own multiple linkages with a unique political culture and a national society. It would be foolish to suggest that analysis in terms of the three elementary forms proposed here can or should eliminate these differences. Nevertheless, and without claiming too much, it may be helpful to look at them while bearing in mind factors which are not purely Moroccan or Italian or Israeli-Arab ones. An analysis in terms of who does what to whom is not comparative, and the reader is left with three distinct impressions.

So: is it acceptable to compare these three incidents? In the Moroccan coup the state bureaucracy is 'patrimonial' – it is an out and out instrument of patronage, and is officially so: only the military seem to have any inkling that it might be otherwise, and the statements they made to this effect were inspired, not only by their awareness of greater Weberianism overseas, and by nascent professional defensiveness, but by the threat which civilian administrators and entrepreneurs posed to their position within the patronage system. When the officers take action they mobilise 'mixed factions' – clientele groups which are largely recruited through ethnic and familial relationships. There is no question, yet, of class struggle, though Waterbury – in an article written before the coup – is prepared to predict it for the future. Cohen recounts an incident in which men reject the opportunity offered by a para-state bureaucracy to act as individuals and to become the personal clients of a class superior. They do not accept the personal claim of 'Uthman and his father to act as intermediaries with the labour organisations. Their method is to present petitions to the bureaucracy itself, asserting their independence of 'Uthman in terms of the bureaucracy's own notions of impartiality – to invoke the official norms of conduct; and also to interest political parties, with votes at stake in a coming election, in this case which they present as exploitative and unjust action by a government agency dominated by the labour party. Their solution is to set up a committee which will distribute jobs *pro rata,* according to

the numerical strength of descent groups which are given equal representation on the committee. It is a beautiful example of rejection
of the differentiation which patronage requires, of the individualisa-
tion of class, and of re-affirmation of the significance of group membership and of the construed, nominal, equality of groups. Finally,
the Losesi, described by Bailey, maintain a distinction between political elections and administrative ones: they, too, reject the attempt to
import state and party patronage into the community: that is the
proper consideration in elections to provincial and central
government, but it is divisive, and it should stop beyond the threshold
of community affairs. The candidates are not presented in party
groups, but in coalitions of those who will and those who will not have
good contacts with the outside sources of patronage: Losesi opt for the
insiders. 'We are all equal here' they say to outsiders.

Now it must be admitted that this is scarcely an adequate analysis:
the reader may wish to modify and even to add new elementary
forms; and more examples are needed to establish how the shifting
kaleidoscopic patterns of class struggle, bureaucracy and patronage
appear within the same political community on different occasions.
This is freely admitted. Nevertheless, poor and gauche as it is, it is
necessary to insist that some activity of this kind is required if
accounts of mediterranean politics are to be comparable one with
another.

The account presented here has been one which attempts to achieve
greater precision of description in the hope that, by introducing
common elements in different ethnographies, communities may be
compared. Anthropology really has no future, scientific or humane, if
all that is produced is a series of good but completely isolated monographic community studies. It is only when this comparative task is
begun, that anthropologists can attempt to answer the questions of
practical men: what about corruption? nation-building? modernisation? political mobilisation? the creation of revolutionary consciousness in the not-yet-for-itself mediterranean proletariat? what about
justice? Each anthropologist will have his own cavils for each of these
questions, but will also recognise that they are not completely
meaningless: will an analysis of this kind help to give answers?

The anthropologist may be able to resist the temptation to identify
patronage with corruption. Kenny started it, with his epigram that
Ramosierra was governed not by bureaucracy but by amigocracy

(1960): for Ramosierra, where the officials are largely disregarded, unintegrated into the community, with no share of the Pine Luck, that phrase seems to capture some truth. But Kenny must regret his joke, for it has not served analysis: the minds of his contemporaries and successors seem deflected by that equation of *amigo* and *bureau,* to the extent that Pitt-Rivers's examples of patronage do not include any rural employment, any connections between *señoritos* and labourers, but only manipulation of courts and offices (above, p. 143 and 1961); to the extent that Boissevain has not one word to say about rustic contracts and oppression (above, p. 142). Nor does Stirling (1968) contemplate seriously the prevalence of partiality in any matters other than those where it is out of place, by his standards. However, it is no use simply saying that patronage is an idiom which anthropologists' ethnocentrism has led them to perceive only where it offends them. Waterbury (1970: ch. 3; 1973b) has shown that it is possible for whole states to be organised on the principle of segmentary clientelistic factions – as Badian (1958) in fact suggests the whole of the Roman mediterranean was once united and then governed by contracts of partiality, both public and private. 'Do not be ethnocentric' is scarcely a sufficient outcome.

The mention of Waterbury is one clue, providing another thread of hope through the labyrinth of community studies. For just as it is true that ethnographers have not looked sideways, to compare their results with those of others, so it is also true that they have not often looked upwards, so to speak, at levels of segmentation higher than the one they study. Partly because it is difficult to collect the information; partly because they have the alibi that Prefects and Ministers are on a par with the Virgin and Saints; partly too, perhaps, because they have tended to think of 'higher levels of segmentation' as more rarefied than the grass roots, and operating on different principles – for these reasons, although they may speak of their communities as being progressively integrated into nation-states, and have divined the local consequences, they have not integrated their local studies into national studies (e.g. among many others, Davis, 1973). Waterbury, who appears to have made only fleeting visits to the grass roots (1972: 108-11 for example), makes two points which are relevant. First, he shows that the higher levels of segmentation, the elite groups as he also calls them, do not necessarily operate on different principles from those observable at lower levels: elite men marry, live in communities, manipulate relationships in the same way as villagers. Although the scale of their operations, the kinds of thing they operate with, and the consequences of their politics may be different, none the less the building blocks are very similar at all levels of political activity, and result in balanced opposition between segmentary units of equivalent structural order – what Waterbury calls stalemate. That is one point. Second he discusses the survival of segmentary stalemate, and comes to the conclusion that 'there are important forces at work that will lead to the gradual regrouping of factions in a more conventional class framework' (1970: 74). He argues that the multiplication of potential elites, through education, without corresponding expansion of appropriate elite positions, will lead to disgruntlement among the excluded: they are most likely to phrase their discontent in terms of class struggle although that does not exclude segmentary factionalism within the class movement, nor eliminate it at grass roots levels (ibid.: 317-21).

Just as Waterbury is the only writer to have used anthropological material to characterise a state entire, so he is the only one to make predictions about the movement of the forces he describes. He does so in terms which are conformable with those used here – the inadequacy of patronage to provide sufficient rewards to secure support, and its replacement by a class idiom. This is because the expansion of education, itself a consequence of increased state intervention and centralisation, creates a category of would-be elite members who are necessarily frustrated. Is this scenario generalisable? Is the movement of all progressing mediterranean societies one from patronage to class struggle? It seems unlikely: Weingrod's analysis is of a movement towards increasing penetration of the patronage system by bureaucratic control and of centralisation of patronage. It seems necessary that if a state is to continue to control patronage, it must have an expanding economy – to allow the continual provision of development resources, for example. It is also the case that centralised patronage is consistent with a pattern in which it is the relatively deprived groups or categories which vote to maintain the patrons in power. Similarly it is possible to characterise some northern states as ones in which centralisation and bureaucratisation of the class struggle has occurred, formalising and administering the interests of one class or another. The combination of class and bureaucracy in Yugoslavia or Spain is paralleled by Waterbury's prediction that class and patronage will combine in Morocco; or Weingrod's insight that the political scientists' kind of patronage (a combination of bureaucracy and patronage) will eliminate the class struggle in Italy. Certainly, the functional organisation of bureaucracy, with offices for this and offices for that, can destroy the hegemony of one or a few local patrons whose position, hitherto vulnerable to peasant revolts, derives from their possession of wealth. When the centralising bureaucracy is open to patronage or encourages clientelism (e.g. La Palombara, 1964: 252-348; Rossi, 1965; Rossi-Doria, 1963), it destroys class struggle.

'. . . We found a plethora of non-corporate social structures (for the most part coalitions) which organised *fundamental* economic and political activities of a quite modern sort' (Schneider, Schneider and Hansen, 1972). Any attempt to predict the changing characteristics of a state must examine the location and scope of such coalitions: Waterbury, for example, makes it clear that the local units of loyalty are corporate groups, rather than coalitions, and that the non-corporateness of the groups increases the higher the level of segmentation considered. Cohen's case suggests that certain kinds of state intervention – what might be called bureaucratic patronage in a time of recession – can re-establish corporate groups at the expense of nascent class formations, just as Bailey's description of the Losa election reveals a community rejecting integration into the provincial and national patronage system. Certainly, the outcomes of movement are varied, and there is no place for what the Schneiders and Hansen have appropriately called 'the optimism of the unilinea[r] model' which predicts the move from traditionalism to modernity, from under-development to development, from feudalism to capitalism to . . . . In Italy the actual sequence continues . . . state capitalism, which manages to centralise patronage, to overwhelm the periphery with development. In Morocco resources are not sufficient to maintain a stable and centralised patronage system. In Portugal, as Cutileiro makes clear, the state managed to control all expressions of class, and to maintain a patrimonial system without a perpetual erogation of funds and public goods.

Appendices to chapter 4

1   *On friendship kinship and patronage in Campbell's* Honour, Family and Patronage *(1964) (see p. 148)*

The reader will remember that Campbell describes friendship (except between first cousins) as instrumental, and as crossing the boundary of the community – it is patronage. The purpose of this appendix is to point out that it is a misreading of Campbell to imagine that (because all instrumental friendship involves an outsider) all patronage involves an outsider: some Sarakatsani patronise other Sarakatsani. 'If through wealth or influence a man is in a position to act as a general protector of his kindred, not only is he expected to do so, but this, in most cases, is his wish' (1964: 99). An outside friend expects Sarakatsani clients to mobilise their kindreds on his behalf (ibid.: 231). Together with the episodes described at pp. 98-9 and 108-9 this suggests that patronage permeates the Sarakatsani's social relations. Companies (*stani*) had two terms of reference: they could also be called *tselingato* 'When the speaker was more concerned with the relations of dependence and co-operation between the *tselingas* (i.e. leader) and his followers' (ibid.: 17). And the ideal *tselingas* attracted 'kinsmen or affines who have no brothers, cannot agree with them, or whose brothers are not sufficiently wealthy or influential to remain together' (ibid.: 93). The consequence of such attraction was to enhance the power (in terms of men and sheep) of the leader. So, the easy equation of friendship and patronage, and their distinction from kinship and equality, do not hold.

2   *On violence, feud and the settlement of disputes*

One of the reasons for the cursory treatment of these topics in this book is that Black-Michaud's monograph arrived after February 1975, too late for its argument and light to be assimilated in the main text. It is a book which examines the theory of feud and warfare using mostly mediterranean evidence. It is on the whole excellent, but should be supplemented by reference to Cozzi (especially 1910a) whose account of Albanian feud is based on his experience of trying to stop killings, and may therefore perhaps be more soundly based than Black-Michaud's main sources; Favret (1968) – whose treatment of debt relations to some extent anticipates Black-Michaud's – and perhaps to Maunier (1927) and Bourdieu (1965) whose treatments of *tawsa* *(taoussa* in Maunier's transliteration) invite the reader to broaden the argument from blood-debt – admirably discussed by Black-Michaud – to debt in general.

Black-Michaud's main ethnographic point is that feud should be defined as a status relationship of perpetual indebtness between corporate groups. It has important consequences for theory and it makes some often obscure ethnography fall into shape. The book should be set alongside the rather inferior ethnographic material on relationships of dispute in other mediterranean societies. V. Ayoub (1965) and Nader (1965b) discuss the role of courts and middlemen (*waasta*) in securing peace (see also Broegger, 1968).

Politics

Balikći (1965) describes institutionalised withdrawal from interaction (see also P. Schneider, 1969: 131; Eugene Cohen, 1972; Bialor, 1968; Wylie, 1964: 196-205) and formal methods of restoring good relations (see also Bialor, 1968). On mafia, Blok's recent (1974) book is the best general survey, though there is little concern with the detailed ethnography of social control, other than on a broad political and economic front. Gilsenan (1973a) provides material on the *apparatus* (enforcers) of Lebanese patrimonial lords which permits interesting comparisons. Boissevain (1966b) gives some material (though he commits the solecism of referring to the Honourable Society at p. 225 – it should be *honoured*). On collective oaths see Gellner (1959) and Durham (1910) in addition to the commoner sources (Gellner 1969; Berque, 1955; Montagne, 1930, etc.).

Finally, on a deliberate attempt to avoid political disputes among kin, see Loizos (1975: 81) whose material should be set alongside the reports of institutions designed to prevent conflict among co-heirs (see pp. 193, 251-2).

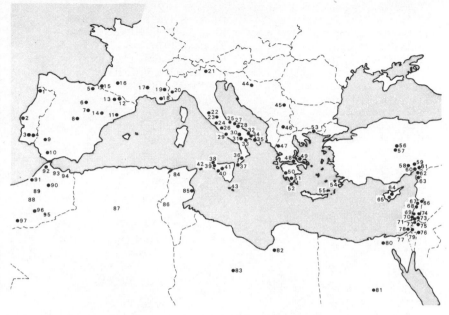

Map   Approximate location of identifiable places mentioned in text.

Key to map

Note: The map shows the rough location of identifiable places mentioned in the text: a point on the map indicates that the name found in the list following is a territorial unit – a village, oasis, town, city; when there is no point the name is of a people. Names which are marked with an asterisk are the real names, others are fictitious and the location indicated on the map is in some cases merely guessed at – though where a guess would have been wild the place and name have not been included. The names of places and peoples are followed by a standard reference to the bibliography. It will be understood that inclusion on the map is no guarantee of ethnographic worth, nor of importance in the argument in the text. Finally, general books on a country or region are also omitted: because some places are unidentifiable, and because some ethnographies cover wide areas, the distribution of numbers on the map is no guide to the ethnographic coverage of the mediterranean.

Portugal

1	Soajo	Callier-Boisvert, 1968
2	São Jão das Lampas	Riegelhaupt, 1967
3	*Beja	Willems, 1962
4	Vila Velha	Cutileiro, 1971

163

Map

Spain

5	Murelaga	Douglass, 1969
6	Ramosierra	Kenny, 1961
7	Valdemora	Freeman, 1970
8	*Madrid parish	Kenny, 1961
9	Los Olivos	R. Price and S. Price, 1966a
10	Alcalà de la Sierra	Pitt-Rivers, 1961
11	*Alto Panades	Hansen, 1969
12	Saburneda	N. Redclift, 1973
13	Gema	M. Redclift, 1973
14	Belmonte de los Caballeros	Lison-Tolsana, 1966

France

15	Auguste	Blaxter, 1971
16	Magnac	Pitt-Rivers, 1960
17	Peyrane	Wylie, 1964
18	Colpied	Reiter, 1972
19	Vallois	J. Hutson, 1971; S. Hutson, 1971

Italy

20	Losa	Bailey, 1971
21	Tret, St Felix	Cole, 1969; Wolf, 1962
22	Colombaio	Wade, 1971
23	Colleverde	Silverman, 1965
24	Collefiore	Eugene Cohen, 1972
25	Cortina D'Aglio	Moss and Cappannari, 1962
26	*Sermoneta	Pitkin, 1959
27	Torremaggiore	Santangelo-Spoto, 1892
28	*Manfredonia	Colclough, 1970
29	*Naples	Parsons, 1962
30	*Grassano	Ambrico, 1961
31	Pertosa	Colclough, 1971
32	Quercio	Littlewood, 1974
33	Pisticci	Davis, 1973
34	*Cisternino	Stirling and Rowland, 1973
35	Calimera	Maraspini, 1968
36	Franza	Lopreato, 1967
37	Montevarese	Broegger, 1968
38	Nicuportu	Cronin, 1970
39	Genuardo	Blok, 1974
40	Leone	Boissevain, 1966
41	Milocca	Gower Chapman, 1973
42	*Pantelleria	Galt, 1974

Malta

43	Hal Farrug	Boissevain, 1964

Yugoslavia
44 *Zelcin   Mosely, 1943
45 *Orašac   Halpern, 1958
46 Veliko Selo   Balikći, 1965

Greece
47 *Zagori   Campbell, 1964
48 Vasilika   Friedl, 1963a
49 Ambeli   Du Boulay, 1974
50 Vergadi   Bialor, 1968
51 Kardamili   Gearing, 1968
52 *Mina   Lineton, 1971
53 Stavroupolis   Photiadis, 1965
54 *Kalymnas   Bernard, 1967
55 Nisos   Kenna, 1971

Turkey
56 *Elbaşi   Stirling, 1965
57 *Sakaltutan   Stirling, 1965
58 *Pozanti   Eberhard, 1953a
59 *Kozan   Eberhard, 1953b
60 *Ceyhan   Eberhard, 1953a
61 *Osmaniye   Eberhard, 1953a
62 *Hassa   Eberhard, 1970
63 *Antakya   Eberhard, 1970

Cyprus
64 Kalo   Loizos, 1975
65 Alona   Peristiany, 1968a

The Lebanon
66 *Bishmizzeen   Tannous, 1941
67 *Tripoli   Gulick, 1965b
68 *Douma   Khuri, 1965
69 Al Munsif   Gulick, 1954
70 *Beirut suburb   Khuri, 1970
71 *Aramti   Khuri, 1967
72 Libaya   Nader, 1965a
73 Haouch   Williams and Williams, 1965
74 'Ain ad Dayr   Sweet, 1967

Jordan
75 Kufr al Ma   Antoun, 1968
76 Al Karak   Gubser, 1973

Israel
77 *Israeli Triangle   A. Cohen, 1965
78 *Rehovoth (Shaurayim)   P. S. Cohen, 1962
79 *Negev Bedouin   Marx, 1967

165

Map

Egypt
80	Sirs	Berque, 1957
81	*Kharga	Abou-Zeid, 1963

Libya
82	*S–W. Cyrenaican Bedouin	Peters, 1960
83	*Sawknah	Dalton, 1972

Tunisia
84	*Djebel Lansarine	Cuisenier, 1964
85	Hamman-Sousse	Moore, 1963
86	*Djerid	Ferchiou, 1968

Algeria
87	*The Mzab	Alport, 1973

Morocco
88	Akhdar	Maher, 1975
89	*Ait Ndhir (Beni Mtir)	Vinogradoff, 1974b
90	*Sefrou	Rosen, 1973
91	*Sale	Brown, 1973
92	Mediouna	Schorger, 1969
93	*Aith Waryaghar	Hart, 1954
94	*Zaio	Seddon, 1973a
95	*Ait 'Atta	Dunn, 1973; Hart, 1973
96	*Zawiya Ahansal	Gellner, 1969
97	*Seksawa	Berque, 1955

5

Family and kinship

I Introductory survey

The mediterranean presents a wide variety of kinds of nuclear and extended family households. There are no matrilineal kin groups, but there are bilateral kindreds and patrilineal descent groups as well as the familiar and probably commoner bilateral groups of kinsmen. The patrilineal areas, chiefly to the south and east of the mediterranean, are well known for their practice of parallel cousin marriage, which has consequences for family organisation; and the Christian areas – and Moslem communities in close contact with Christians – are noted for their extensive use of godparenthood to extend the range of familial obligation between adults of the same generation.

These, then, are the themes of this chapter: kinds of family, kinds of kinship, kinds of family-like tie. It is often said – indeed, there is scarcely a study from the northern shore which does not say it – that 'the family' is overwhelmingly important in the social organisation of mediterranean communities. But that is not a theme to which much attention is paid here, for it presents the familiar quandary: it would be a rash man who asserted that the family was equally important in all mediterrean societies; on the other hand, the only study which attempts to discuss the importance of the family in a precise way is by Farsoun (1970) and it is not comparative. Otherwise the articles and monographs are loose and vague, claiming (say) that the development of industry (Pizzorno, 1960) has 'weakened' family ties. Of course, imprecisely and on the basis of intuition and sympathy, a careful reader may come to some appreciation of the variation which satisfies him. In any case he should beware of a trap: it seems that many ethnographers have emphasised 'the importance of the family'

167

in mediterranean societies taking their own society, even their own family life, as the standard of comparison. It might be that less emphasis would be made if mediterranean families were compared to those of parts of sub-Saharan Africa or the Far East. Rather than an attempt at such a grand comparison, here is a sketch of the necessary groundwork: an examination of the many different kinds of relationship which may be, undoubtedly are, weakened, strengthened, by a variety of forces. For, in the mediterranean as elsewhere, everybody has a father and a mother, most have siblings, most have wives and children. The experience of these relationships, however, must surely vary: paternal authority is exercised and experienced differently in nuclear family house-holds and in extended family ones – where father is either subordinate to another man, or superordinate over other families. Similarly, evidence from Italy suggests that relations in nuclear families where property is transmitted at the marriage of children, are significantly different from those in families where it is transmitted only at the death of the owner. Again from Italy, it is suggested that uxorilocal residence affects the composition of typically co-operating groups (a man with his father-in-law and wife's sisters' husbands), and that this affects the relations men and women commonly have with their brothers. That contrasts with virilocal residence: certainly, reports from Sicily make some play of the difficulties which a young wife experiences when she tries to detach her husband from her mother-in-law. In those areas of the Balkans where young women are imported into extended family households, and have to earn acceptance, it is probable that the experience of family membership is very different from either of these.

II Kinds of domestic group

The first theme of this chapter is the organisation of domestic groups. It is first because it is so easy, and so misleading, to invest the words *father, mother, brother, sister* with generic social meanings; yet the composition of households, in which a persons's expectations of these roles are created through experience, is not always and everywhere the same. It is not merely a question of temperamental fittedness: some parents are, indeed, inept. Nor is it simply that society can demand standards of behaviour from men and women which it may cruelly deny them any chance of achieving (Parsons, 1962, 1964; Lombroso, 1896). The fact of the matter is that there are broad

differences between fatherhood (say) as it is in nuclear family households and as it is in extended or joint ones (where there are several
fathers, only one with final control). Put like that, nothing could be
simpler: the ethnographer has to ask how many nuclear families there
are in how many households, and then tries to make statements about
the social nature of biological relationships. But some qualifications
and distinctions must be made, in order to present a true picture and
to make comparison possible.

For example, Stirling (1965: 37–43) distinguishes the ideal and the
statistical norm. In the two Turkish villages he studied everyone
wants to live in an extended family household or even be head of one,
but at any given time about three-quarters of households are not
extended. Such departure from the ideal is explained in part by the
revolutions of the domestic cycle: there may be an interlude between
the division of a major agglomeration of nuclear families and the
establishment of new ones: a young married couple may eventually
establish an extended group but until their sons are married and have
brought their wives in, the household appears as a nuclear family one.
Some people, moreover, suffer demographic failure, and do not beget
enough sons to be able to achieve the ideal. Demographic failure may
also prevent Sarakatsani from achieving their extended family norm
(Campbell, 1964: 297) – and in this case the failures seem to attach
themselves as supernumerary members of more successful companies: co-operation in production is thereby assured, even if such
attached men and women are not, strictly speaking, members of a
household.

The Balkans provide the ethnographic literature with the institution of *zadruga*, but with few first-hand accounts of its internal organisation, or of assessments, based on observation, of the quality of
relationships within one. While the zadruga has fascinated European
scholars – and discussion of it was bound up with political relations
between Germans and Slavs – it seems that the term itself means
'co-operation'; so Mosely (1940) records that ' "to live in zadruga"
means "to live in concord" or "in harmony", not "to live in a
zadruga" '. Erlich, writing in the 1930s, reports that zadruga means
association or community (1966: 32); Hammel, that peasants normally contrast extended and joint fraternal households with nuclear
family ones by qualifying the word house *(kuca)* with the adjectives
big *(velika)* or small *(mala)*. 'The peasants themselves now call an
extended or joint family a zadruga, but probably because the term has

169

come into the folk lexicon from ethnographic, historical and folkloristic writings used in the elementary schools' (1968: 13). The word is also used for agricultural co-operatives. Barić, indeed, contrasts the *velika kuca* of the Dinaric coast with the zadruga of Croatia and Slavonia. The former was an agnatic corporation with property and political obligations; the latter was a collective with an agnatic core to which non-agnates might attach themselves (1967a: 5; 1967b: 256). As for the distribution of extended households in the Balkans, it is clear that they were not common, in the 1930s, on the Adriatic littoral. Erlich reports the highest proportion of villages with extended households – 50 per cent – in Western Macedonia. Montenegro, parts of Christian Bosnia, Hercegovina and Serbia also manifested the institution, the proportion of villages with extended households varying between 15 per cent and 25 per cent. Her survey does not include Albania: there, the ethnographers – admittedly more concerned with describing an exotic type than with differentiating social forms – have drawn material mostly from the hinterland of Shkodër, towards the Montenegrin border, and give the impression of unrelieved zadrugadom. Who were the members of a zadruga? What were relations between them? How was the head *(gospodar)* selected? Two main sources are accessible. One is Mosely's study of the Varžić zadruga in Zelćin, Slavonia (1942): it contained twenty-six members, of three generations, the agnatic male descendants of a common ancestor and their wives: there were thus twelve adults and fourteen children. The *gospodar* was in fact two men, brothers, the eldest males. With extensive property, derived in part from an earlier inheritance, in part by purchase, the zadruga seems to have been relatively prosperous. 'The affairs of the zadruga are decided by all the married men together . . . "After supper we talk over the work we shall do on the morrow. As we all decide, with our sons, so we work." It is not clear whether or not this was an unusual dispersal of authority within the household. Three younger men (sons of the gospodar) looked after the horses; one married man (Mikola) and his unmarried brother looked after the pigs, with assistance from Mikola's son and their nephew in school holidays. In addition to special duties they all turned out on major routine tasks such as ploughing and harvesting. The women's work was supervised by the wife of one of the gospodar, and her official title was 'cook': assisted by a young girl, the other adult women took turns of a week each to fetch and carry and wash up. Although the Varžić zadruga employed permanent labourers these lived on an outlying farm: otherwise, everyone who was a member was an agnate or a wife of one; and every living descendant of the common ancestor was a member, apart from three women who had married out.

The other source is Valentini. He was a Jesuit priest sent from Rome to Albania to judge the correspondence of local custom to Canon Law; he wrote an illuminating article on family organisation (1945). It is a commentary on the code of Gjecov (see Appendix 1) supplemented by other sources, and by three anecdotal case histories (two of them of troublesome betrothals) in an appendix. Valentini assumes throughout a household consisting of a complete agnatic group and their wives, and says the supreme authority of the household is vested in the family council – not in the executive head *(xoti i shpi)*, who could be deposed. In fact, as his first case history shows (1945: 188-90) a good strong *xoti* was immune from anything more than grumbles behind his back. Only the senior woman's control approached his, and her independence was marked by her licence to work while she listened to him – the others had to sit still. Cozzi (1912: 324, n.2) reports that the *xoja* was usually but not always the wife of the *xoti*,[1] and that she retained her position after the *xoti's* death. The authority of the male head was not constant, throughout the Balkans. Durham seems to contradict Valentini when she says '. . . The house is ruled by the *xoti i shpis,* and all the household obey him like dogs' (1910: 462) – but she did not know Albania as well as Valentini. Karanović (1929-30) describes two Bosnian zadrugas. One, of forty-eight people solely occupied in agriculture, seems to have been formal and hierarchical: for example, meals were served to six tables, each seating a category of members: the smallest children, the ten-year-olds, the shepherd boys, young men and women, grown women, and grown men. The head was accountable to no one. In another, where the men were cabinet makers and masons who went into Serbia each summer for work, the head was much more of a *primus inter pares*. He was elected biennially, by all married men; he did not go out in search of work, but he fixed the contribution which each migrant member should make to the common funds from his wages, and presented annual accounts.

The writers on Balkan zadrugas often assume that Slav society, left to its own devices, would have eliminated the zadruga. Where it survives, they say, it is the consequence of an Ottoman brake applied to natural Slav development: the zadruga survives, preserved in the amber or gravel of Ottoman indifference. Erlich (1940; 1966: 26-30) says the areas of Yugoslavia most recently liberated from the Turks (where the most villages with zadrugas were) represented the past of the other areas. There is an unmistakable assumption that Balkan primitiveness – tribal, feuding, with extended families – is a survival of ancient conditions. When writers discuss the disappearance of the zadruga they do so in terms of modernisation: an industrial cash economy, a socialist republic, labour migration – all these things militate against extended family households, and aid the growth of efficient, conformable, nuclear family ones (Durkheim, 1898b; Erlich, 1966; Halpern, 1963; Halpern and Anderson, 1970; Mosely, 1943). The decline is self-evident: extended families are 'natural', and they give way in the face of modern conditions.

However, it is not wise to assume that mediterranean extended family households are always survivals from a disappearing past in which peasant landowners combined in natural units to farm plentiful land. The existence of the *zadruga* as a familiar institution no doubt gave the marcher lords of the Austrian border the idea of granting land to zadrugas in return for military service (Mosely, 1943; but cf. Barić 1967a: 8; 1967b): these were not 'natural' units. In Italy, in the period 1946-51, at an absolutely minimum estimate there were two million people living in extended family households engaged in sharecropping for landowners – not a tribal society, not peasant landowners, but extended family households none the less. Moreover, the households were not 'natural': membership was not genealogically ascribed, but people were recruited *ad hoc* to provide a sufficient labour force for however much land was taken in tenancy, and the family was thus created after negotiation – with the landowner on the one hand, and with potential members on the other. Pitkin (1959c) even records that land reform settlers in Sermoneta were setting up extended family households – though perhaps only in response to the sort of pressures which Silverman noted (above, p. 66). (Stem families exist at the fringe of the mediterranean in Portugal (Callier-Boisvert, 1968: 96; Willems, 1962), in the Italian Alps (Cole, 1969), and these are associated with the expressed need to keep a family estate intact, which seems reasonable. The only discrepant note is struck by Santangelo-Spoto (1892): admittedly his account of landless, labouring, stem families in Torremaggiore dates from the last century, but it is none the less enough to cast a deeper shadow of doubt over the common connection of non-nuclear households with property and with primitive agricultural technologies.)

Before turning to the Arab and Berber shores of the mediterranean it may be helpful to interpose a short note on the terms used. For it is quite common for ethnographers, in particular those who have written about the Lebanon, to use the term extended family to refer to the use of kinship ties in state politics and in business. They are chary of *kinship* because it can connote *lineage* which may also be important in other contexts. Farsoun (1970) thus refers to 'the functionally extended family', pointing out that 'it is not residentially nucleated'. Seventy-five per cent of the households he discusses were nuclear family ones, but they all had intense relations with other households. *Extended family* may serve admirably to refer to such relations, except that people may be confused if the term is also used for proper extended family households. In this book, therefore, *kinship* is used where ethnographers of the Levant often use *extended family;* the cost of this practice will be that some readers will have to be careful not to confuse kinship and lineage. It is, however, necessary to record that native idioms do not always accord with these usages. In Italy *famiglia estesa* is used to signify a far-flung family with many members: it is translated kinship here. In Hogar people refer to *'espiritu de clan'*, and mean the solidarity of a group of people closely related to the head, living under his roof perhaps in several domestic units but working together as one productive unit: *'clan'*, here, would be translated extended family (Adams, 1971: 168-9). In Al-Karak district one word *('A'ila)* can signify either an extended family or those same people who do not in fact happen to live under one roof (Gubser, 1973: 50). Some anthropologists' usage cannot be justified at all, however: Cronin's use of 'invisible clan' in Sicily (1970: 55-7; cf. Davis, 1976a, n. 38), is a case in point; and Rosenfeld's 'jointly held extended families' (1968) is also suspect.

So much for terminologies. It is now proper to admit that the relation of household and family in the Maghreb and Middle East is not well studied, and that what is known appears much more complex than it does elsewhere in the mediterranean: the overall impression is extremely tantalising. In some cases it makes best sense simply to understand nuclear family households (e.g. Gellner, 1969; Schorger, 1969; Sweet, 1967; Aswad, 1967). In other cases the information is fuller. Hart (1954) makes it clear that agnatic solidarity among nuclear family household heads can be expressed by fathers who retain control of property: nuclear families are created without an individual property basis, in other words. Similarly, extended families in Bint el-Hudūd may formally divide but continue to co-operate, a father offering fruits and facilities to his sons. Even when households are divided, Cohen says, the families may continue to live in the same house (A. Cohen, 1965: 54-5, 58-9). The Seksawa do not usually divide the property of a living father, though they may divide harvests; and even when there is more than one nuclear family in a household (what Berque calls *'famille souche'*) they are not usually commensal except when the head is extremely prestigeful. Some groups (e.g. the Ait H'adduyws) had more extended family households than others (Berque, 1955: 35-7).

The best account is of Cyrenaican Bedouin, by Peters (1965 – but see Appendix 2). Their households – tent-holds – have two distinctive characteristics. The first is that they commonly contain agnates, not necessarily all the close ones, who attach themselves to the core married couple: of six tents whose composition he describes, only two contained spouses and children and no others; one also included the husband's mother and two brothers; another, the husband's mother, his half-brother and father's brother's son (who was also his wife's parallel cousin). These are apparently patrilineal agglomerations around a nuclear family core, but Peters suggests that in some cases the core is not so much the male head of the family as his mother. Certainly, in the group which Peters describes, relations between tents were of great importance: 'the elementary family is subject to far too many vicissitudes to exist on its own' (ibid.: 140): the description of political identity, production and consumption involves consideration of the camp as a whole, and the boundaries of households are permeable, necessarily and easily crossed. This is the second way in which the household organisation of patrilineal endogamous semi-nomads does not fit the general categories 'nuclear', 'extended' and so on.

To conclude this brief survey of the kinds of extended household distributed round the mediterranean shores, Lineton's discussion of what he calls potential households may usefully emphasise the fluidity of household composition, and the possible misleading nature of the standard categories which anthropologists are apt to use. Lineton (1971) studied Mina, in Inner Mani, from which most people had emigrated – to Athens and to nearer towns (see above, p. 31). 'A proper family, a proper house' is thought to consist of parents and their children and sons' wives, but only ten of the 123 households met this ideal. Nevertheless to establish a new household at each marriage may prove extremely inconvenient for the two families of origin, and in any case, the new household as well as the two depleted ones were likely to be precariously self-sufficient: so the period immediately following a wedding may be one in which the separation of the newly-weds from their parents is masked and shrouded in an elaborate to-ing and fro-ing. Moreover, men who, for example, marry before their sisters do, still have and meet obligations to their household of origin. Lineton argues that households are not identified by simple straightforward co-residence; faced with the deliberate masking of household separation, with the continuation of obligation between members of families, he wishes to regard households as bundles of rights independent of common residence (ibid.: 77-83). Lineton argues very carefully that households are not so much physical entities as moral ones, and invites his readers to call 'potential households' those groups which recognise common obligations to provide income, support, dowry, for their members and which could at any time re-assemble. 'Many of the obligations of family/household membership could be fulfilled without co-residence' (ibid.: 84) and even if most of the members of the family were away the presence of, say, an aged parent kept alive the claims of the potential group *vis-à-vis* other potential groups of the same depleted kind. Lineton's claim that the group scattered by emigration should be regarded as in some sense a household is not likely to be accepted by many other anthropologists. They may think that households are precisely defined recognisable things and, perhaps, that Lineton's argument springs from an insistence that domestic units can only be dissolved in particular ways – by death, marriage, divorce. If none of these has taken place, why – the household still exists. But his data are quite clear: households fragmented by emigration are reunited from time to time; other households are extended, and some of the obligations recognised within those are also recognised by people who live in Piraeus or Athens, behaving towards inhabitants of Mani as if they shared a common roof. The moral impetus is sometimes actually associated with a household, sometimes not. Lineton thus leads his readers to contemplate the indistinctness of the formal boundary between nuclear and extended households: it is due to the ability of Maniots to dissolve and re-create households at necessity and will, and to accept obligation to kin regardless of whether they share a common purse or not. Anthropologists have long recognised that the normal process of the life-cycle can change the structure of domestic groups; Maniots show that a structure of obligation can be maintained when the domestic group does not exist: that is why Lineton calls it a potential household. If the reader agrees that the word household, however qualified, should not be applied to such a group of scattered kinsmen, he must probably argue that what makes the difference is the experience of childhood, fatherhood, motherhood in such homes: whatever the sense of obligation, the experience must be different. It is worth noting another similar case – Vasilika. There only three of fifty-one households had two married couples, and none had more than two (Friedl, 1963a: 19); nevertheless 'the mental construct ... [is] ... that several married farming brothers will live together': extended and joint households remain as a 'latent principle' (ibid.: 64). Another argument against applying the term 'household' to a group united by a principle and purpose rather than by a roof and purse is that life within households is coloured and shaped by expectations of how the unit will break up: units which have already broken up, however 'unnaturally', do not create such expectations among their members. But the dispersal of property and persons from households is a large and complex topic, requiring a section to itself.

III Division of households, dispersal of property and persons

All households divide sooner or later. It is the thesis of this section that the ways in which they divide have important consequences. The experience of being a son or a daughter, a father, a brother, is shaped not only by the kind of household a person lives in but by the expectations he has about how it will break up. The pattern of division, the way in which people and property are disposed, also has consequences for the composition of neighbourhoods, for the way old people are treated, for the structure of the local economy. Indeed, the reader is asked to bear in mind, through the sometimes dry technicalities which follow, that these experiential and mechanical consequences are what justified the labour. For once again it must be said that the ethnography is not complete – in some cases through negligence, in others through lack of interest, in others through lack of precision. So the discussion which follows may sometimes seem divorced from hard evidence: but that may inspire ethnographers to re-open their notebooks to achieve refutation; and it may direct the attention of future researchers to questions which, they may be convinced, are important.

Take societies with nuclear family households first: logically, where such households are the ideal, marriages occasion the dispersal of persons from their parental home. In general that is indeed what happens, even though there are exceptions of various kinds. For example, in Pisticci (Davis, 1973) the last daughter to marry may bring her husband to live in the parental home; in Nicuportu (Cronin, 1970: 45) newly-weds also sometimes live with the parents of one of them. This is similar to the practice of having a widowed parent live with a married child, for in both Pisticci and Nicuportu a new household is created: the property in the house is transferred (in Pisticci to the daughter – Cronin does not say to whom) and the headship of the household passes to the husband. Another kind of exception occurs when there are no houses available (Pitt-Rivers, 1961: 99-102; Lison-Tolosana, 1966: 160; Wade, cited in Davis, 1976a). It is important to distinguish these exceptions from stem family succession where co-residence with parents carries exclusive rights to immovable property. The only other exception to the general rule is the bizarre Alona where each pair of parents supplies a house to the newly-weds – in such a poor community that seems inexplicable; indeed, Peristiany does not explain it (1968a).

So the general rule is that marriage creates a new household. Particularly when this is further associated with bilateral inheritance everything seems to fall into place, and to go together as naturally as could be. But there are qualifications and distinctions to make. The main one is about the word 'neo-local' which is often applied to residence in these communities, for in fact the *locale* of the new households is not usually new: in most of these societies the rule is that the house the new couple will live in shall be provided by the parents of one of them. Because the information about which houses are available reaches neighbours first; or because, if building has to be done, it is easier to build close rather than distant; or because parents like their children near them – for a multitude of reasons the houses which parents provide are likely to create clusters of brothers and their wives, or sisters and their husbands, even if there is no specific rule which says that this ought to be so. Such clustering has consequences for relations within and between families and for the composition of neighbourhoods. So far as family relations are concerned, the evidence is as follows. In Nicuportu where a bride moves to her husband's neighbourhood she is said to have difficulty in detaching her husband from his mother (she does it by insinuating that her husband's mother *loved her other children more than him* – a discrimination, this, which recurs in more mundane terms when wives discuss property arrangements) (Cronin, 1970: 76-80). In Los Olivos (Price and Price, 1966b) a bride is enjoined to break relations with her mother, and the same seems to occur in Peyrane (Wylie, 1964). In Hal Farrug, Boissevain says that there are problems wherever a newly married couple lives (1965: 35-7; 1969a: 36-40), and these passages should be read in conjunction with Buxton's account (1921) of the transmission of nicknames: on Malta, the wife takes her husband's name; on Gozo the husband takes his wife's. Lison-Tolosana gives good detail on the kind of accusation and counter accusation made in Belmonte de los Caballeros, but does not say who provides the new house (1966: 158-9; see also Pitt-Rivers, 1961; 101; Gower Chapman, 1973: 111; Cutileiro, 1971: 112-13). Neighbourhoods, too, are affected: there is no rule of residence in Vila Velha, but by 'inclination' newly-weds try to live near the bride's parents, creating a cluster of kin related through women. 'Restricted as they are to mothers, daughters and sisters these networks [used for visiting and mutual aid] form the only operative groupings based on kinship found in this society' (Cutileiro, 1971: 126-7). The in-marrying men may be considered good partners for co-operative enterprise (Pitt-Rivers, 1961: 99-102; Davis, 1973: 67-9) and the husbands of sisters may co-operate in the maintenance of a common honour (Davis, 1973: 63). More generally, neighbourhoods are gossip centres, run by women, deserted for the most of the day by men: it is in neighbourhoods that reputations are made. The composition of them is therefore of considerable importance: if a bride's parents have to provide her with a house, she is likely to have at least some sisters near by, members of the same gossiping, reputation-maintaining group; if the bridegroom's parents provide the house, it is her husband's brother's wives – all with different interests – with whom she co-operates. Littlewood (cited by Davis, 1976a) has written that in Quercio, a town of 10,000 inhabitants, a mother does not really mind where her daughter lives, since she can get anywhere in a few minutes (married daughters do generally live near their mothers, however); but this should not lead anyone to minimise the importance of neighbourhoods: Quercio mothers do gossip with their neighbours. The other extreme is perhaps described by Kenna: the village of Nisos has 320 inhabitants, and it takes less than five minutes to walk through it. Nevertheless, Nisiots recognise no less than six distinct neighbourhoods, and some women had never visited some of the neighbourhoods. The composition of neighbourhoods *is* important; it *is* affected by rules or practices of residence at marriage, and it is largely neglected in the ethnographies. So much for residence patterns: 'neo-local' often conceals a bias within the apparent impartiality of 'bilateral': and it is an important bias.

The dispersal of persons cannot really be discussed outside the context of the dispersal of property. It is not too much to say that the dispersal of property among new nuclear family households presents a genuine structural dilemma: each society has had to find a compromise in response to the dilemma; and each compromise carries with it consequences for relations within and between households. The dilemma is itself the result of two contradictory ideals: a nuclear family should be independent of others, particularly in livelihood; and children should receive equal shares of their parents' patrimony. So far as the first of these is concerned it is so much a commonplace of the ethnography that people have begun to fail to record it properly (e.g. Davis, 1973); but both the exaggerated respect owed to fathers in a way which symbolises submission and inferiority (Freeman, 1970: 54-7; Lison-Tolosana, 1966: 151-3; Broegger, 1971: 104-5; Davis, 1973: 50-1; Cronin, 1970: 105-8; Cutileiro, 1971: 114-15; Gower-Chapman, 1973: 68-87; cf. Parsons, 1962, 1964; Lombroso, 1896), and the association of full adulthood with headship of a household and with independence – these are well attested. The head of a household has the chance to establish himself as a good and rich man – to make alliances, to pursue the interest of his family, to establish his own reputation – from which may accrue further advantage. So that a good marriage settlement – the dispersal to a son of part of his father's patrimony – not only demonstrates his new independent rule in a household, it is also a crucial initial stock, a start in life on which he can build and can show that he is a responsible man. Independence, adulthood, the simultaneous dispersal of persons and property, these go together in highly competitive not very differentiated peasant communities.

On the other hand there is the principle of equality of division between children. Sometimes there is differentiation between sons and daughters: in some societies daughters clearly get larger shares than sons; in others, sons get larger shares than daughters. Curiously – and significantly – there are no reports at all of quarrels among sisters about inequality; but sons are invariably reported as seeking equality of division of the patrimony: this is partly a matter of basic bilateral ideology; partly – and more directly – a matter of jealousy if one brother should have a better start in life than another.

These two principles demand different patterns of dispersal of property: full independence at marriage requires dispersal of property at marriage – a man should get his birthright and his life-chances then. The principle of equality is best achieved by dividing an estate when the owner dies. That is because in most families there is more than one child, hence more than one marriage. In large families the children's marriages may occur over a span of twenty years; the estate to be divided, and from which children will draw their portion *seriatim,* is likely to change in value. For the parents themselves can inherit; they may have a stroke of good fortune – a series of good harvests, for example, enabling them to purchase more land. A stroke of misfortune (prolonged sickness, in contemporary southern Europe where the wonders of modern medicine are known and charged for, can cripple a family's finances) may deprive younger children of endowments equal to those already made. A sibling may die before he has received any share, altering the number of children a partially dispersed estate has to be divided among and throwing out earlier calculations of equity. As children move out of the home the size of the domestic labour force shrinks – and this has consequences for the saving and investing capacity of the parental household. In times of change and development the structure of local economies changes, producing consequent changes in the relative value of resources. All these things affect the size of the estate in time, and make the calculation of equality very difficult.

Moreover, marriage settlements are not like fixed prices in a retail trade: they are negotiable. Of course, if a rule says that there is a community-wide rate of endowment, the negotiation would not affect relations between siblings. But there is only one report of this, and that concerns bridewealth – which is not an endowment of a new couple (Rosenfeld, 1968: 268). As it is, a parent meets with another parent, and they negotiate. A prospective spouse's future parents-in-law are not in the least concerned with achieving equality among his or her siblings; they are there to see their own child as well endowed as possible. If they make a settlement, they do so to force the other family to match it, and it may be that to match it they have to provide more (or perhaps even less) than consideration of strict internal equality would dictate. In any case strong extractive pressure is applied by the negotiating parents, and this is another and very important factor, which makes it difficult to achieve equality of endowment in a series of marriages from a fluctuating patrimony (see e.g. Friedl, 1959a).

The alternative is to wait until the parent's death. People are still disgruntled often enough by what they get: this is sometimes because a father has used the capacity to make a will favouring one or other of his children. But with this method there are greater possibilities of achieving equality. Nevertheless if people disperse at marriage, and property is dispersed at death, men may to spend their most productive and reputation-forming years without land, dependent on their parents or an employer for a livelihood: they observe their parents, moreover, becoming more aged and incompetent as they preside over a patrimony which has to support fewer and fewer people. There is thus a real incompatibility between the two principles of independence and equality; they are best achieved at different points in the domestic cycle; and to pursue one of them necessarily diminishes the possiblity of achieving the other.

To turn to the ethnographies is to discover a variety of solutions to the dilemma; these are not solutions in the sense that they eliminate conflict, or by some magic or illogicality permit people to do inconsistent things without consequences. The devotee of subtleties of the kind which Pitt-Rivers has produced in his essay on honour (allowing Spaniards calmly to derive ought from is and back again, for centuries, with impunity) cannot expect them here: there is no sociological let-out, no play on words, which resolves the inconsistency or absolves people from the consequences of desiring incompatibles. Indeed, it is because the various solutions do have characteristic consequences that they are worth writing about. The 'solutions' are in fact compromises; people accept conflict in some relationships in the hope of avoiding it in others.

A new household is most usually endowed with furniture, equipment and linen. Even when the house is rented (Pitt-Rivers, 1961: 99-102; Cutileiro, 1971; Price and Price, 1966b) basic equipment is provided by one household or the other, or by both. Generally speaking the bride and her family provide linen, but there is considerable variation in the allocation of responsibility to provide other goods (e.g. Riegelhaupt, 1967: 117; Friedl, 1963a: 57-8; Freeman, 1970: 76; Davis, 1973: 36). There is a possibility that the whole complex of provisioning – house and furniture and linen – fits with rules about paying for the wedding; and that the allocation of responsibility to provide particular goods symbolises something about notions of conjugal roles, but information on both these points is hard to come by. In any case the extent to which the bride or bridegroom are personally responsible for the goods they provide is often unclear. The amount of linen required for a decent marriage can be enormous by English standards (Broegger, 1971: 95; Davis, 1973: 35; Friedl, 1963a: 57-8; Pitkin, 1960), and to collect it together may take a decade or more. It is common for a girl's mother to help prepare the linen, but the girl also usually practises the essential skills of embroidery and sewing. The embellishment of linen is an obvious expenditure of money, time and skill, and a large bottom drawer thus indicates something of the prestige of the family: displays of it are often made (Pitkin, 1960; Davis, 1973: 34-6; Cutileiro, 1971: 95; Freeman, 1970: 73-4) but presumably the girls of Los Olivos, said to embroider their initials on sanitary towels, derive mainly private satisfactions (Price and Price, 1966b: 312, n. 4). Lambiri seems to indicate that Megaran girls working in the linen factory provide all their linen themselves (1968: see above p. 68): and Cutileiro says that young people who have incomes from employment provide their family's share of the basic equipment (1971: 95-6).

There is now an irritating terminological problem to be settled: what is the basic equipment to be called? The commonest usage is *trousseau,* but only the Prices (1966b) are bold enough to refer to the bridegrooms' *trousseaux.* The issue is important because in some cases the goods are accounted against eventual shares in inheritance (e.g. Freeman, 1970: 73-4). Cutileiro is inconsistent: there is 'no dowry' apart from a trousseau of linen (1971: 95); but, when it comes to inheritance, a son who married when his parents were more prosperous than they were at the time of other sons' marriages, may have that fact taken into account. That seems to imply that sons too receive some goods when they marry (ibid.: 125). Riegelhaupt (1967: 117) remarks, 'none (of the trousseau) is looked upon as a "dowry" '. As soon as the problem of what to call the basic equipment is tackled, the area requiring definition expands, for further confusion arises from the colloquial and legal usages of the word dowry: colloquially it may mean property which comes with a wife; legally the term designates property of a particular status – one in which the right to alienate is restricted during the life of the wife. Ethnographers have tended to slip from one contrast to another: linen may be contrasted with dowry (restricted property); but it may be assimilated with dowry (property transferred at marriage) and contrasted with inheritance (property transferred at death). In the context of particular ethnographic accounts everything usually becomes quite clear; but such semantic slides must be eliminated from a comparative study, as this one is, which has also to accommodate difficult cases of dowries in the legal sense which are not accounted against inheritance (Cronin, 1970: 46; Broegger, 1971: 95). The distinctions which have to be made are as follows, and they are accompanied by a suggested terminology.

Any property which is transferred at the death of the owner can safely be called inheritance. If it is transferred at the marriage of the recipient (not necessarily the owner's child), then brides have to be distinguished from bridegrooms. So far as a bridegroom is concerned, property which he receives, the value of which is deducted from his share of the inheritance, can safely be called a settlement; if it does not disqualify him from a full share in the estate it might be called a marriage gift. So far as brides are concerned, property which cannot be alienated without permission of a court or consent of the donor may be called dowry, and it should be noted clearly whether or not it disqualifies her from inheritance. Property which a girl brings to her marriage and which has no legal restriction on alienation is quite often designated by a local word (e.g. *corredo* in Italy or the special use of *roukha* in Greece); if there is no local word, then the Roman-law *paraphernalia* may be used, as it is in Italian law, provided that the girl is not disqualified from inheriting to its value: in that case marriage settlement is advisable. To summarise: a *settlement* is property which is given to either a bride or a bridegroom by any donor, subject to no legal restrictions on use or alienation, and which disqualifies the recipient from inheritance. A *dowry* is property given to a bride by any donor, subject to restrictions on use and alienation; it may or may not disqualify her from inheritance. *Paraphernalia* is property from any source given to a bride, subject to no restrictions, carrying no disqualification from inheritance; *marriage gift* is the same as paraphernalia in all respects save that it is given to a bridegroom. These distinctions are set out in Figure 2. Any anthropologist who works in a single community, and without comparative intentions, will find many of these distinctions are otiose: but in fact a careful specification of what rights are gained, what forgone, is a great aid to the student who wishes to compare one ethnography with another. The reason for making such a comparison is not mere legalism: rather, there is an evanescent suggestion in the ethnographies that the particular rules of any community regarding the dispersal of persons and property have

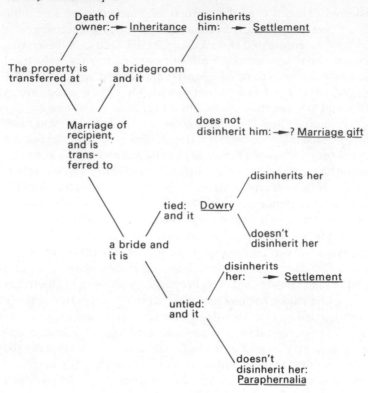

Figure 2   Suggested terminology for property transfers

consequences for the quality expectations, and experience of what it is to be a father, a brother to a brother or to a sister, Of course, questions of temperament, of general economic conditions and of religious ideas, may also play an important part.

Before discussing that, it may be useful to set out some of the broader patterns which seem to be associated with the various practices. The first is that settlements and dowries are usually made to both bride and bridegroom unless it is the sons of the family who are territorially concentrated: where sons stick together after marriage it is the usual practice for them not to get property until their father's death. For example in Vasilika sons do not generally get property when they marry; but when a son gains educational qualifications and moves to the city the expense involved is considered his share of the patrimony. Compare Alcalà (Pitt-Rivers, 1961: 99):

Neither (the bride nor the bridegroom) are likely to have any property from the parents while the latter are still active though the new couple may be given charge of a farm or mill belonging to one of the parents. If any dowry is given, which is rare, it represents either a share of the inheritance of the girl's parents or a free gift on their part.

The Alcaleños seem to keep all options open: it must be associated with their similarly flexible rules of residence (Pitt-Rivers, 1961: 100-3). The concentration of sons is of course most obvious in extended family households, and it may – where there are nuclear family households – perhaps be recognised as a bias towards family extension. It is thus the case that where daughters are dispersed and sons concentrated at marriage, property is dispersed to daughters at their marriages, and to sons at their father's death. So, Vasilikan girls get land if they marry farmers, city house sites if they are rich enough, while sons wait till their fathers die, unless they too move to the cities.

But the converse is not true: where property is dispersed at marriage daughters always get some: sons may get some as well, but there is no case in which sons get property and daughters do not. Friedl must be given credit again for providing an explanation which may be generalisable: 'My suggestion is that among the farmers in the Boeotian countryside, male honour depends not only on male protection of the chastity of women, but also more explicitly and obviously on the provision of adequate dowries for their women . . . the action is also an expression of [their father's] masculinity' (Friedl, 1963b: 133). Honour is not merely sexual, it involves the complete range of domestic roles: setting up a daughter in a decent marriage (with a dowry) is one sign that a father has not been found wanting: someone was prepared to marry her, and he has done his duty. Contemplation of this success has – in Vasilika – a specific verb: *kamarono* (Friedl, 1963a: 19). In Cyprus women sing praise songs at weddings to celebrate the qualities of their children and their own achievements. Peter Loizos recorded the following song composed impromptu by Mrs Stella Pipis at the wedding feast of one of her daughters, and has kindly given permission for it to be printed here.

185

The astronauts today
can go to the moon
praised be my Maker
who has given me such joy.

I've had six children
and they're all educated
not one below the mark
they're all outstanding.

I've had six children
and not a wrong'un;
one is an auditor
one a land-office man.

And may God help Prokopis [a] to come
who gave us the houseplots
and brightened this district

And deep in my heart
today is great joy
now my Maroulla's come [b]
my highschool teacher

My two daughters
are better than the rest [c]
I've a highschool teacher
and a primary teacher

Welcome my Dimitris
for paying the musicians [d]
I ask my Maker
may he live a thousand years.

It was the wish of God
that these two should be one
and she built her house
with her golden hand.

Notes to poem:

(a) Prokopis, her brother, resident in England who gave up part of his inheritance to provide building sites for his sister's daughters.
(b) Another daughter, studying in Athens.
(c) I.e. better than all other village girls.
(d) To pay the musicians is a compliment to the singer: a skilful singer responds immediately with a verse.

Translation does justice, for once, to the deep pride of a parent to whom raising and setting up six children is an achievement like sending men to the moon.

Pisticcesi do not sing impromptu songs, nor do they have a special verb for contemplating the successful conduct of a family's most important affairs, but they know the pleasure, and boast that they experience it: indeed, they claim to derive it from having set up their sons in marriage, with settlements, as well. Pisticci is fairly typical of societies where both sons and daughters receive property at marriage: daughters get parapherns and a settlement or dowry consisting of a house, or rent for a house, and land if possible. Whether it should be a settlement or a dowry is negotiable between the contracting families. Dowries are increasingly unpopular because of the legal restrictions on use. Pisticcesi, however, continue to call the property a 'dowry' even if it is only a settlement (Davis, 1973: 34. n.5): in this they are like some ethnographers. Sons normally get a settlement of land if the parents have any. In addition to this dispersal of property at marriages, Pisticcesi, like most other people who make settlements on both sons and daughters, keep a parental reserve for their lifetime: this, they say, is to make sure that their children treat them well in their old age, and also to allow for any possible re-adjustments: if the settlements they have made during their lifetime turn out to have been unfair, equality can be achieved when they die. The other societies in which a parental reserve is kept to redress inequalities and to protect the parents from their children are Alona (Peristiany, 1968a), Milocca (brothers concentrated), Villamaura (brothers concentrated) (P. Schneider, 1969; J. Schneider, 1969), and Vergadi (Bialor, 1968). The societies in which most property is dispersed by inheritance, children receiving only parapherns or marriage gifts, are São Jão das Lampas (Riegelhaupt, 1967); Vila Velha (Cutileiro, 1971); Alcalá (Pitt-Rivers, 1961) and Los Olivos (Price and Price, 1966a). In Nicuportu (brothers concentrated) daughters get parapherns which may be discounted against inheritance if they are valuable (Cronin, 1970: 46); in Montevarese daughters get para- pherns and a dowry or settlement which is not discounted against inheritance: but Broegger's discussion raises doubts about whether what he calls dowry (which could in any case be a settlement, since he is not specific) is not in fact usually paraphernalia (Broegger, 1971: 94-6). Finally, in Belmonte de los Caballeros a son should have a settlement, and if he does his bride may get a dowry of land in addi- tion to the usual paraphernalia (Lison-Tolosana, 1966: 160).

What are the possible consequences of these patterns? The evid- ence is so thin any answer must be utterly tentative, and such confid- ence as it may carry must be derived from the certainty that family relationships differ among other things according to the property relations and residence patterns which local custom provides for. If the question appears at all in such a summary book as this it is because some sense must be given to the repeated statement that family feel- ing is strong or important in mediterranean countries: as a general impression that seems to be both true and inadequate for scholarly investigation; and it is by introducing distinctions, by suggesting where family feeling may be stronger and weaker, that substance may be given to the sensed truth of it.

Take as a first line of inquiry the expectation of fraternal enmity commonly recorded in the ethnographies. It is very difficult to say that brothers quarrel more bitterly in some societies than in others, but it may be possible to say that, within the same single society, brothers quarrel more among themselves than they severally do with their fathers: the observation – still requiring delicacy and scepticism – may be easier if what is compared is not brothers in this society and in that, but brothers and sons in the same society. The guess might be, then, that when a father distributes his property among his sons dur- ing his lifetime, at their marriages, they are likely to be content with him, but discontented with each other: partly guided by their wives they compare the settlement they have each received, and will be likely to find them unequal. They then quarrel about the division of the parental reserve patrimony – reserved precisely to redress imba- lances: an easily recognisable sign of this is the prolonged existence of small parcels of land under multiple ownership, which have not been divided because the siblings cannot agree on the division (Davis, 1973: 131-3, 133-6). Conversely, when fathers do not divide property during their lifetimes, but leave it all to be inherited, expect quarrels

between fathers and sons, relative amity between brothers. The signs
to look for are, first, old people treated with contempt when they own
property which they cannot farm (e.g. Cutileiro, 1971: 120; Gower
Chapman 1973: 47; Cozzi, 1912); and second, devices for the division
of an inheritance which randomise unfairness. This broad association
of dispersal of property at marriage with fraternal discontent, of
dispersal of property at death with filial discontent, is of course
modified by the pattern of dispersal of persons at marriage. Take the
concentrated brothers-dispersed sisters pattern as normal: then the
relations within a neighbourhood will vary in part with the pattern of
property dispersal. But where brothers are dispersed and property is
also dispersed largely at marriage (and in fact where brothers do
disperse they always take property with them) it seems likely that
fraternal discontent will be exacerbated. Of course, other factors still
affect the relations of family members. The size of the town, village or
hamlet is important. The general state of agriculture and of the economy as a whole is important. For example, it is likely that brothers,
waiting to inherit, will become more impatient if innovations are
being made in local agriculture generally: where agricultural innovation can increase incomes and values, and old men are not taking
advantage of the new opportunities, as they often do not, sons may
strengthen their impatience by adopting the posture of would-be
agro-businessmen thwarted by the conservatism and selfishness of an
older generation. Similarly, since diversification of local economies
usually has the effect of devaluing farm land and making farm incomes relatively less desirable, because more hardly won than others,
there may be a calming effect on family stress.

   All this is highly speculative, and it is as well to turn quickly to
another but related matter. No ethnographer of the mediterranean
has recorded either a general expectation that sisters will quarrel
about property, or even any isolated cases. True, they have not said
that sisters never quarrel, so the evidence is as purely negative as
could be; but supposing it is the case, what might the explanation be?
One element must be the general position of women in society:
women are neighbourhood-bound and are excluded from wider
arenas of competition. Moreover, the provision of a competence is
generally speaking a component of male honour rather than of
women's prestige: competencies, got largely by competitive behaviour, are in the male province. Women appear not to take part in the
negotiation of their own dowries and, when they have inheritance

rights, they are represented by their husbands. When women are
scattered by marriage they are widely reported to sow dissension
among residential groups of brothers. Cronin reports that Nicupor-
tesi attribute fraternal quarrels to in-marrying women: 'the foreign
sex enters in', they say: not the *other* sex, but the (female) sex which is
identified by the fact that it comes always from another place. In this
case, women work through their husbands to establish and maintain
their own separate identity within a group dominated by men, and by
their mother-in-law. Where sisters are concentrated they stand
together against the other women of the neighbourhood: they are kin,
the others are just neighbours, and hostile: the interest of the group of
sisters directs them towards solidarity. Explanation for the apparent
absence of quarrels among sisters, then, seems to require consideration of the greater involvement of women in neighbourhoods, of
different kinds, created by different patterns of dispersal at marriage.

The Nicuportu phrase 'the foreign sex enters in' is echoed round the
shores of the mediterranean: family quarrels and the dissolution of
extended family households are usually attributed in the first instance
to the women who marry the men of the household. In Turkish
gelin means young wife, fiancée; etymologically it means 'she who
comes', and the intrusive woman is a mediterranean-wide character.
Consider Campbell (1964: 65-9):

> During the early months of marriage the young husband gives
> the minimum of overt public attention to his bride ... he does not
> make conversation. For her part, a bride will never address her
> husband before other members of the family. If she requires
> anything, she arranges it through her husband's brother .... In his
> general behaviour the husband attempts to deny the importance
> of his exclusive sexual relationship with his bride, and he makes
> every effort to conceal the occurrence and frequency of sexual
> intercourse.

Campbell continues: while the bridegroom's family is anxious that he
should give proof of his manliness they think that once he has vindi-
cated the family's reputation of masculinity further interest in the
bride is disruptive: after a few weeks he must return to his sheep and
make no more visits home than he did before, since everything should
appear the same. The bridegroom makes 'secret' visits to his bride,
sleeping in the family hut:

Stories are told about grooms who tripped over milk cans as
they entered the pitch dark hut or failed to convince the dogs of
their true identity. They are considered to be hysterically funny;
perhaps an indication of the ambivalent feelings which this
conflict of loyalties provokes.

Compare Peters's account (1965) of Bedouin fathers who – together
with all the bridegrooms' senior agnates – ignore their sons' weddings: a nuptial tent is set up, and the father ignores it; the bridegroom, showing reluctance, is forced into it by lewd bachelors, and his
father ignores it; guns are fired 'volley after volley' when the bride is
discovered to have been *intacta,* and the father ignores them. After
the seven-day wedding, ignored throughout by the father, the newly
married man leaves his bride early in the morning to feign to sleep by
his father's side 'as he always had done in the past'; and he continues
to eat with his father – a sign of solidarity and acceptance of authority
– perhaps for several years (cf. Bourdieu, 1965: 224).

Such formalities are not simply the expression of the quite common
resentment of the rising generation by a declining one: throughout
the mediterranean men express dissatisfaction at their waning
powers, their lost youth, the vigour of sons eager to play their role. The
maturity and marriage of the sons of an extended household foretell
the division of a close-knit group and its associated property, and that
is why heart-felt charades are played to conceal the inevitable, and to
prevent mutual recognition of the end (cf. Lineton, 1971, above,
pp.174-6). Moreover, there are some reports of less symbolic devices
to prevent the growth of separate interests within the household. The
twenty-six members of the Vařzić zadruga, described by Mosely
(1943), were clearly anxious to maintain their community, which they
saw threatened not only by the normal structural tendency to division, but also by the common trend of the time: they saw zadrugas
collapsing all round them as they succumbed to the pressures of
'modernity'. The collapse of other zadrugas, moreover, had a domino
effect: when they were divided the property was partly transferred out
through the women, who, from an on-going household, normally
received only marriage chests of linen and clothes. But the existence
of propertied women marrying in to a zadruga creates a focus for
sectional, nuclear interests, and strengthens the tendency to fission.
The Varžić household must have observed the consequences in other

households; three of their six wives had brought property, and others
were expecting to inherit (Mosely 1943: 160-1):

> Thus, apart from the zadrugal property, which is owned and
> used by the household as a unit, its various members have
> acquired, or have expectations of acquiring, substantial amounts
> of individual property of the Roman-law type. The members are
> not permitted to spend any time working their own land or looking
> after their own cattle; all their time is devoted to the work of the
> zadrugan except for the sewing and embroidery of the women ...
> 'What she [a wife] has there [at her father's] we do not admit into
> our zadruga.'

The Varžić practice was to put individual property out on half-and-
half sharecropping contracts, a deliberate attempt to mitigate the
consequences which followed from the decay of pure zadruga practice all round them (cf. Barić, 1967a: 7).

Women who bring property set brothers at odds by creating sectional loyalties and interests. In São Jão das Lampas they say that
siblings would quarrel less but for the 'daughters-in-law' (Riegelhaupt, 1967: 121); in Pisticci brothers who wished to maintain a
partnership in business made an agreement that their wives should
play no part in their enterprise (Davis, 1973: 56-7). Both these communities, like Nicuportu, have predominantly nuclear family households, but people who live in extended families say the same. Rosenfeld found, in his study in Lower Galilee, that women have 'personal,
status and economic reasons' for urging the division of property:
'Forty men would eat from the same tray if it were not for the women';
but women want independence of each other within the household,
the standing to treat with other women outside the household, and the
ability to save and to manage on their own account. In fact of the
seventeen extended families he lists, only three contained more than
two married couples: all the rest were composed of a father and his
only son and their wives. Rosenfeld makes the point, which rings true,
that it is not only intrusive women who dislike working for others and
getting a disproportionate reward: when one son has more children
than the others, and the product of equal labour is put into a common
store, the others see themselves contributing more to his keep than
they receive (Rosenfeld, 1958). In fact, of course, it is otiose to lay the
blame for the disruption of fraternal harmony on either the fathers or
the mothers of growing families within the household: it is an auto-

matic process, in which both sexes collaborate. Brothers who have lived together do perhaps feel nostalgia for the days when they had no separating interests; and Barić makes the telling point that when there is an imbalance between the component families in the household it is the women who notice it most: men do not necessarily work any harder as the household grows – they store less, or sell less, but women look after the children and cook and clean: the labour of food-processing and domestic maintenance does increase significantly, and certainly more than productive labour does. It is therefore comprehensible that women should complain first (1967a: 7).

One other point should be made on this topic of intrusive women: it is not only sons' wives who are perceived to be intruders. Both Cuisenier (1976) and Rosenfeld (1958) have noted that a father's remarriage or second marriage can disrupt the harmony of an extended family household, particularly if the father divorces his sons' mother in order to remarry. In Lower Galilee a father's second marriage is said to cut the property; in the Djebel Lansarine in northern Tunisia Cuisenier identified three ways in which an extended family customarily breaks up: it may be divided by the sons on the death of their father; or by the father either when his eldest son wishes to establish a separate household (cf. Marx, 1967: 107-8) or when he himself remarries and makes a grant of land to his ex-wife to which she takes her children.

The equal division of a patrimony among brothers who have collaborated for many years, and who have not received settlements from it, seems to be done with greater amity than it is when brothers have been separated for some time, and when what they divide is a residue to redress long-standing inequalities. The sign which may justify the judgment of greater amity is the existence of rules and procedures which recognise the impossiblity of achieving absolutely perfect equality, but which make sure that it is in no person's interest to strive for inequality. The existence of such rules, that is, may betoken fundamental agreement; and conformity with what they prescribe may indicate a willingness to submit self-interest to control, to maintain properly good relations among brothers: certainly it contrasts with the bitter quarrelling, the refusal to accept a set of binding rules, characteristic of some other societies. Such rules are of three kinds: the device reported by Friedl from Vasilika (1963a; discussed also by Levy, 1956; see below, pp. 251-2) accepts the inevitability of some inequality, but randomises its impact: the various kinds of property are divided into the right number of shares, and lots are drawn by a child or neighbour. On Nisos (Kenna, 1971: 259-61) the youngest son divides the property into shares and the others each choose their share, in age order beginning with the eldest. This procedure constrains the divider to make the shares as equal as possible. The third kind of procedure is to invite a respected and acceptable outsider to make the division: this is done when Yugoslavian and Albanian zadrugas break up, and in Portugal (Cutileiro, 1971: 125) and in Turkey. Stirling (1965, 122-3) records a device, used to deal with brothers who dispute the divider's judgment, of extraordinary subtlety: 'If one of the heirs claims that the valuation of an article [allocated to another person] is too low, then he is asked to value it himself and accept it as part of his share at the higher valuation.' Thus the argumentative heir is constrained to act in good faith, to object only when he really means what he says. Valentini (1945: 138-68) provides an account of the rules of division in northern Albania which illustrates in detail the distinctions made between kinds of property when an extended family's patrimony is divided: some common rights are not divided at all; some goods are divided among adult males 'by gun'; stores of food are divided 'by mouth' – women and children have shares; land is divided 'by brother' – by segments of the household. The division was usually made by the council of the household. Some idea of how this might work out in practice may be got from Mosely (1943, 165-8), though it should be remembered that this account is from a different region of the Balkans. It is useful, finally, to call attention to a unique article by Cuisenier (1967) in which he reports the result of a survey of property transmission in Yugoslavia and Turkey: knowing the law, he asked – is it observed? He found that of 224 inheritances 31 per cent, were illegal – some heirs were deprived of their rights by one prepotent heir among them; 9 per cent, involved a will and legacy, and 60 per cent, were in conformity with the law, but were not necessarily made with regard to the law – a distinction which may escape some readers. But in about a third of these Turkish cases someone deprived his co-heirs of their rights, and in 84 per cent, of those cases it was mothers and sisters who were deprived. A similar tendency to exclude women from their legal rights was noted in Yugoslavia. Cuisenier's article also considers the transmission of property at marriages; he concludes that transmission 'par alliance' is much less significant than transmission by descent, and that customary rules to provide dowry and bridewealth are

194

ignored about as often as legal rules about inheritance. It is difficult to make much of this meticulous article. Although the rate of infraction must surely vary from community to community, Cuisenier's article is unique, and there is no explanation of the facts he details other than the very general ones, that it is not only capitalist landlords who are greedy and prepotent about vital resources, but also brothers and sons; and that peasants tend to ignore state laws when it suits them and can do so with impunity. Indeed, it is Cuisenier himself who says, in a later article (1976), that rules are not primary: Tunisians who inherit ask 'with whom *must* we share?' and then seek rules, among all those available to them, which most fit the dispositions they wish to make. An ethnographer who wishes to follow in Cuisenier's steps, therefore, should put rules about transmission of property in a context of all state rules, as well as in a context of power relations and manipulation.

These two sections have reviewed the evidence about household composition and the dispersal of persons and property from households. The two are obviously related: all households of whatever kind, except stem families, are created by the dissolution and dispersal of others. The key movement, the mainspring of the domestic cycle, is marriage: in the case of nuclear households the marriage of either sons or daughters brings about the dispersal of persons and of some property; in the case of extended family households, the marriage of daughters disperses them, and the marriage of sons, apparently bringing new recruits and property to the group, presages dissolution in delayed action. The experiential differences between nuclear family households and extended family ones are considerable; but a close examination of property relations and the mechanics of dispersal suggests a continuum. At one extreme is Pisticci, with sororal clusters in neighbourhoods, matrilineal inheritance of houses, and associations of men married to sisters maintaining a common economic and sexual honour, dispersing property to both sons and daughters at marriage. Then there are communities where either daughters or sons or both may get property at marriage, and the rules appear to achieve maximum flexibility. Alcalà seems to be an example. Such societies contrast fairly sharply with those where – as in Nicuportu – daughters get property at marriage, sons have to wait until their parents die, and there are neighbourhood fraternal clusters; although people in these communities expect to live in nuclear family households, the brothers may co-operate and collaborate for some time in ways which are like those of extended family systems; when they begin to co-operate less they blame 'the foreign sex'. Then there are communities of the kind described by Lineton and Friedl where although people live in nuclear family households they behave as if they lived in extended ones, and they use elaborate and subtle devices to divide joint property without disrupting fraternal co-operation. Finally there are the patrilineal, patrilocal extended families of the Balkans. These, too, are subject to division, the seeds of which are sown by marriage. Variation in fraternal and filial relations is related to this continuum: fraternal disharmony may be related to serial dispersal of property (which itself may be associated with dispersal of persons) to brothers at their marriages; while filial discontent is associated with dispersal of brothers and paternal control of property.

Some of the preceding argument is highly speculative. When the evidence is inadequate it is sometimes necessary to take the merest hint as the basis for inferences which are strictly speaking illegitimate. No apologies are offered, for the way to ensure that future monographs will include the necessary evidence in sufficient detail is to insist now on comparison. The common assumption seems to have been that families are much of a muchness and do not require detailed study, particularly when an ethnographer finds that nuclear family households are the rule in the community he visits. If the speculation is dubious it may none the less lead future ethnographers to a higher awareness of variation in family relationships, even if they wish only to refute or qualify what is said here.

The argument here has been based on the assumption that anthropologists must try to capture something of the variety of human experience. The differences in experience of being a mediterranean father, mother, child, are the consequence of the composition of the domestic units in which people live, and of rules and expectations about how it will break up. The various methods which people have devised with ingenuity and suffering and joy (felt equal to landing on the moon) to disperse persons and property are themselves solutions to the dilemma posed by the pursuit of incompatible aims of independence and of equality. Any solution carries with it typical patterns of amity and hostility, even if these are masked by elaborate pretences that nothing has changed nor ever will.

In conclusion, it is worth noting that the notions of independence and equality are variable in content and application. It is always important to ask – equal among whom? In some societies daughters get larger shares than sons do; in others, smaller ones; the rules for dividing the property of a zadruga specify that different kinds of property shall be divided equally among different categories of person – with varying numbers of persons in each category. Moreover, domestic groups of whatever kind have a variable autonomy. While it is clear that neither Sarakatsani nor Cyrenaican households can survive without perpetual co-operation with others – so much so that it is difficult to speak of 'households' at all in some cases – these are only the most striking instances of an interdependence which is manifest in all the societies under discussion. The interdependence may be embodied in associations and co-operatives, as the Varžić zadruga's was (Mosely, 1943); or it may be expressed through kinship and spiritual kinship, binding households together in wider associations: but what Sahlins has called the domestic mode of production, typified by absolute autonomy, does not exist in the mediterranean any more than it does elsewhere.

So far the discussion in this chapter has been of relations within households, and between the households which are produced by the dispersal of persons and property. It is now time to place these units within their context of kinship relations.

IV Systems of kinship, patterns of marriage

The households and families discussed in the two previous sections are embedded in systems of kinship and alliance of various kinds. Broadly speaking the north-western mediterranean is bilateral, without kin-groups – although, as has been seen, residence rules and practices cause groups of kin to come into existence *de facto*, and these groups may have a core or a 'bias' (the term is from Callier-Boisvert, 1968) towards the matriline, or patriline, as the case may be (e.g. Campbell, 1963: 81, 91; 1964: 55-7, 300; Kavadias, 1963). The north-eastern mediterranean is, broadly speaking, patrilineal, usually without kinship groups, though these are known to have existed and to have been vigorously engaged in political and economic activities in the past. In Greece the studies available are all of bilateral societies with varying degrees of residual patriliny (Friedl, 1963a; Lineton, 1971); the only study of a bilateral kindred is Campbell. The rest of the mediterranean studies – the whole of the eastern and southern sections – are of patrilineal societies with a preference for endogamy.

All this is 'broadly speaking': it should give the reader a rough guide to what he should expect when he reads the ethnographies. It is a curiosity of kinship studies that they have not achieved the same depths of analysis and subtlety in the mediterranean as they have elsewhere. So far as the bilateral mediterranean is concerned, kinship studies have suffered from the all-too-easy assumption that a kinship system so familiar requires no further exploration and writers have been tempted, and have often enough succumbed, to elaborate the themes of what kinship and relationships are for, even what kinship relations are like, without paying the proper preliminary attention to what the system is. So kinship is bracketed with friendship and clientage and becomes an aspect of corruption, of networks; it becomes a link in the chain of influence, a negotiable instrument whose specific characteristics and dynamics are swallowed into the maw of manipulation, meretriciousness and mobility. So far as the patrilineal mediterranean is concerned the problem is rather different: the subtle advances of kinship studies of recent years have been made on the basis of material from societies with cross-cousin marriage and rules of exogamy. The Islamic pattern of preferential marriage of parallel cousins, of endogamy, has been neglected: there has been an 'espèce de tabou ethnologique qui frappe le monde arabe'; preferential marriage with the *bint 'amm* (father's brother's daughter) 'a complètement dérouté les ethnologues parce qu'il les éloigne sensiblement des notions fondamentales auxquelles ils sont habitués' (Chelhod, 1969b: 39). In these circumstances not much has been done on mediterranean kinship, and this section is therefore confined to a résumé in barest outline.

Peters (1960: 1967) describes the lineage organisation of Cyrenaican Bedouin camel herders, and they may be taken as a model, representing an extremely pure type of patrilineal segmentary grouping in which descent is a principle of political organisation. They are called pure because they are most like the sub-Saharan peoples with segmentary systems, and provide several points of contrast with them. But many of the mediterranean patrilineal peoples are settled, not nomadic or semi-nomadic, and these provide examples of one kind of variation on the patrilineal theme (Hart, 1954: 1957: 1970: 1973). Another variant is provided by patrilineal groups with a claim to saintliness (Gellner, 1969); and still others by urbanised or commercial or trading groups (Waterbury, 1973b). To say that these are less pure variants on the patrilineal theme is not the same, of course, as saying that group membership is determined by kinship *plus* some other extraneous principle: all these peoples use descent groups, and alliances between them, for some purpose or other; but the formal characteristics of patriliny appear to vary from context to context. Campbell provides the only account of kinship *plus* another principle, and the Sarakatsani whom he studied are strictly bilateral. Patrilineal organisation on the northern shores of the mediterranean has not been rigorously studied, and it is in any case on the wane (Stirling, 1960: 1965; Hammel, 1968; Lineton, 1971).

To take Peters first: the Cyrenaican Bedouin have a fully fledged system of descent groupings. The descendants of Sa'ada, an ancestress who migrated to Cyrenaica it may be in the eleventh century (Peters, 1968), are grouped in nine tribes named after the great-grandsons of the heroine. To these tribes are attached two other kinds of person: adopted lineages (*leff* lineages) which acquire genealogical legitimacy in the course of time, and client families *(mrabtin assadgān,* see pp. 135-7). The adopted lineages are grafted into the validating genealogy at the third level below the tribal level of segmentation: that level also defines the day-to-day political group, the smallest political unit, which does not usually contain more than 200 people. It is to this group, too, that clients attach themselves.

Any Sa'adi can trace his descent from his ancestress in about twelve generations. In the first descending generation from her he distinguishes Sa'adi living in the ecologically quite different eastern and western parts of Cyrenaica; then, in the next generation and in the western half (Evans-Pritchard, 1949: map facing p. 35), those living in mountains from those on the plains and foothills. At the third generation he distinguishes tribes and then, successively, primary, secondary and tertiary sections of tribes: he can thus identify his minimal political group in six steps; and this group has a genealogical depth of another five or six generations. The top six generations of the genalogy are common to all Sa'adi – they are public property, and exhibit a symmetry which contrasts markedly with accounts of segmentary organisation from sub-Saharan Africa (e.g. Evans-Pritchard, 1940: ch. 4, passim; especially pp. 140-1, 195-203): this public genealogy accounts for the major blocs of Sa'adi settlement, each with its distinctive ecological features (Peters, 1960: 365-6); group boundaries are drawn so that each group has some land of each of the kinds available in that territory (Evans-Pritchard, 1949: 57-9, and map).

Below this level, the genealogy is private: Peters noticed that when Bedouin recited their genealogies to him, disputes between the reciter and the bystanders usually broke out at this point in the recitation which constituted what he came to recognise as the fifth ascending generation area of ambiguity and argument (cf. Peters, 1960: 368, n. 7). Khuri (1970) notes the same ambiguity in the genealogies of Lebanese Muslims, partly urbanised. The genealogies also cease to be symmetrical at this point: Peters recorded a range of from two to twelve tertiary sections within secondary sections (1967: 270, 276) and the tertiary sections themselves may have from four to thirteen component lineages (1960: 365, 380). Peters's explanation of this is that people could not adjust the genealogy to the realities of alliance and support at any higher level of segmentation, for members of collateral tertiary sections would have to recognise and accept adjustments if they were to be made in the public sector of the genealogy (Peters, 1960): groups which are in daily rivalry would have to agree about genealogical manipulations which were designed to strengthen one of them against the other (Peters, 1967; see also Appendix 5). On the other hand, grafting in new lineages at any level lower than the fifth ascending generation would bring them within the reach of memory. So new groups become assimilated gradually, over a period of from seventy to a hundred years, at the end of which they are full agnates with proper genealogical credentials. It is also at this level of segmentation that ancestors and their lines are lost, the genealogy is telescoped, with resultant confusion and argument among those who recount the history of local groups.

Hart has pointed out the apparently important differences between settled and nomadic or semi-nomadic groups, but has not yet published full details. Settled farmers do not usually identify their local groups with genealogical ancestors, but by geographical names; where lineages claim common descent and are fairly numerous they may give their name to the territory they occupy. More often clans are scattered, having pockets of territory, and local groups are extremely heterogeneous. The Berber Aith Waryaghar, for example, occupy the territory from the Jbil Hmam mountains to the alluvial plains behind Al Hoceima on the coast: they say that they came from the mountains, and pushed north to the sea; indeed the distribution of lineage groups suggests almost that they tumbled down off the mountain, imprinting a pattern as they rolled over and over: each group in the mountainous area is settled also in the foothills and on the plains, and the pattern of neighbours is replicated over and again in the three areas (1970: 19-25). But the clans whose topographical relationships are thus reduplicated are 'thoroughly heterogenous . . . and descent from common ancestors must be considered as largely fictive', and in fact Hart estimates that the Aith Waryaghar tribe is no more 'Waryaghar' than the USA is Anglo-Saxon (ibid.: 25). In these circumstances the contrast with Peters's Bedouin must be that the Aith Waryaghar are more 'fictive' than the Bedouin (see Figure 3). 'The question of descent, on [the] tribal level, from a putative common agnatic ancestor is

I Tribe (*dhaqbitsh*)	agnation 'quite irrelevant'
[II Fifth (*khums*)	clans and agglomerations of clans – Hart sometimes does (p. 17) sometimes does not (p. 11) count this as a level of segmentation. See also Hart, 1966a:76-81.]
II [III] Clan (*ar-rbaᶜ*)	agnation claimed, 'largely fictive'.
III [IV] Sub-clans (*ar-rbaᶜ*)	agnation claimed, not traceable.
[IV [V]? Sub-sub-clan	Hart seems to contemplate seven levels of segmentation. From p. 12 it is clear that there may be, in some real cases – i.e. the question is not, as with fifths, one of Hart's indecision – an extra segmentation here.]
IV or V [VI] Lineage (*dharfiqth*)	agnation claimed and traced.
V or VI [VII] Sublineage (*jajgu*)	agnation claimed and traced.

Figure 3   Segmentary organisation of the Aith Waryaghar, after Hart, 1970

quite irrelevant' (ibid.: 11): it is at clan level (the next descending one) that agnation becomes not 'quite irrelevant' but 'largely fictive'. It is only at the fourth level of segmentation, where sub-clans are distinguished into lineages, that the Aith Waryaghar do actually trace common descent (ibid.: 12). Hart's one analysis of a local community (1970: 46-58) concentrates on a lineage – the Imjjat – who trace their descent from a man who moved into the sub-clan area of Aith Turith

in the 1850s. Imjjat has a genealogical depth of three or four generations; there is no indication of the depth of longer-established
lineages, and a comparison with Peters's Bedouin on this point is not
possible. Perhaps it would be superfluous: the Aith Waryaghar do not
seem to graft their immigrant allies on to their genealogies; Hart
indeed refers to the common Rifian happening 'of individual or
lineage A packing up its belongings and *moving* to locality B, which
may be in a different tribe entirely. The name of the old lineage is,
however, invariably retained in the new locality' (1970: 47, n. 38). He
wishes to call this procedure scission: when people move out and
retain lineage affiliation he says the term fission is inappropriate.

Gellner provides an account of Berber saintly lineages which contrasts neatly with those of Peters and Hart. Saintliness passes in the
male line, and is acquired by descent from the Prophet Mohammed's
son-in-law. Not all the descendants in this line are saintly – they are in
varying degrees laicised. Saintly groups, even laicised ones, are
nevertheless quite distinct from lay tribes, for they retain genealogical
association with sanctity. Lay tribes have what Gellner calls Occamist
genealogies: the genealogy has just enough depth to account for
actual alliances and territorial distribution (see, for example, Hart,
1973 for an account of the semi-nomadic Ait 'Atta). By contrast the
saintly genealogies are 'Veblenesque': the saints have lines of descent
which are prolonged to include prestigious ancestors which identify
the line of maximum saintliness, and which relate the saintly lineages
to segments of the clan which have lost saintliness and are laicised.
The saintly genealogy has thirty-four generations from Sidna Ali,
Mohammed's son-in-law, to the heads of households in 1960 (Gellner, 1969: 179-200, 261-75). The Ihansalen, the saints of Zawiya
Ahansal, are distinguished from all other descendants of Mohammed's son-in-law by descent from Sidi Said Ahansal who moved into
the Central High Atlas in the late thirteenth century, it is said, and
who founded the line which accounts for all the saintly and laicised
groups in the area. Sidi Said Ahansal comes almost in the middle of
the genealogy: he is in the eighteenth generation descending from
Sidna Ali; and the first local segmentation occurs immediately in the
next, the nineteenth: a group of laicised descendants (the Ait Tighanimin), strive to achieve recognition for saintliness, and claim descent
from one of Sidi Said Ahansal's sons. This claim is disputed by those
who are recognised saints (ibid.: 157). The next point of segmentation
is in the twenty-second generation: a laicised village group is de-

scended from a son of Sidi Lahcen u Othman. The line continues from another son of his, and other holy lines – rivals to the saints at Zawiya Ahansal – are attached in generations twenty-two to twenty-five.

The twenty-sixth and twenty-seventh generations in the genealogy (seventh and eight ascending) provide the key figures who account for the internal structure of Zawiya Ahansal. Two brothers in the twenty-sixth generation define membership of the two main groups within the lodge and their sons – seven in all, 'sometimes referred to as seven brothers' (ibid.: 271) – define effective saintliness: that is, the descendants of Sidi Mohammed n'ut Baba are either effective saints or closely associated with them; the descendants of his brothers provide minor lines within the lodge.

It is clear that this genealogy differs from Maghrebian economical ones: the differences are the consequences of holiness, which is a valuable asset. For example the outstanding saint in generation thirty-three, Sidi Mulay, had two brothers whose children are currently heads of households. They describe themselves as direct descendants of Sidi Mulay, not collaterals, and this illustrates the point that holiness has an attractive power. It is quite common to find that weak lines in a segmentary society may alter their point of attachment to the genealogy: brothers may become sons as their descendants associate with a more powerful group, and so on. But in fact the groups in Zawiya Ahansal who are not descended from Sidi Mulay and who claim descent from him seem to be demographically as strong as their saintly cousins, and Gellner describes one such household as rich. This kind of manipulation is best understood by referring to another example of it at a higher level of segmentation: the descendants of Sidi Yussif, in generation twenty-two, live at Amzari, half an hour's walk from Zawiya Ahansal. The Ait Amzrai are laicised: they are not internally stratified into more and less saintly groups (ibid.: 157); they feud; they are at odds with the saintly lineages at Zawiya Ahansal; they have 'Occamist' genealogies (ibid.: 217-23). They are like lay tribes, except in one important respect: they do not take part in the wider confederations of local groups because their genealogy does not attach them into lay groups: they are laicised saints, and when they are involved in major disputes they cannot ally with other warring segments. They have no segmentary allies because there are no segments of a higher order: the Ait Amzrai have to rely on the saints for protection (e.g. ibid.: 219-20). They have all the internal characteristics of lay groups, and undergo most of the vicissitudes of lay life, but have no place in the lay segmentary system.

The Ait Amzrai are descended from Sidi Yussif in the twenty-second generation; this is known, it is common knowledge. But Yussif is *not* 'the symbol of the unity of the village of Amzrai': although he is the apical ancestor, and defines the Ait Amzrai exclusively and almost exhaustively, he is 'just a name' (ibid.: 266). Rather, the Ait Amzrai define themselves by reference to Yussif's father, Sidi Lahcen u Othman, an undoubted saint, transmitter of sanctity to Zawiya Ahansal: his shrine is in their village, and they give his name as their founder. Such a departure from economy in genealogy is related to the isolation of laicised groups. 'By stressing their special connection with Sidi Lahcen u Othman . . . the Ait Amzrai keep a kind of genealogical hold on all other Ihansalen who are . . . also descended from him' (ibid.: 267): it is a striking discrepancy, that a proudly laicised group should define itself by reference to someone other than their apical ancestor but, given their ambiguous independence, the Ait Amzrai have no choice. The same kind of manipulation is apparent in the claim of the potential founders of laicised groups within Zawiya Ahansal, that they are sons of Sidi Mulay, not his brothers' sons: they can never become lay, can never be fully assimilated into the over-arching structures of lay tribes, and must therefore cling to saintliness.

A fortiori, what has been said of laicised groups applies to saintly lineages: these do not ever combine into larger groups to gain weight in political disputes. 'The genealogy of the Ihansalen is and is not an example of a segmentary system' (ibid.: 273): on the one hand, it does represent the relations between local groups with an agnatic genealogy which embodies social distance on a putative time-scale. On the other hand, as Gellner points out in the passage immediately following that just cited, it is an assymetric genealogy: saintlinesss causes branches to grow longer. The saints are keepers of frontiers and are settled on them without any possibility of massing together in attack and defence; they rely on God to preserve them. Indeed, collateral branches are in a state of rivalry for reputation; and although that is more or less true of all low-level segments, lay or saintly, for the Ihansalen it is a perpetual rivalry which they never put aside in the interests of segmentary agglomeration. Moreover, the saintliness of the line prevents complete break-away by groups which would normally have 'lost the name': laicised groups are inhibited by even their remote connections with saints from full participation in the secular segmentary tribes, and must therefore manipulate the genealogy – even at quite remote levels, as the Ait Tighanimin do – to maintain some defence in their state of exclusion from full secular existence. The cause is not realistically attributed to a faint hope of acquiring the perquisites of saintliness, but rather to weakness *vis-à-vis* the wholly lay tribes. Ambiguities and disputes about the genealogy are thus liable to be at levels remote from those which affect day-to-day business – even though the seeds of such ambiguities are sown in the relations of contemporary Ihansalen households, and in their manipulations of genealogy.

The last of these case studies is provided by Waterbury (1972) whose account is of Swasa grocers and appears to suggest two lines of inquiry. One is that most Swasa are concerned to get tribal prestige with the profits from retail trade: that is to say the majority do not become fully involved in urban affairs, nor in trade, but try to achieve targets of expenditure which will impress rivals at home: in the 1860s, when involvement in trade first began, a good gun and a good pair of slippers sufficed; now it appears to be houses – a man builds himself a villa, defeats his rivals, and is content. The other line of inquiry is into the way the patrilineal framework provides a Soussi with his partners and rivals: it is, typically, a man and his brother who go into business together. The stories of partnerships and rivalries which Waterbury recounts have the *dramatis personae* of any account of lineage fission. Uncles arc bound to help young men to set up in business and then to compete with them; half-brothers set up in friendly co-operation and then become bitter rivals (1972: 231-2):

> It has not been threats from hostile 'out-groups' alone
> that have driven the Swasa on to commercial success. Rather more
> importantly, their drive has been a function of their own internal
> rivalries and conflicts . . . Their success would be impressive enough
> if one could explain it all by their solidarity and group identity.
> But this explanation takes much away from the far more ingenious
> arrangements they have devised to allow them to engage in fierce
> internal battles for prestige all the while maintaining something
> of a common front towards outsiders.

Waterbury's account leads his readers to wish that there was more information about the formal characteristics of kinship. For if Peters's account is of 'pure' patriliny, Hart's of patriliny modified by sedentary agriculture, Gellner's of patriliny modified by saintliness, it could only be satisfactory to have an account of patriliny modified by commerce: by the use of kinship obligation in commerce, by the use of commerce to pursue rivalries and competitions set firmly in a patrilineal framework. Waterbury, alas, does not provide more than hints (1972: 37-50).

If the formal characteristics of Maghrebian lineages are insufficiently explored, with only one good account, there is a wealth of documentation and argument about patrilineal endogamy, much of which seems incoherent: replies, rejoinders and refutations appear tangential to each other (e.g. the case noted by Hammel and Goldberg, 1971), and it is not unknown for a writer's arguments to be reproduced by his critic in the guise of points which he has failed to consider. In short, patrilineal endogamy, father's brother's daughter marriage in particular, has become the object of typically academic argument. The topic needs the application of a first-class mind; but in the meantime it may not come amiss to provide a commonsensical survey of the issues. These are: is there a rule or preference for father's brother's daughter marriage? How can rates of such marriages be explained? How can the rule itself be explained? To indicate the arguments and evidence on each of these issues in turn is sufficient to cover the field.

The first issue arises out of the observations that, on the one hand, people say that they should marry their father's brother's daughter, and on the other, that some peoples who say this do not have a particularly high rate of such marriages. The second of these observations can be held to one side, while the evidence for the first is reviewed. The fact is that there is no Koranic authority for enjoining or preferring FBD marriage. To some, that is enough: all rules of Islam are Koranic; this is not Koranic, therefore . . . . Another argument is that there cannot be a rule which says that people must marry someone from a particular category, there can only be a 'preference', for it will happen from time to time that no suitable spouse exists within the category. The point here is that most social rules are conditional: 'If such is the case', they say, 'then it follows that . . . .' And most statements of the rule follow this formula: if a girl marries her FBS he does not have to pay bridewealth, but other men do have to (Barth, 1954; A. Cohen, 1965: 121, etc). If an outsider asks for a girl who has an eligible FBS who has not made it clear whether or not he is interested in her himself, her father must reply 'seek her hand from her uncle' (A. Cohen, 1965: 121). If a girl marries someone other than a marriageable brother's son, the latter is 'bought off with a few sheep (about five) and some articles of clothing' (Peters, 1965: 132). If an educated and wealthy girl refuses to marry her illiterate and loutish cousin she will cause a tremendous fuss, but if she is strong enough she may eventually succeed (V. Ayoub, 1965: 14). If a man wishes to prevent a girl's unsuitable marriage to an enemy, he casts around to rustle up a cousin with a prior claim (A. Cohen, 1965: 71-93). The examples could be multiplied – is it really possible to say that there is no rule? It is like all rules, flexible (that is, breakable), useful, and conditional: if a Sarakatsanos is sufficiently powerful he can contract an incestuous marriage (above, p. 95). Another argument is that the rule of FBD marriage is the epitome of a general principle of endogamy: people should marry within their lineage, clan, congregation, village – and this is neatly expressed and summarised by saying a man should marry his FBD (Keyser, 1973). That may be so, and indeed for some cases it expresses the appearance of the data admirably. But it would be wrong to show that FBD marriage can be subsumed under a general category, and then to argue that therefore the rule itself does not exist: that is just sleight of mind: it is valuable to be reminded that endogamy means marriage within a specified group, not marriage to a person in some particular category; but that should do no more than make people cautious when using the word endogamy – it does not affect the status of the word rule in this discussion. Finally, a statistical argument and a positivist one: some elegant minds (Gilbert and Hammel, 1966; Goldberg, 1967) have produced ingenious calculations to show that observed rates of FBD marriage are indeed higher than random selection of spouses would produce, but that they can be explained by propinquity – there is no need to invoke a rule. So when Hammel and Goldberg (1971) reject Khuri's (1970) critique of their positions they turn a statistical cheek for him to attack, saying that Khuri's own data seem not to be susceptible of an explanation from propinquity, and that they would be more impressed if he developed that line of attack. The statistical argument misses the point, however: the straightforward question is whether or not there is a rule; the point is not that computers and ingenuity can devise alternative explanations of observed behaviour. That raises interesting further problems, for if there is a rule but it produces behaviour which is no different from the behaviour which could be produced by some other rule, that gives an indication of the place of rules in human affairs, but it does not support the claim that there are no rules, or that rules are irrele-

vant in the study of society. The same argument must be directed to
the admirable and thorough Marx. He 'would deny that there is
endogamy at all among the Bedouin of the Negev' (1967: 222-8).
True, just more than 11 per cent, of his sample of marriages joined
patrilateral parallel first cousins; true, 'a member of the section is
thought to have prior claim to its women but . . . may not always insist
on marrying them' – nevertheless, Marx denies the existence of
endogamy because he can explain each marriage in terms, not of rule,
but of the material and political advantages it brings to the group or
groups involved. As the statisticians have done, so has Marx – he has
discovered another principle which can explain the phenomena; but
the issue is whether or not there is a rule. Marx may accept a mild
caricature of his position because it has didactic value: he seems to
think that a rule exists only when it constrains people to act against
their self-interest, and if he can show self-interest then he can dispose
of the rule. Two points must be made: it is not an essential quality of
rules that, like medicine, they should be nasty if they are to do any
good. Second, the 'principle' of material and political interest is very
abstract, very remote from the luxuriantly detailed specification of
the particular advantages got by each marriage which Marx analyses:
it would be odd if a marriage carried no advantage, and it is dangerous
to proceed from a demonstration that each marriage has some, to the
creation of an abstract general principle that marriages are arranged
to meet individual or group interests. Rather than adopt an observer's
generality so rapidly, it is better to proceed more slowly – to say, for
example, that the Bedouin of the Negev have a conditional and flexible rule . . . Whether or not there is a 'rule' of marriage in any particular society is an empirical question, to be answered by asking the
people concerned. Whether the ethnographer wishes to call it a rule or
a preference is partly an empirical question, partly one of judgment:
on the whole British anthropologists would call something a rule if it
establishes claims: what happens if a girl is to marry someone else?
What happens if she refuses to marry a man specified by the rule (or
preference)? It is then possible to ask the question – does this rule (or
preference) have any consequences for the kinds of marriage which
are contracted? It really should not surprise an anthropologist to
discover that a rule can make no difference at all to people's behaviour: certainly, it should not lead him to discount the rule, for his task
is, among other things, to investigate the relation between consciousness and behaviour. In Haouch, for example, sixty-three adolescents

were asked if they thought one should marry a patrilateral parallel first cousin: 63 per cent of the girls and 66 per cent of the boys thought that it was better to do so – but the actual rate of such marriages was much lower (Williams and Williams, 1965): people do not and sometimes cannot always do what they want.

Rates of marriage have to be measured before they can be explained, and that has been done in a surprising variety of ways. One problem arises from the fact that the term *bint 'amm* (father's brother's daughter) is usually a category term as well as a specific one: the commonest categories are *parallel cousin* and, by anticipatory fulfilment of the rule, *wife:* thus V. Ayoub (1965) notes that *bint 'amm* is used of all village wives, but a term adopted from the French, *madamti,* was used to refer to his own wife who could not be categorised even fictitiously as a father's brother's daughter. In the village most wives are the daughters of men who fall into the category father's brother – for that term is also extended in use. Most anthropologists seem aware of the dangers of asking 'Is your wife *bint 'amm?'* but Khuri suggests that some 'incredibly high' rates of FBD marriage can only be explained by the simplicity of the investigator (1970: 617, n. 1). It should be noted, incidentally, that the categorical use of *bint 'amm* and other similar terms is not uniform: different relationships are included (Marx, 1967: 222; A. Cohen, 1965: 107; M. R. Ayoub, 1959; V. Ayoub, 1965; Khuri, 1970: 617, n. 1). Another problem of an elementary kind is that some investigators have based their calculations on a census of people present rather than on genealogical inquiry. Because people who have moved out of hearth may go out of mind, and because perhaps such people are more likely to marry outsiders than those who stay at home, a household census can produce inflated rates. This point is made by Peters (1963: 177, n. 3) who has culprits in mind but names no names. Peters also argues, and rightly, that it is useful to calculate two rates, one for men and one for women: in the Lebanon, he shows, women's rates are higher partly because fewer of them marry. Since 1963, too, and perhaps because Peters suggested it, anthropologists calculating the rate of FBD marriage in a village or other community have distinguished FBD marriages joining two villagers (two people, one marriage) and those joining a villager to an outsider who is also a father's brother's child. These are all elementary precautions against distortion, and they concern the identification of FBD marriages. Another set of problems concerns the universe: a rate has to be calculated as a percentage within a universe, and it is possible to define universes in ways which make them greater or smaller, with corresponding effects on the rate. The simplest way is to take a sample of couples and to count the FBD marriages (e.g. Marx, 1967; Keyser, 1973). Khuri has calculated FBD rates on a universe consisting of all marriages between kin (1970). The most sophisticated statistics, recommended by Peters (1963), are those which take the number of possible FBD marriages as the universe and then calculate the rate of actual marriages. That has been done by Goldberg (1967) who studied Tripolitanian Jews in Israel: there were a limited number of people who stood in the right relationship; there were rules, too, about the right age for marriage, as well as rules about the age differences between spouses. Moreover, some potential spouses had overlapping FBD pools, so that the marriage of one of them diminished the chances of the others. Goldberg took a sample and calculated that of fifty-two men who got married twelve could have married an FBD, and four did. This produces a rate similar to that produced by Gilbert and Hammel with a computer programme (1966), and they agree that the FBD rate, calculated on this universe, is higher than the rate of marriage between any other kin calculated on a corresponding universe.

Explanations of rates can be mentioned briefly: when they are divorced from explanations of the rule, they take two forms. The first is propinquity which appears as a special kind of general 'endogamy': people marry people who are like them, and who live near them; in the natural course of events some children of brothers will marry. Gilbert and Hammel think that propinquity will explain the rates; other writers (e.g. Keyser, 1973) think that a rule or preference may exist which enjoins 'endogamy' – perhaps no more than 'marriage with a person who is close in kinship or religion' – and that FBD marriages occur as a result, not because there is a rule. The second kind of explanation is based on demographic calculations, and, at the pen of Barth (1954: 131-2), is used to explain why the rate is no higher than it is: Barth in fact counted nine FBD marriages out of twenty-one, giving a rate of 46 per cent. This is in fact the highest rate calculated in modern times, and deserves to be treated with some scepticism: it is important to know more details about the universe and the method of collecting data. In any case, the demographic explanation can be invoked only to explain why there are not more FBD marriages: it would not explain why there were fewer than the population could provide.

It is now time to turn to the various explanations for the rule itself. Khuri (1970) has reviewed the literature, and it is convenient to start from his article. He classifies the explanations as cultural or functional. The cultural arguments have been of the kind which relate a man's marriage to his father's brother's daughter to his father's brother's concern for the girl's honour. The misbehaviour or mistreatment of a spouse reflects poorly on her father, and if he can marry her into the family, he maximises control over her and her husband. Not many people have proffered this argument: it ignores the girl's parallel cousins' right to give permission for the girl to marry out; and as Khuri says it assumes that no girl wants to marry her first parallel cousin and that a husband loses no honour if his wife misbehaves. The functionalist arguments are of three kinds: parallel cousin marriage prevents the dispersion of property (but Khuri, echoing Barth (1954: 131), points out that Koranic laws of inheritance are usually ignored, so why should FBD marriage be necessary?); parallel cousin marriage strengthens the position of individuals within lineages; and, finally, it has value for the solidarity of the group. Khuri does not deny that an individual may consolidate his position by marrying his daughter to his brother's son but he does say that such cases are very rare in his experience. His argument against the explanation in terms of value to the lineage is simple: the value attributed to patrilineal endogamy is that it results in segmentation along patrilineal divisions rather than along affinal ones; but Khuri again echoing Barth (ibid.: 128) states that segmentation occurs whatever preferential marriage rule is followed, and therefore preferred endogamy cannot have particular value.

Khuri is undoubtedly right when, echoing A. Cohen (1965: 120, n.1), he suggests that any single explanation of patrilineal endogamy is unlikely to meet all the cases – though why he should then reject explanations because they do not fit the data he collected by interviewing a large number of Lebanese established in the suburbs of Beirut, is hard to understand. What is exceedingly valuable in his essay is his exploration of the coincidence of roles before and after marriage: 'FBD marriage does not create conflict of roles as marriage within the same nuclear family would do, nor does it create affinal but tense relationships associated with out-marriage' (1970: 607). When a man marries his father's brother's daughter various roles are superimposed: his paternal uncle becomes his father-in-law; his paternal uncle's wife becomes his mother-in-law; his father becomes father-in-law to his niece, and so on. Khuri's argument is that these roles are in all important respects the same, and that superimposition of an in-law relationship on close collateral ones of various kinds creates no conflicts, nor demands sharp and sudden changes in behaviour. So a girl's father's brother ought to treat her with stern reserve always: before her marriage anything else would lead her father to think that his brother had designs on her mother. After marriage, her husband, particularly if he is her father's brother's son, would construe any sign of affection as a sexual approach. The coincidence of roles smooths over the difficult adjustments required at marriage (see Peters, 1965), and the only people who seem to suffer are the spouses themselves: cousins of opposite sex are expected to show extreme indifference to each other; and such displays may hang over into married life: 'the husband's expected demonstration of his potency and manliness and the wife's [expected] satisfaction and freedom, are forsaken for the purpose of achieving modesty' (1970: 613). 'To preserve the solidarity of the family, it is necessary for its members to suppress their individual interests' (ibid.: 614).

Khuri's argument is fascinating and it makes a valuable contribution to anthropology, but it is eccentric. If a people did practise FBD marriage – or any other kind of close marriage – on a large scale, it would be odd if the roles of the *dramatis personae* before and after marriage did not come to resemble each other. Where marriage is not a means of changing relationships – of making alliances – clearly it must be a means of keeping them the same; and if there is a diffuse awareness of the possibility that men generally may become the fathers-in-law of their brother's daughters it is not unreasonable to suppose that they should anticipate that change, and so eliminate it. If that seems an unduly intuitive argument, it is considerably less so than Khuri's, which is that the coincidence of roles *causes* ('explains') the marriage rule. It is much more likely that the coincidence of roles occurs because men anticipate and hence try to eliminate change.

Khuri's account of roles recalls the indelible picture painted by Peters of the Bedouin father ignoring his son's wedding, and of the son leaving his wife in order to lie by his father's side at dawn (above, p. 191), just as he did before he got married. Peters explains that in terms of household solidarity, of the maintenance of a community of interests, just as Khuri explains the suppressed sexuality of spouses. Not only does Peters's account show that Bedouin households are less independent of each other than the Beirut suburbanites (who 'live in scattered apartments', have diverse employers), Peters also provides an exacting account of marriage with people other than members of the spouse's patrilineage: endogamy is put into a context with all marriages, and it is clearly shown that exogamous marriages are not simply, as it were, failed endogamy, a lapse from principles, but are patterned and politic.

Remember that Peters describes tertiary sections of agnatic tribes as having about 200 people, and a high rate of endogamy. These are solidary groups in various ways: they collectively have clients (1968); when blood-money is divided among them it is divided equally, not in proportion to degrees of kinship (1967); they name their sons after men who have died without male descendants, to keep the name alive, and, if they have inherited from such a man, they will marry a wife for him to perpetuate his line: this they do within the tertiary agnatic group (1960). Parallel cousin marriage, however 'creates small nuclei' of people within the group who are cognates as well as agnates. A man who marries his first parallel cousin will be marrying his remoter cross-cousin traced in another line. A man who marries his first cross-cousin marries his agnate in a remoter line. All affines are also agnates. As Peters says (1965: 133; cf. M. Ayoub, 1959: 266, n.2):

> ... with parallel cousin marriage present in the corporate
> group, men referred to as agnates are not agnates only; each and
> every one of them is the centre of a bundle of roles, each role
> potentially as important as the other[s]. It would be false to argue,
> moreover, that the complexities of relationships can be unravelled
> by analytically separating them. . . .

It is not clear from Peters's accounts whether such marriages, creating nuclei, were repeated within the nucleus from one generation to another. The only information remotely bearing on that point is in Rosenfeld (1968: 257): he found in Lower Galilee that nine of 255 married adults were people whose parents, grandparents and great-grandparents had married within the *lineage* (it is not clear that all eight grandparents and sixteen great-grandparents had so married). However, to return to Peters, about half of all Bedouin marriages are within the tertiary section, and he says that there is a high rate of parallel cousin marriage (1967: remember that Peters's careful cal-culations are on the data collected in the Lebanon, while his theore-tical contributions relate to Cyrenaican Bedouin). The effect of

213

parallel cousin marriages is to create lines of division within the tertiary section. Although Bedouin claim it is an undifferentiated unit, in fact, in time of trouble, the section may polarise round two or more of the nuclei (1967: 272-4). Peters argues that the pattern of marriages within the group can only be understood by referring to marriages outside the group: almost as many people marry outside the tertiary section as within it, and exogamous marriages are contracted with groups of another secondary section, never with the collateral tertiary sections of ego's own secondary section. 'Once established these external links are perpetuated by cross cousin marriages in successive generations' (1967: 274). Such links are valuable because they give a group some access to resources in areas fairly remote from its own: the 'mother's brothers' who have a prior claim to water over that of clients, and for whose sake clients may be discarded (Peters, 1968: 176; above, p. 136), are surely (though Peters does not say so) men from other secondary sections, in whose territories water has failed. Climatic vagaries are such that a man is prudent to establish claims outside his own territory. Links with collateral tertiary sections are not useful in this way: those groups share some of the same resources, and otherwise more or less the same kinds of resources; in times of scarcity it is precisely these groups which are in shared straits, precisely these groups which are likely to come into conflict. So cross-cousin alliances, repeated over the generations, have a utility which the Bedouin themselves perceive.

They also have consequences which Peters discerns and which, he states emphatically, the Bedouin do not. For their model of their system of alliances is one in which collateral tertiary sections have greater solidarity than groups belonging to different secondary sections; indeed, since any killing across the boundaries of secondary sections is automatically defined by them as 'feud' and, since there are such killings, the Bedouin themselves conceive secondary sections as permanently hostile – a hostility which is, they say, forgotten only when war breaks out and secondary sections combine for the duration. In short, the Bedouin model is that of a patrilineal segmentary system of the classic kind, exhibiting balanced opposition between segments of a like order.

But this is not what happens. The tertiary sections are not balanced; secondary sections contain from two to twelve (unequal) subsections. When leaders gather armies, secondary sections do not mass together as the genealogical theory says they should. Although according to theory secondary sections are in permanent feud the reality is that only some tertiary sections of each group behave as hostilely as they should, while others prosecute not the feud, but cross-cousin marriages. In fact Peters says that such marriage alliances are an indirect means of expressing hostility towards collateral tertiary sections.

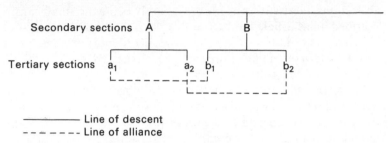

Figure 4   To illustrate Peters's argument on cross-cousin marriage alliances.

Where A and B are nominally feuding, and a_1 a_2 and b_1 b_2 are nominally solidary, actually rivals, a well-established cross-cousin alliance between a_1 and b_1 can allow a_1 to pursue its rivalry with a_2 by inciting b_1 to the attack. Peters refers to such cross-cousin marriages as 'leap frogging' and sees in them a means by which collateral tertiary sections can pursue indirect competition (cf. A. Cohen, 1965: 136-8). The Bedouin are not reported as saying what they very well might say: 'We marry those our rivals fight', for they are unaware of the implications of their cross-cousin marriages, and live by a model of their system which is closer to Evans-Pritchard's model of the Nuer system. What Peters explains structurally, by reference to cross-cousin alliances, the Bedouin explain as contingent lapses from the ideal of segmentary solidarity. It is worth noting that Peters's account rests on an ecological base: it is because resources are scarce that Bedouin quarrel with their minimal sections, ally with people in control of other resources, and use those allies to pursue *sub rosa* quarrels. Favret (1968), in another context, has put a slightly different emphasis on cross-cousin alliances: if no alliances were permitted outside the lineage all competition would be confined to the lineage arena; the ability to make alliances outside reduces internal tension. There is no particular reason this structural argument should not be combined with Peters's ecology.

Peters's model of the Bedouin system is of corporate agnatic groups which take on clients and engage, as groups, in some political activities (1968); which proliferate segments at the tertiary level; which incorporate new groups in the area of genealogical ambiguity between five and six generations ascending from the current household heads (1960); which polarise around nuclei of endogamously married sub-sections, these sub-sections presumably being the small camps described in his article on the family (1965), and which marry-out about half their children, to cross-cousins, in order to pursue interests against those of other like groups with which they are formally allied (1967).

Peters is the only writer who talks about endogamy in the context of all marriages (Marx, who discusses all marriages, 'would deny' that endogamy exists among Bedouin of the Negev, see p. 208) and who presents a reasonably complete, if scattered, account of a Bedouin society. That is not to say that other writers have not discussed marriages in general, and noted sanctions and interests which affect the practice of parallel cousin marriage. Families with high prestige tend to follow the *bint 'amm* rule more than weak or stronger groups do: in Lower Galilee the range was from 23 per cent in the strongest lineages, to 8 per cent in weak ones; and as lineages became internally differentiated the wealthier families restricted their marriages even further (Rosenfeld, 1968: 252–5). The effective saints of Zawiya Ahansal took women from the lay tribes, but gave no women to them; they also secluded their women, as most other residents did not (Gellner, 1969: 140, 182, 191). The Bedouin and peasants of the Negev are said by Marx (1967) to regard marriageable people as a scarce resource, and they allocate them to unlimited ends: these are chiefly maintaining the solidarity of co-liable groups; getting access to water and grazing, and gaining protection: this last has declined in importance as general security in the area has increased (ibid.: 131). It follows from Marx's analysis that the marriages of groups in different political and economic circumstances will be distributed differently, and indeed they are. Peasants, for example, have insignificant property interests to bind them together; from time to time none the less they need to concert the action of co-liable groups to meet political threats: solidarity can only be maintained by marriage alliances, and peasants should therefore show a higher rate of endogamy than Bedouin. They do, for those whom Marx studied were 57 per cent endogamous, compared with Bedouin, only 24 per cent of whose marriages were within the co-liable group. In the Abu 'Ābed peasant group, for example, all four marriages were within the group, all four in the closest permissible relationship (three parallel cousin marriages, while one man married his father's brother's son's daughter) (ibid.: 119). In some circumstances this peasant strategy may be abandoned: the seven Qlā 'īah co-liable groups established alliance between themselves, and in 1961 were able to take some action against their Bedouin landlords (ibid.: 121). The Zullām Bedouin, who do have property, use their marriages to secure access to kinds of land held by their tribe: so the Gwe 'id contract marriages between the plains and the hilly winter pastures marrying members of other tribes in some cases (ibid.: 134-8). Marx reckons that of their thirty-six current marriages, seventeen were 'economic', the rest 'political': they were to maintain links between sections, and were exhaustive – repeated in each generation, every section was linked to every other section.

Parallel cousin marriage thus has different rates in different groups, and has a different purpose. sixteen per cent of male peasant marriages are FBD, while only 8 per cent of Bedouin marriages are (ibid.: 246): that is related by Marx to the landlessness of peasants, and to their lack of other interests to consolidate. In relatively large Bedouin sections such marriages consolidate clusters of men who can then more easily exercise control over peasant tenant groups, and some marriageable people will be allocated to that purpose. Relatively landless Bedouin have no such surveillance needs, and their rate of parallel cousin marriage is correspondingly lower; weak and small groups use their marriages to ally with strength. Peasants all use their marriages to strengthen the group, and in small groups that will necessarily entail a high proportion of father's brother's daughter marriages, and a lower proportion for the larger groups (ibid.: 228-33). It must be said that Marx's analysis – marriage by marriage – is very detailed. He is quite properly concerned to break down the notion of endogamy into its constituent units – a procedure which allows him, eventually, to deny that there *is* any endogamy. That is salutory; but it is also sometimes difficult to see how he re-groups marriages into new categories: not endogamous and exogamous, but consolidating in a small group, or in a larger one; political or economic; aiding surveillance or aiding alliance. The principle is rationality (opposed to rule-bound behaviour) – but that is a remote and abstract principle; and the very detail of the evidence raises the doubt that it is always those particular interests which Marx seizes on among others, which are the determining ones. Nevertheless, Marx's contribution to the discussion of FBD marriage is invaluable: like Peters he argues that multiple motives underlie such patterns; like Peters, he puts FBD marriages into a context of all marriages; with Peters's argument and Marx's evidence it is now clearly inappropriate to look for an explanation of FBD marriage: 'There can be no single sociological explanation of this kind of marriage . . . [it] can be found in diverse social systems with diverse combination of factors (A. Cohen, 1965: 120, n.1).

In no society is marriage disinterested. In societies with patrilineal organisation *and no rule of exogamy* (to put the case in its mildest form) patrilateral parallel cousins can marry each other and sometimes do. When they do, there are often consequences which can be related to the logic of kinship operating in a particular social environment: the formation of nuclei within large herding patrilineages is one such consequence. In a different environment – such as Beirut suburbs – those consequences may not follow. Parallel cousin marriage may reinforce the solidarity of small groups whether these are weak (as Negev peasant sections) or dominant (as the Learned Families in Peters's Lebanese study); as categories within a community gain or lose power, so their marriage patterns may alter (Peters, 1972); as basic structures change, so may the overall rate of parallel cousin marriage (A. Cohen, 1965: 9). In societies with a rule of this kind there are always marriages which are in breach of the rule: the FBD marriages gain significance from that kind of context as well: in one known case (the Cyrenaican Bedouin) the other marriages are also patterned (and interested), and clear consequences of a kinship logic kind follow from the existence of two rules of marriage. In all societies with an expectation that particular kinds of marriage may occur the crucial roles of affinity and parenthood are likely to resemble each other. These are all aspects of patterned marriage which can be investigated fruitfully, on the basis of sound statistics.

European patriliny has disappeared in the last century. There may be signs of what once was, but corporate patrilineages no longer exist. Mina still has the towers which were the refuge of privileged Niklian lineages and attached Achamnomeri client groups (Lineton, 1971: 36-40, 245-75; Stahl, 1974: plate facing p. 7) but these are no more important than the towers of San Gimignano. Yugoslavians may call their pretend uncles *strič* (father's brother) rather than *ujak* (mother's brother) because it is more complimentary to imply the closeness which, forty or sixty years ago, came with agnation: but that is now scarcely understood (Barić, 1967a). The level of corporate patrilineal groups in European societies has been stripped away, leaving bare that 'substratum' of kinship relationships which is common to all societies (ibid.: cf. Marx's discussion of kinship, 1967: 163-4). The Sarakatsani are the only other well-described people in the mediterranean who recognise groups defined by kinship alone. These are exhaustive but not exclusive, for they are bilateral, peculiar to each individual, and thus overlap; only siblings share the same kindred. Campbell says that the Sarakatsani think of these groups as extensions from their own nuclear families, and coins the phrase 'equivalent bilateral extension' to express the way they identify members of the group: they trace through both sides of the family from themselves, and include second cousins but no remoter kin; they do not refer to an apical ancestor or ancestors: what results is a group, but it is not a descent group. A Sarakatsanos knows that he can trust a kinsman so defined, and that he cannot trust any other Sarakatsanos. Such groups are, obviously, scattered: the core of each individual is his own family, a corporation owning rights to land, animals and religious articles. It is a corporation embedded in a number of kindreds – each sibling group represented in the family has a different kindred. A man uses his kin for collecting information about market prices, or about available grazing; they provide information about prospective marriage partners, for the kindred is exogamous, hence alliances are made with hostile families, and only kinsmen can be trusted to provide honest information about the standing of unrelated families. They may also call upon each other to give aid in trouble: to make loans, to use influence – provided that they do not harm the interests of their own family in so doing. They are expected, too, to give moral support in conflicts in which their kinsmen are involved: though they never pull the trigger they encourage an offended kinsman that it is right that he should. When two unrelated men quarrel, a third party who is a kinsman to each is expected to remain strictly neutral, and the quarrellers are expected to moderate their conflict from regard for the awkwardness of his position (1963: 75-80). Finally, poor Sarakatsani join richer kinsmen in day-to-day herding. A company (*stani* or *tselingato*, see above, p. 24) usually includes only members of a family, but five of the eighteen companies whose members Campbell lists included men from the leader's kindred (ibid.: Appendix A; see also

Appendix 4 to this chapter).

The formal characteristics of the Sarakatsani kindred are that it includes second cousins but no remoter kin, and that kinship is traced in both lines. So most of the members of a person's kindred (totalling perhaps 250 people altogether) are his second cousins: their children, however, are not kin to him. His first cousins' children are his kin, but their grandchildren are not. His siblings' grandchildren are his kin, but their great-grandchildren are not. He is most likely to be dead when his own great-grandchildren are born. So the majority of an active adult's kindred is composed of men of his own generation: in ascending generations the range narrows, the number of persons decreases to his eight great-grandparents; in descending generations the range similarly narrows, because of the cut-off at six degrees of kinship. The restriction of the kindred in descending generations, Campbell says, is conformable with the way in which men, as they get older, cease to need to rely on a far-flung group of trustworthy allies, and become more absorbed in the affairs of their own children and grandchildren, in the affairs of their nephews and nieces. As they marry their children off, as their sons begin to take active roles in the management of affairs, so their interests are focused, and so their reliance on kinsmen is diminished. The shape of the kindred thus reflects the vicissitudes of the domestic cycle: a man lives with his brothers at least until his father dies, often longer; his marriage creates his separate and distinctive interests.

There are no other well-described groups of kin round the mediterranean shore, and it is time to review briefly what has been written about kinship of other kinds. It was suggested in the last section that rules of residence at marriage can establish groups of different kinds – brothers and their wives, sisters and their husbands – who regard themselves as kinsmen. That is they take their kinship to be their defining characteristic and distinguish themselves by the frequency of their interaction from other people who are also kin. But there has not been much discussion in the ethnographies of groups thus formed by kinship *plus* some other principle. Most of what is written about bilateral kinship is concerned with selectivity and instrumentality. In relatively small communities people know that they are related to a lot of fellow-members, even if they are unable to trace the precise relationship; and they recognise that there are obligations between kinsmen. It is widely reported that people tend to select particular kinsmen among all possible kin, for instrumental reasons: they want to exercise claims against them, in order to gain advantage or security. Sicilian peasants, says Boissevain, see themselves in a hostile world, surrounded by bureaucrats, competitors, landlords, each of whom is at best indifferent, at worst activated by unbridled malice (e.g. 1966b): in these circumstances they select particular kinsmen who may be useful to them, and interact more with them than with others.

The discussion of residential patterns has perhaps made it clear that such selection, which undoubtedly occurs, is not wholly motivated by self-interest. And for this reason, perhaps, the kin relationships which they use may not be chosen wholly at random: there might be a bias in association, derived from the bias in the dispersal of members of families and in the association between newly founded households and their households of origin, which, over a period of time, is extended into a wider area of remoter cousinage. In Pisticci, for example, men who wished to maintain solidary relations among their sons and to deny the impartiality of bilateral inheritance, would live in the country, would set up quasi- or pseudo-extended households, and might assert that their aim was to keep 'land with the name', that is, in the patriline. The deliberate deviation of a few men, recognised and recognising themselves to be eccentric, can be very revealing of the regular long-term bias in the kinship and residence system (Davis, 1973: 120–3). More substantial information comes, as it often does, from Campbell. His careful analysis of Sarakatsanos kinship leads him to coin the term equivalent bilateral extension. And yet Sarakatsani derive prestige in the male line: a man derives his kindred relations in both lines, but the one which immediately identifies him is the one which gives him his name: 'if he possesses the surname of one of the leading families, or is directly descended, preferably in the male line, from a famous *tselingas* of the last century, this also is a significant element in a man's reputation'. When a man with a famous name of this kind behaves in ways which are inconsistent with it, other people substitute another name – they do not accord the (patrilineally derived) name and reputation to the unworthy (1964: 300-1). There is no question but that the Sarakatsani are 'fundamentally bilateral': what is clear, though, is that the process by which a man's kindred shrinks and his interest is focused on his descendants and closer collaterals as he grows older, can be perpetuated after his death: his *post-mortem* value as a source of prestige is mainly to his agnatic descendants. To say this is to do no more than to assert a bias in fundamental bilateralism: it is clearly related to the composition of extended family households, just as, indeed, equivalent bias is likely to be found in Vasilika, say, where neighbourhoods have fraternal cores. All this is to some degree speculative: it is dragged out of rather recalcitrant material by the aprioristic judgment that some bias is inevitable-in even the most self-consciously bilateral society, and that such a bias in households and neighbourhoods is likely to produce remoter consequences in the broader arena of kinship association. The reason for dragging it out is to question the current fashionable assumption that all interaction between kin in the north western mediterranean is rational, and hence random. Look for patterns which derive from the application of rules of residence and inheritance.

This injunction gains persuasiveness from other considerations: if men are self-interestedly using other men to acquire security or income, why should they use kinsmen? Exchanges of sociability between kinsmen should be no different from exchanges between non-kinsmen: but the relatively high incidence of kinship in Boissevain's anecdotes (1966a, 1966b, 1969a, 1969b, 1974: 1-3), for example, or in Blok's account of mafiosi (1974, especially Appendix C, diagrams 3, 5, 7, 8) does suggest that kinship carries with it some extra value which makes association with kinsmen more desirable than with others. Some of the more fantastic calculations of kinship over several generations and affinal links (e.g. Davis, 1976a) must be explained in this way. The relations may well be instrumental, but why are they cast in terms of kinship relations? The answer is that kinship carries with it obligations for fair-dealing, trust, honesty, which other relationships do not carry. Obligations are often enough ignored. Trust may be betrayed, the relationship itself denied, but it is nevertheless true that men who wish to attract the support and co-operation of others will do so in the name of prescriptive obligation – and will express an even greater sense of betrayal than if they are let down by an acquaintance or friend. This argument would be reinforced if it could be shown that men consciously create kinship for future generations by contracting marriage alliances. It is not enough to show that they wish to see their sons and daughters well married, to equals or superiors; it is necessary to show too that they take a long-term view of the probable general usefulness of the new connections which their children and grandchildren will enjoy. The evidence for this is scanty (Davis, 1973: 139-45; Freeman, 1970: ch. 5), but merits further comparative investigation.

V Godparenthood

One reason the notion of a rule of patrilineal endogamy comes under attack is that, naïvely understood, such a rule could be understood to eliminate alliance from marriage. Part of the argument in the last section shows that some communities do have a rule, which they break to make alliances, others have a preference which is ranked with other preferences. In the Christian, European, mediterranean studies of marriage-strategies are few and patchy (e.g. Willems, 1962; Davis, 1973: 143-5) and are concerned with property relations, with capture by marriage: the chief exception is Blok (1974) – but his material is not focused on the marriage alliance between groups of *mafiosi*.

If this chapter now moves from kinship and marriage to god-parenthood it is because godparenthood is used in the Christian mediterranean as a way of making alliances. That is to say, in some cases it is part of a system by which corporate kinship groups are brought into permanent relation to each other. In others where there are no corporate kinship groups the relation is established on a less permanent basis, though still often a long-term one, between families. That is one reason for writing about godparenthood and marriage: in the area of alliance, the two institutions overlap. In other ways there is connection: godparenthood is an achieved relationship, ideally never-ending – like marriage; it is created in a church, and sanctioned by God – like few relationships other than marriage. Indeed marriage is one of the two sacraments at which godparenthood is normally created (the other is baptism). Godparenthood, like marriage, creates kinship – an injunction to amity, a prohibition on sexual intercourse and marriage. So apart from cases in which it creates alliance, god-parenthood also has more obvious features in common with marriage and with kinship: these features are no doubt why it has variously been called spiritual kinship, synthetic kinship, quasi- and pseudo-kinship – even 'a kind of spurious kinship' (Pitt-Rivers, 1961: 107). Those usages can seem casual, and could dull the mind or conceal nuances: in this book it is called godparenthood. That has the disadvantage of implicitly denying the claims of those who say that god-parenthood is a Christian form of a much more ancient mediterranean institution, apparently not associated with God at all: the denial, properly qualified, is therefore made explicit in Appendix 6 at the end of this chapter.

Start, then, from the observation that the Christian sacrament of baptism creates a relationship between a child and its sponsors, and between the sponsors and its parents. The relationship includes duties of spiritual guidance laid on the sponsors *vis-à-vis* the child, and a diriment impediment to marriage between a sponsor and both the child and its parents. In the vernaculars people often have words for these relationships which combine parenthood and a modifying suffix or prefix: 'co'-parent, 'little' parent; in Italian, a word which is also used for grandparent (*nonno, nonna*); and so on. People (all Christians and some Muslims) can create relationships with these characteristics (guidance, impediment, amity and a modified kinship terminology) on other occasions than baptism, but no other occasion is common to them, and only those characteristics are common to them all. In this sense baptism is a lowest common denominator, and so it is convenient to start with it: but do not think that baptism is the seed from which all the other sometimes luxuriant growths have sprung – there is no evidence for that.

The only monograph on mediterranean godparenthood is a masterpiece (it is perhaps the only such produced by an anthropologist working in the mediterranean). It is Hammel's short book *Alternative Social Structures and Ritual Relations in the Balkans* (1968) and it reconstructs and analyses the most elaborately systematic godparenthood yet recorded: godparenthood, affinity and agnation are mutually exclusive structural alternatives. Hammel had got enough idea from the literature to produce a research project and to get to the field to ask the right questions; but he was then blessed with a good informant who, after more or less fruitless conversation, suddenly said 'Now, young fellow, I think I see what you want to know, and I will tell you. We have kinship, alliance and godparenthood' (ibid.: 4). Agnatic groups, defined by shared respect for a patron saint (*slava*) at the outmost limits, by knowledge within them, might establish relationships either of marriage or of godparenthood with other similar agnatic groups. The godparenthood relationship was certainly systematic in the sense that it was unilateral ('members of one line were godparents of those of a second, who were godparents to those of a third, and so on' (ibid.: 1)) and Hammel thinks that affinal relationships may have been so too (ibid.: 31-2).

In Serbian the man who sponsors a child at baptism or haircutting, and the child's father, address each other as *kum* (the child is addressed by the sponsor as *kumce,* and reciprocates with *kum*). The terms are extended to all members, male and female, of each man's 'entire household or wider agnatic group', and the relationship between the groups continues for as long as the groups do. That these are statuses which are assumed by one group *vis-à-vis* another group is evidenced by repetition and by substitutability: people who have once sponsored a child from another household (zadruga) continue to provide men to sponsor further children of those families. And at ceremonies requiring the presence of a *kum* any man from the household of the actual godfather could discharge that household's obligation. The expenses of sponsorship were met from zadruga funds and, although the reciprocating gifts were given to and kept by the actual sponsor, the leader of a well-run zadruga saw to it that each member had his turn at officiating as representative of the corporation. The units involved in *kumstvo* were normally zadrugas, occasionally larger agnatic groups. These were liable to divide every two generations or so: if a sponsoring zadruga split, the various *kumstvo* were divided among the new segments – as was other property; if a sponsored zadruga split, individuals within the sponsoring group took special responsibility for particular segments. Where division of the zadruga was substantially incomplete, and considerable property was still held in common, the *kumstvo* might also remain undivided. In fact the similarity between property and *kumstvo* relationships of sponsorship was greater than that, for sponsorship status might be given away or sold. 'Once . . . I came on a peasant farmstead and announced to a most suspicious woman that I was interested in . . . *kumstvo*. A gleam of avarice appeared in her eye, and the reply shot back, "Do you want to buy one?" ' (ibid.: 45-50, especially 48, where there are examples of successful sales).

So the evidence is, allowing for regional variation, that *kumstvo* was, is, a status relationship between groups, divisible as the group was, and transferable. However, the reconstruction goes further than that, for it is also clear that *kumstvo* was usually unilateral, that it was part of a wider system of exchanges, and that it was exclusive of the other statuses of agnation and affinity – broadly speaking always, and allowing for regional variation. The evidences for unilaterality are twofold: in spite of the reciprocity in terms of address, the roles of the sponsoring and of sponsored groups were different. And they were incompatible since to accept the status of sponsor to another group was to accept some not very explicit superiority over it; in fact, because a group seeking a sponsor looked among its social superiors, the notional superiority of status was often validated by actual differences in wealth and prestige – for example, Gypsies would ask Vlachs, and Vlachs would ask Serbs, to be *kumstvo* (ibid.: 77-9). However, there are some examples of reciprocated *kumstvo*, and Hammel never found that the circle of relationships was closed by unilateral links. For example, in the series of groups A-B-C . . . X, where A sponsors B, B sponsors C and so on, he never found that . . . X sponsored A. Rather, the circle was short-circuited by an exchange of *kumstvo*: A sponsors C, C sponsors D, D sponsors B, and A and B sponsor each other. There might, in a community of seventeen or ninety patrilines (ibid.: 74-7, gives an example of each), be one or more cores of reciprocal *kumstvo*, the reciprocating groups each having links with different patrilines in the community. In fact it was rare for zadrugas to reciprocate: the normal pattern appears to have been that zadruga 1 of Lineage A would be *kumstvo* to zadruga 2 of Lineage X, while a different zadruga of Lineage X would be *kumstvo* to a different zadruga of Lineage A. With these exceptions *kumstvo* was not exchanged reciprocally, but was offered in exchange for peace, to placate hostility. Hammel cites a Montenegrin case: one child killed another by accident. His mother took a young baby to the dead child's family and asked them to accept *kumstvo*, whereupon they realised that some serious trouble had occurred. 'A drowning man, seeing someone on shore, may cry out "in the name of God and St. John accept *kumstvo*" . . . A man caught in the act of theft may make a similar request. . . . It is said that offers of this kind cannot be refused' (ibid.: 82). Because the offer of godfatherhood cannot be refused, and can avert trouble, people kept some children long-haired and unbaptised until the age of ten or so, in case they should be needed in an emergency (ibid.: 94). Less dramatically, *kumstvo* may be offered to solicit a big favour, or in recognition of one received, and in these cases the notional superiority of the sponsoring group is undoubtedly also actual (ibid.: 82-5).

The unilaterality of *kumstvo* relationships, with the exceptions noted above, is related to their incompatibility with agnation and affinity. A formal relationship implying inequality may fit uneasily with the solidarity of agnatic equals: Hammel, in his extensive collection of *kumstvo* records, found only two cases involving parties who claimed agnation. In both cases it was distant, and the patrilines were in the process of fission, and it therefore seems reasonable to accept that the two systems were dissonant. If a man may not marry his godchild and if this impediment is assumed by agnatic groups on each side in perpetuity, it follows that there will be no affinity between the two agnatic groups. The prohibition on such marriages was strictly observed until the Second World War, and Hammel records cases where *kumstvo* was created to prevent marriage; and where marriage followed the fission of an agnatic group and the division of *kumstvo* – marriage that is, between the segments where *kumstvo* no longer lay. By logic and in practice the statuses of affine and of *kum* were incompatible.

Hammel is careful not to claim too much for the system he describes: he is even exaggeratedly careful to record his doubts and the weaknesses in his evidence and to qualify what others may see as the discovery of a double system of alliance – marriage and *kumstvo* – not overlapping but working in tandem, the one between equals, the other between unequals. He says that these features of Serbian godparenthood, in a patrilineal system, make it unique in the mediterranean, and it is true that only hints come from other patrilineal Christian societies. In Albania, for example, Cozzi says, affinity and godparenthood (including the 'St John' – Sh'Njon created by haircutting) are impediments to marriage – but he does not say between whom (1912: 316). Durham says that siblings and descendants of couples joined by godparenthood are disbarred from marriage (1909: 23), but she does not say that groups are implicated. A year later (1910: 459) she wrote:

> it has been the almost universal practice to take a wife from
> the tribe next door and to marry the resultant daughters back
> into it . . . among the Moslem two tribes will go on exchanging
> daughters backwards and forwards for generations . . . and it
> has only very recently been checked among the Christians
> (cf. Whitaker, 1968).

The syndrome appears to rise even from the racy language: exchange marriage between groups, impediments to marriage between the people directly involved in godparenthood and between some of their kin – it is possible that Hammel is too cautious.

Godparenthood is always established at baptism; in some communities marriage witnesses, best men, or marriage sponsors are also regarded as standing in some special relationship to the spouses: when this occurs it is often associated with the right of marriage witnesses to be godparents to the first child of the marriage. In the Roman Church a sponsor is required also for chrism, but this sponsorship is not often used to establish special relationships (e.g. Cutileiro, 1971: 208n). On the other hand there are a number, sometimes abundant, of customarily recognised life-crises, attended by rituals, which the churches do not recognise: first haircutting, first nail-cutting, ear-piercing (for girls), and so on (Durham, 1909: 22 seq.; Valentini, 1945: 39-50; Hammel, 1968: 8; Anderson, 1956; Gower Chapman, 1973: 119-22; Davis, 1973: 60-1). At this level of luxuriant flourishing what is apparently a quintessentially Christian rite overlaps with rituals used in non-Christian communities which also create special relationships (see Appendix 6). There is fuzziness at the boundary between religious communities; there is fuzziness at the boundary between canonical and other rituals within Christian communities; there is fuzziness at the analytical boundary between Christian godparenthood and the possibly similar kinds of relationship which may be created in Islamic communities.

Instances of the indeterminacy at the boundary between sacramental and non-sacramental rites are provided by popular attempts to impose sacraments on ecclesiastical doctrine. Albanian tribesmen, Durham reports, distinguished the generic *kumarii* into *kumarii i pakzimit* (baptism) and *kumarii i floksh* (haircutting). Valentini remarks that 'the common people has tried to sanctify [haircutting] without any support from the clergy, with the name Shnjon'. Where baptism is thus explicitly called 'the St John' (as in 'to give the St John') people do often use the term for the relationships which they establish extra-canonically. Contrariwise, people do not always recognise sacraments which are recognised by the church. Vila Velhans do not recognise sponsors at chrism as compadre; and the Sicilian Milocchesi refused to call compadre the person who performs an emergency baptism even though, should the child survive, the canon law imposes a bar on marriage between the baptiser and the child (Gower Chapman, 1973: 120). Finally, people may recognise sacramental bonds in a religious context which are not recognised by their church. Durkheim (1898b) cites Ciszewski to the effect that people who have been baptised in the same water, or who have met on pilgrimage, enjoy *kunstliche Werwandschaft*.

The extension of terms of address is widely reported (e.g. Davis, 1973: 60-1; Kenna, 1971: 228) and one sample will suffice (Cutileiro, 1971: 210, where another example is given):

In Vila Velha a fairly wealthy landowning family employed a
young servant girl whose sister was the . . . goddaughter of
one of the nieces of the landowner's wife. Instead of addressing
them as *minha senhora* and *Senor X*, as her status as a servant
required, she consistently called them and their sons *padrinho* or
madrinha, to the point of causing them embarrassment in the
presence of guests.

It may be that the term 'extension', in so far as it implies any grad-
uality, is misleading. With the act of baptism, it appears, all the
members of the families on each side begin to call each other by the
appropriate terms. Similarly, performance of the roles in the ritual
creates an impediment to marriage not only between the parties but
also between some members of their families. The range of the prohibition in any particular community is co-extensive with the prohibition on kinsmen, with a few exceptions. If a man may not marry his
own cousin, so he may not marry his godparents' cousins. The charts
showing degrees of prohibited kin and degrees of prohibited godparental kin can usually be superimposed on each other, with godparents in the place of their godchild's parents. Durham mentions
that godparenthood impeded marriage; and while Valentini (1945:
58-60) says that there was an impediment to the marriage of all
agnates and godparent's agnates (offenders were fined and their
houses burned by tribal authority), the rules prohibiting affinal marriage, also reaching to 'the four hundredth degree' (according to
Gjeçov) were not applied with so much 'rigour'. Indeed, as Valentini
says; they could not be so applied since affinity was an attribute of
agnatic groups, and in short time there would be no permissible
Albanian marriages. Hammel says of Montenegro that local practice
was more restrictive than ecclesiastical law in the male line, less so in
the female line; so Orthodox Montenegrins who wished to marry
close uterine kin got themselves married by a Moslem judge. Valentini (a Roman Catholic) notes some Albanian marriages between
affines which the canon law prohibits; but he thought that in general
the old canon law degrees were respected (1945: 60-1). Kenna says
that households between whom there is *koumbaría* cannot intermarry (1971: 228 seq.) and that godchildren of the same godparent
may not marry each other; Friedl (1963a: 72) that *koumbaría* carries a
prohibition on marriage to the same degree of kinship as cognation
does. Campbell says that copulation is incestuous if it involves the

families of parties to a ceremony of baptism (1964: 221). Similarly, terrible tales were told in Milocca about couples who offended St John (Gower Chapman, 1973: 117) and in Beja their offspring were said to be werewolves (Willems, 1962) Cutileiro reports (1971. 208) that 'the rules of incest' used to apply, but do so no longer, and, moreover, that people who are engaged or courting are never asked, even now, to be godparents to the same child: a prohibition, not imposed by the church, on marriage and copulation between the godparents themselves.

The two schedules of impediment are coterminous: whatever the prohibited degrees of kinship may be in a local community, the same degrees are applied to godparents; in this sense godparents and parents occupy similar structural positions – are structurally identical – and may not therefore marry each other. Callier-Boisvert remarks that, in Soajo, 'entre parents par alliance, on trouve une appellation qui surprend: compadre, comadre, termes reservés en principe au compère et a la commère' (1968: 97): it is possible that the common element of impediment has allowed Portuguese terminology to slip, as it were, from one schedule into the other.

In all communities the combination of obligatory honesty and trustworthiness, with a prohibition on copulation and marriage, creates relations of easy-going familiarity: *compadri* may freely visit each other's households, where people lacking the bond of god-parenthood would generally not. A compadre is above suspicion and may therefore visit freely. On an analoguous freedom between affines (*cognati*) and hence between godparental affines Valentini remarks: 'Tant' è vero che tra famiglie cognate v' è gran libertà di tratto, uso di frequentar le case gli uni degli altri e passarvi la notte . . . senza eccessivi reguardi fra ragazzi e ragazze, il che purtroppo in realtà da luogo a dolorosi fatti insanabili' (1945: 61). It is quite common to hear that the status of *compari* is treated ambiguously and is the subject of ribald jokes at weddings: lovers also visit freely, and in Pisticci a lover seen to enter a house frequently is euphemistically or ironically referred to as a *compadre*. A man may refer jokingly to his mistress as his *commare*. In a personal communication Dr Loizos has said that the proverbial Cypriot phrase 'the *koumbaros* puts it in from the left side' may refer to any action from which a person is disbarred by his status: when he does what he ought not, he does it the opposite of the correct way. When godparenthood is associated with patronage (above, p. 92), the sexual connotations of the relationship may be even more explicitly recognised. The ambiguity which attends the relationship is also encapsulated in the unique report by Ciszewski (cited by Durkheim, 1898b) that southern Slav spouses might declare themselves to be *kum* and *kuma,* or to be brother and sister, and live chastely together if they have evidence that God has cursed their marriage – for example, from a series of still-births.

The points which emerge from this discussion are first, that ties between people can be created by participation in sacramental life-cycle rituals, and that there is a mediterranean tendency to regard as sacramental those other acts creating ties which local custom has added to ecclesiastical doctrine. Second, that participation in the rituals, in ecclesiastical law, creates an impediment to marriage between the parties; this, too, is found in the 'folk-sacraments'. Third, that the status of godparent and godchild (and of the folk-analogies) is extended to include the families of the parties concerned. Fourth, that where local systems of kinship reckoning deviate from the strictly bilateral ecclesiastical ones, it is the local custom which prevails: marriage is, in these cases, usually more extensively impeded than the canon law requires. Fifth, that the local prohibitions on marriage between spiritual kin are coterminous with the prohibitions between kin: if the two charts of prohibited degrees are superimposed one on the other, with godparents in the place of parents, then the boundaries coincide. Sixth, that the relationship is often a sexually ambivalent one.

Finally, consider the point raised by Hammel: godparenthood implies unequal status between the parties. That, too, is widely reported from the Christian mediterranean. In some communities the association of godparenthood and superiority is extremely close. Kenny remarks on the semantic connection between *patrono* (patron, employer, patron saint) and *padrinho* (godfather, marriage sponsor and second at a duel). In Vila Velha '. . . a child may have a spiritual *madrinha* in the person of a saint. . . . This happens when delivery is difficult' (Cutileiro, 1971: 206-7): when a saint is godmother superiority could not be clearer – the connection is more than semantic. The same must apply when godparenthood is used to terminate hostility (Gower Chapman, 1973: 118), and in the many reported cases where men have chosen important men to be godparents to their children. These cases are too numerous to cite, but it is worth noting that although important men can therefore have numerous godchil-

dren, not everyone succeeds in persuading them to sponsor their child
(e.g. Campbell, 1964; see above, p. 144). The commonest solution is
probably represented by the Nisiots, who say that each child should
have at least one influential godfather (Kenna, 1971: 257). Vasilikans,
like most people, select marriage partners and *koumbari* 'whose
wealth and position will be a source of potential help to themselves
and their children' (Friedl, 1963a: 72): it is on record that they do not
all succeed. One exception to this general practice of seeking out
patron-*padrinhos* is Valdemora: there, godparents are usually
kinsmen and that 'speaks for the adequacy of kin-based networks'
(Freeman, 1970: 143; cf. Boissevain, 1966b: 203). Callier-Boisvert
makes a similar point, more sharply, when she suggests that rich and
wealthy people can afford to choose close kinsmen – they do not need
patrons, or, their kinsmen *are* patrons – and draws the contrast with
the poor: for them godparenthood is '. . . un moyen . . . d'obtenir la
protection des gens bien placés'. She also puts the phenomenon of
extension in a new light when she recalls that in rural areas, where a
great landowner may be the natural godfather of the community,
'parfois tous les enfants appellent *padrinho* le parrain d'un des
enfants' (1968: 99).

Pitt-Rivers has, absolutely correctly, emphasised the spiritual,
sacred nature of godparenthood, a theme which did not receive much
emphasis again until Gudeman's structuralist essay on godparenthood (1971). Gudeman acknowledges his debt to Pitt-Rivers, but
does not pursue the distinction between 'sacred compadrazgo' and
'profane kinship'. That is a pity, for it is difficult to see the *shnjon* as a
profound or pure religious experience, or even as the touching manifestation of the simple faith of honest peasant folk. What is clear in
general terms is that Christian mediterranean societies provide direct
special and specific spiritual sanctions for only two kinds of created
relationship – those concerned with sex and honour (marriage), and
those concerned with power (patronage). Perhaps that should lead
some future ethnographer to look more closely still at those societies
where people commonly choose kinsmen to be godfathers, and at
claims that this is because kin-based networks are adequate. But in
any case sexual and power relationships are singled out for special
religious sanctions, and indeed are sometimes confused in the figures
of the godfather who is an incestuous lover, the lover who is called
godfather, and the patron who loves his employees' wives and
daughters, and makes that a condition of employment.

VI Conclusion

Godparenthood has been called pseudo-, quasi- and spurious kin-ship, 'like marriage' (Lineton, 1971: 39) – and the best account, although it may be a unique case, demonstrates that it can be an alternative to both marriage and agnation. It is certainly related to kinship: godparenthood utilises the words of parenthood, and creates impediments to marriage. It is certainly like marriage in the way it is sanctioned, in the way it permits the creation of alliance, and then spreads out among the kin of the individual most directly concerned. But it creates no rights to inherit property, it does not disrupt a household immediately nor, by introducing a foreign sex, does it presage the dispersal of persons and property, and it is contracted often enough between unequals.

Mediterranean men and women have reached and institutionalis-ed various compromises to cope with the dilemma posed by the con-tradictory ideals of independence and equality within the household: the ideal of love and amity is undermined by marriage; the ideal of married independence, adulthood, full participation in the stratified world of men, is in conflict with the prescription of equality among the children of a household: societies offer amity and the easy perform-ance of duty in some spheres, at the cost of denying it in others. God-parenthood is not always sacred, nor does it always contrast with profane kinship: for, on the one hand, it can be an expression of submission to secular demands of patrons – and perhaps such sacredness as it may still possess is then a check, keeping submission and prepotence within bounds. On the other hand, godparenthood can be created to coincide perfectly with profane kinship – though perhaps in that case profane kinship is more fraught with danger and conflict than it is elsewhere. However, some parts of godparenthood do represent a recombination of elements of kinship and contract which, divorced from the movements of the domestic cycle, may embody those ideals without contradiction: procreation without succession; holy alliance without marriage – independent choice and contract, association, without threat to the equality of the household; (god-)children who do not supplant their parents; people who may behave familiarly, may freely enter a house, without danger to honour, without a hint of interest: neither strangers nor kinsmen. So although godparenthood is an idiom of relationship which draws heavily on the terminologies and institutions of kinship and marriage,

Family and kinship

and may indeed overlap with them, and is an idiom in which sacredness can connote hierarchy (as most religious symbolism is ambivalently hierarchical and egalitarian) none the less it is an examination of the contrasts between godparent and parent, godchild and child, *padrinho* and *patrono* which reveals . . . Well: not the *true* meaning of the institution, for there probably is none; but certainly the most moving, compassion-arousing aspect of mediterranean family behaviour – the search for amity untainted by interest, for protection uncontaminated by prepotent exploitation.

Appendices to chapter 5

1 *On versions of the laws of Aleksander Dukagjini, and other Albanian matters*

Dukagjini, a fifteenth century 'legislator', is credited with the formulation of a code of laws which are fundamentally those of self-help within a tribal organisation of limited powers. The code was not written down until the nineteenth century, by Gjecov, an Albanian compilator of oral traditions. For contemporary expert opinion see Whitaker, 1968. Hasluck (1954) gives an English account of the 'unwritten' law; but Kastrati (1955), reviewing the sources and providing details of the attachments and perspicacity as well as the research procedures of their authors, casts doubts on the reliability of Hasluck: he prefers Durham (1909, 1910, 1928, 1935, 1941). Certainly, Durham's work was not produced by a literary executor, as Hasluck's was; but Hasluck has a much more professional 'feel' than the jumbled and enthusiastic work of Durham (and see Hammel's 1957 comments on the Albanian kinship terminology recorded by Durham). Neither lady, Kastrati says, spoke any form of Albanian perfectly. Perhaps the best source to rely on in an accessible language is Dodaj's (1941) translation of Gjecov. Kastrati discounts Valentini's aspersions (1945) on Dodaj's accuracy but, in view of the conjunction of Italian translation and invasion, it may be as well that the reader treat all sources circumspectly. Valentini's book, referred to by Kastrati, appears to be a separate edition of the article cited here: it is probably more easily obtained in article form.

2 *On a corrected version of Peters's article, 'Aspects of the family among the Bedouin of Cyrenaica' (1965) kindly communicated by the author (see p. 174)*

This article contains the only modern account of the composition of relatively free (in contrast, that is, to Bedouin of the Negev) Bedouin. So apart from its predictable structural elegance it has considerable ethnographic value. Unfortunately, the version published contains a number of discrepancies between the diagram on p. 142 and the text on that and the following page. The following notes will permit readers of this book to correct the 1965 version.

p. 142 diagram: resurrect n. 16, wrongly shown dead in one edition.

       text: 14, read – 'the niece of (3)'

                    15, read – 'with his elder brother who'

                    19, read – 'wife's aunt's (3) flock'

p. 143:   5, read – 'sister of (3) and aunt (6)'

                    12, read – 'blind, was a close patrilateral cousin of both, but his sister was also 10's mother'.

3 *On Sarakatsani marriages*

Campbell provides little information about marriage alliances: affines are neither kin or non-kin, and are considered suitable for co-operation but not particularly trustworthy (1964: 38, 146); some Sarakatsani seemed uncomfortable at the thought of second cousins becoming affines through the marriage of their children: hence, of 121 marriages 'in recent years' only nine were between third cousins (ibid.: 131-2). Thus marriage usually 'joins strangers while it separates those who are already kinsmen' (1963: 86; 1964: 40). So, since Sarakatsani do marry only Sarakatsani, and since they usually marry people from families regarded as hostile, with 'mutually destructive' (ibid.: 75) interests, Campbell argues that the pattern of marriage identifies the Sarakatsani community and maintains its boundaries (1964: 147). Interestingly enough one of the 'two notorious instances' (ibid.: 111) of marriage between second cousins was arranged by an exceptionally prestigeful man (ibid.: 267; see above, p. 95); it would be interesting to know whether the other incestuous marriage involved a powerful man (the incident described at p. 172 seems to be the same marriage as at p. 267); and indeed what was the social standing of the eighteen second cousins who arranged the nine marriages between their children.

4 *On the kin ties between component families of Sarakatsani stani (see p. 219)*

Campbell, 1964: Appendix A is the source. The list gives details for 18 *stani*. Six included only members of the leader's family. A total of 27 families had attached themselves to the other 12 leaders. The heads of 11 of these 27 families were brothers to the leader of their *stani*. Seven of them were close affines (e.g. the leader's father-in-law), 4 of them were more distant affines, and 5, as stated in the text, were members of the leader's kindred.

5 *On Bedouin segmentation (see p. 200)*

Peters's insistence that Bedouin manipulate their genealogies at the fifth and six generation level (where the persons were not known to living members, but where the genealogy is still private) is the basis of his long and subtle *prise de position* towards Evans-Pritchard's statement that the Nuer proliferate segments at *any* level of the genealogical structure.

Peters's argument is diffuse and technical, but one item may be summarised here. If legitimating genealogies are to remain of constant depth then *either* telescoping must occur, *or* apical ancestors must be pushed out into limbo: 'extrusion of ancestral names must take place at the apex of the genealogy'. If the proliferation of segments at lower levels has, as it were, a peristaltic effect on the *whole* genealogy, and the apical ancestor is shot into limbo, then the descendants of the lost ancestor must change one of their identifying names:

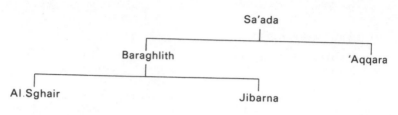

If Al Sghair and Jibarna are promoted (due to strength of numbers at lower levels) then Sa'ada herself may be squeezed out by Baraghlith, who would thus become the founder of the whole group. The people claiming descent through 'Aqqara would take the name of the group from whom, formerly, they were distinguished and to whom, in some respects, they were opposed. Since it is impossible to imagine this happening, and since Bedouin genealogies do have a constant depth of twelve generations, the extrusion of ancestors must necessarily occur at some point in the genealogy where public recognition by opposed groups is not required – and that is precisely at the sixth generation from Sa'ada. It is an intricate and ingenious argument (1960: 360 ss). Peters suggests that Nuer conditions of expansion could permit such looseness, though he clearly regards this as a remote possibility. A point he does not mention is that the Bedouin appear to place much more virtue in their founding ancestress (descent from whom, after all, justifies their privileges against client groups) than the Nuer do in corresponding figures. Indeed, it may be a characteristic of North African tribesmen generally to start their identificatory references 'from the tribal or clan level and [to] work down towards the smaller units' (Hart, 1970: 12; cf. Chelhod, 1960a): the Nuer appear not to do this – see e.g. *The Nuer* (*cit.*), p. 195.

6 *On non-Christian godparenthood (see p. 223)*

Hammel suggests that godparenthood is only accidentally Christian, that pre-Christian forms of association were taken over and modified by the churches. That is not central to his argument, and so it is not a topic which merits discussion in the main text; but the idea is an interesting one, it is contested by Gudeman (1971: 46), and it raises questions of method and theory which can be indicated here, to be taken up again in chapter 6. Hammel, like Gudeman, refers to Mintz and Wolf (1950) and also to Filipović (1963). The former give a brief history of the development of sponsorship from Roman law to its use by the early church as a safeguard against *agents provocateurs,* and associate it with Greek and Jewish distinctions and terms. That is an acceptable procedure, but it would be necessary to provide rather more history than they do, and to argue the case more sharply. It *is* significant and interesting that latin *Sponsio,* 'a contract enforced by religious rather than legal sanctions', should provide modern language with both sponsor (as of a child at baptism) and spouse: but anthropologists have not yet devised criteria for weighing etymological 'evidence'.

Another kind of argument is institutional. If godparenthood is pre-Christian what sort of institution was it? Filipović speaks rather diffusely of blood brotherhood, also mentioned by Mintz and Wolf, and the implication is that this institution is the precursor of Christian godparenthood. The argument requires elaborate safeguards against the rather too easy move towards calling *any* method by which people make alliances a precursor of godparenthood. For the reasoning could be of this kind: godparenthood has certain functions and is Christian; the same functions in pre-christian times were performed by blood brotherhood; therefore blood brotherhood is the precursor . . . and so on. It is illegitimate to switch from functions to origins; and the selection of *which* functions to take to be the important ones, in the hands of an enthusiastic rather than scrupulous mind, can be somewhat arbitrary. Or perhaps not quite arbitrary, for the functions selected often exhibit a materialist bias: there is no one who argues, for example, that spiritual guidance and care, which is one function of godparenthood, were formerly provided by some other institution.

That said, the reader may relax severity for a while, to contemplate the following snippets, culled from the literature.

(i)   Balkan Moslems could enter into *kumstvo* relationships by sponsoring a Christian, or by accepting the sponsorship of a Christian at circumcision rituals (Hammel, 1968: 10-12). Filipović (1963) says that Christians who were converted to Islam retained their *kumstvo* ties. People in a zone of religious transition were often able to maintain a spiritual identity in each religion (e.g. Durham, 1910: 456). These are cases of a general indistinctness at boundaries. There are no easily discovered reports of similar indistinctness in the Lebanon or Egypt where substantial minorities of Christians live among Moslems, although Chemali mentions godparenthood in the Lebanon (1915-16: 915, 933).

(ii)   Blood brotherhood is said by some writers to be established 'like godparenthood': it is a means of 'artificially extending kinship ties'. Halpern says that in Orašac it was created on consecrated ground (by a grave) and was sealed '. . . before God and St. John'. The children of blood brother might not marry (1969: 163). Valentini says that blood brotherhood creates an impediment between a man and the women of his blood brother's house, and that is a means of making a peace (1945: 39-50).

(iii)   Milk motherhood is reported from Turkey and Syria. The relationship of wetnurse to child creates a relationship of brotherhood and sisterhood between the nursed child and the nurse's children, and an impediment to marriage (Suzuki, 1964; Stirling, personal communication). Dickson (1952: foreword) records that his mother's milk dried up, he was suckled by a 'Anizah woman and this gave him 'a certain "blood affinity"‸(*sic*) with the 'Anizah; for to drink a woman's milk in the desert is to become a child of the foster mother. This fact has been of assistance to me in my dealings with the Badawin'. In Turkey, a child's *göbekadi* (umbilical) name is the name given by a male relative as the midwife cuts and ties its umbilical cord – but Spenser (1961) does not say whether that creates any special relationship. *Tafargant* pacts are created by Ait 'Atta when lactating mothers from two groups exchange milk: *tafargant* carries an injunction to amity and an impediment to marriage (Dunn, 1973: 97). On the various kinds of pact possible between Berber groups (*Tada* – also *tata*; *amur* and *taymat*) see Vinogradoff's succinct compendium (1974b: 72-5), Dunn's article (1973) and Maunier (1937).

These rather random bits and pieces do not justify any claim that god-parenthood is pre-Christian. On the contrary, they suggest that the mediterranean displays a variety of ways in which men may make alliances, with equals and with patrons (e.g. *amur*). It is interesting that these so often impede marriage; interesting that they often carry spiritual sanctions, but these common though not universal characteristics should be related to general features of mediterranean social organisation, and not be ranked in any historical causal or original sequence.

7   *On some Iberian inheritance systems*

This appendix is merely to note a state of indecision among ethnographers: some say that they describe a system of 'equal inheritance', by which all heirs divide equally, but none the less only one will take on the land, and will pay off his co-heirs in due course (e.g. Freeman, 1968a) while others refer to the same system as one of primogeniture (e.g. Codd, 1971: 189; Hansen, 1969). Callier-Boisvert says that while the law is for partible bilateral inheritance, it was common for one child to inherit the estate, taking on an obligation to help his siblings (1968). Future ethnographers might care to distinguish state law from local practice; but perhaps they should use the term primo- (or indeed ultimo-) geniture only where inheritance by one person is associated with corporate households – stem families, such as those described by Cole (1969), where property, a house and a line are associated in perpetuity.

6

Anthropologists and history in the mediterranean

I   Oxford and the anthropology of more complex societies

Saki wrote a short story which epitomises the problem: a rising politician drives his wife to suicide by making bad jokes. The last straw was a Commons debate on the Foreign Office vote in which Arlington Stringham remarked, 'The people of Crete unfortunately make more history than they can consume locally.' It is a remark which might be made about almost any part of the mediterranean, without of course accepting the implicit definition that history is what causes present expenditure. Indeed, a student who surveys the ethnographic literature for a definition of history will not find one, nor several, but none: and he is reduced to looking not at 'history' but at a series of facts about the past as they are presented by anthropologists. In this broad sense there is a a lot of mediterranean history – facts about Greece, Rome, Islam, Judaism, early and late Christianity, Egypt – the mediterranean is a major producer of history. How have anthropologists used it?

Part of the interest of this question is that when Evans-Pritchard gave his controversial Marrett lecture in 1950 (1964), throwing off the mantle of Radcliffe-Brownian scientism, inclining to the view that social anthropology was properly one of the humanities, he predicted that anthropologists would shortly be confronted with intellectual and analytic problems which would force them to resolve the issue. For they would move more into complex and civilised societies (ibid.: 22) and, he thought, would begin to see that anthropology and history were divided in practice only by 'emphasis' (ibid.: 24), by 'technique, . . . emphasis and perspective' (ibid.: 25). The interest of this prediction lies in the fact that, as he spoke, he had a number of students in the complex field, or on the point of departing for it. Stirling was in Turkey. Peters, who had followed Evans-Pritchard from Cambridge, retraced his steps to Cyrenaica. When the Marrett lecture refers to Bedouin Arab tribes (1964: 21) exemplifying the new studies in the civilised field, it is presumably Peters's work, as well as his own (1949), which Evans-Pritchard had in mind. (1949: v 'I thank Mr. E. L. Peters . . . for help in preparation of the maps.' This acknowledgment is dated April 1948.) Stirling and Peters took their doctorates in 1951; Pitt-Rivers was in Spain in 1950 and, by the time he had completed his thesis in 1953, Kenny had been in the field for a year. Peristiany lectured in Oxford at that time; his autobiographical notes (ASA, 1969) do not record his switch of interest from Kipsigis to Greeks until much later but Campbell, who arrived in Oxford in 1953, recalls that discussions on honour, to result eventually in the essays Peristiany edited in 1966, had already begun.[1] It is clear then that Evans-Pritchard's theoretical statement of 1950 had some reference to empirical work. His own book on the Sanusi was out, and the Oxford institute contained a number of young men who would consume still more history: they studied Greeks, Turks, Spaniards, Bedouin, complex and civilised peoples who were to be an object lesson to his colleagues. How did they go about it?

II Historic landscapes

Perhaps the most charitable way to begin is to observe that those pupils were thrown in the deep end. For all the appearance of planning and intention, the gathering of mediterraneanists at Oxford in the late 1940s and early 1950s was in fact largely accidental: 'programmes' of research had not then been invented and, it might be thought, Oxford was the least likely place for them to be introduced. Evans-Pritchard's essay accuses the functionalists of throwing out the baby of real history with the bath water of speculative history; there was nevertheless enough water in the mediterranean for his pupils to flounder unless given guidance. And what guidance did they have? Their teacher had told them to look not for laws but for 'significant patterns'; he had told them to read literature and history; and Marc Bloch, Fustel de Coulanges were held before them as examples. But how were they to use 'facts about the past', how to combine them with the techniques, emphases, perspectives of anthropology? These were men who had been sent to the field – they were not to sit in libraries and emulate Fustel by producing an anthropology of some relatively discrete historical time-island – should they then use Fustel as a *source*? (See above, p. 133.) What status should a fact about the past have in order to qualify for inclusion in an ethnography? Should it be a *cause* of some current process or situation? Should it give an *insight*? Should it disclose *development* of institutions? Evans-Pritchard's own work on the Sanusi of Cyrenaica (1949) is quite inexplicit about the procedures to be followed. It explains the success of the Sanusiya order (as opposed to other orders) by the way in which the Grand Sanusi and his successors matched the organisation of Lodges to the structure of tribes. It explains the gradual conversion of a religious order founded in 1835-7 and which a century later had become a military and political organisation, by the way in which confrontation with Italian, Turkish and British representatives called forth consolidation at a national level – how national unity and self-consciousness were created by the assumptions of those who insisted on negotiating with a leader. But most of the book is fairly straight history of a kind which Evans-Pritchard and, before him, Durkheim (1898a: iii) had repudiated: treaties, personalities, international constraints, theatres of war – it is only by reading widely and with a well-disposed heart, in Evans-Pritchard's book as a whole, that the contribution of anthropology is more than a chapter of analysis of segmentary organisation, of saintliness, and of clientage: even with that effort anthropology is rarely more than a nuance in the history, a barely explicit backdrop against which a succession of facts appears in a perspective of irony. Indeed, Stirling and Campbell refer only to *The Nuer* (1940) in their monographs; Pitt-Rivers to *Witchcraft, Oracles and Magic* (1937); Kenny to *The Institutions of Primitive Society* (Evans-Pritchard, 1956). *The Sanusi of Cyrenaica* is necessarily mentioned by Peters: he quarrels with Evans-Pritchard's figures (1968: 169, n.3), but his critique of Evans-Pritchard's account of the feud (1967) is directed at *The Nuer* (ibid.: 261, n. 1) not the *Sanusi* which is mentioned only on the last page of Peters's article (ibid.: 281, n. 1). The earliest of Peters's articles, in fact makes no mention of *The Sanusi* at all, and all references are to the books on the Nuer (1960: 369 n.8, 372 n.10, 376, 377-8).

The young men at Oxford were pitched into fields which had histories, about which a lot of old facts were known: they did not get much guidance from Evans-Pritchard, in any explicit sense – they were not told 'this is the way to do it'; nor did they get much help from the example of *The Sanusi,* or none they acknowledge. Schapera (1962) suggests that this is because *The Sanusi* did not seek to explain the present in terms of the past, and that is true. Schapera's address is also vague about the explanatory value of the past, and how it is to be utilised – it is a matter of 'explaining the development and present characteristics of the social system [the anthropologist] observes' (ibid.: 148). 'With the aid of oral tradition and such written records as are available [the anthropologist], may be able to enrich his interpretation of those institutions by showing when and how they came into existence, and why they feature as they do in modern life' (ibid.: 154). *But how is it to be done?* How did these men use facts about the past?

Take, first of all, the work of Pitt-Rivers. His book, *People of the Sierra* (1961), has a first chapter called 'The boundaries of the community' in which the history of Alcalà is sketched: the name is Arab in origin; the town was once a Berber stronghold; Napoleon's troops committed sacrilege nearby; the nicest houses are eighteenth century; Alcalà has been in decline for several centuries – the history is over in two pages. Look up Anarchism in the index: do you then, even in this concentrated dose, receive the impression that Alcalà was a centre of Andalusian revolution? That the 'class' structure so elegantly described here and elsewhere (1966) had been the object of violent contention for a century before 1938? The place of history in Pitt-Rivers's book is in the occasional revealing footnote (e.g. p. 125) and in the Appendix: 'where I have referred to the more or less distant past I have done so haphazardly . . . I have . . . resisted the temptation to prove anything observed today through a reference to its historical origin or to explain any historical facts through an analogy with the present' (ibid.: 211). He goes on to give an account of the past in terms of the tension which exists between local and central sanctions on behaviour, the contact between pueblo and government from 1752 to 1952 (ibid.: 213-22). The weight of analysis in the main text is on a timeless, functionalist survey, which can be applied, too, to past stages in the history of the society. The analysis is extremely elegant and sensitive, and quite abstracted from the present and the past – an abstraction which is accentuated by the fact that the book does not mention at any point when the research was done. (It was 1949-52; see ASA 1969.)

Pitt-Rivers is not unique. Kenny's book is graced by an introduction from Evans-Pritchard, again using the familiar phrases about complexity and history, civilisation and literature (1961: 1). But

Kenny's four pages of history are only slightly more illuminating than
Pitt-Rivers's two. The Ramosierrans' Pine Luck is their most famous
institution, and it is old, dating from a donation made by King Juan II
of Castille in the fifteenth century. Already in the sixteenth century
tensions between foresters and herdsmen, which exist today, were
apparent: the evidence is that a forest fire in 1537 was attributed to
cattle-owners who needed pasture. That is scarcely an elaborate use
of historical evidence, but it is perhaps the embryo of a theme which
becomes more important in other later writings (including Pitt-
Rivers's); history is used to show that things have been as they are for
a long time.

Stirling, like Kenny (1961: 14), worked in an area which had little
recorded history. But Stirling is the only one of this first batch of
Evans-Pritchard's mediterranean pupils who gives causal status to a
defined historical process: he argues that the present system of land
tenure is what it is because in the past there had been a growth in
population: that present difficulties were caused some time in the
past. This, too, is scarcely more than an embryo; but it is a more
significant one, for it gives a quite explicit explanatory status to past
events. With some irony Stirling also gives an account of a negative
case: the Atatürk revolution had had scarcely any consequence in the
villages he studied (1965: 7-11; see also 1958). The question 'what
events have no consequences?' is clearly as important as the other
('what features of contemporary society can be linked consequen-
tially to known past events?'); but, interestingly enough, Stirling
attempts a sociological explanation only in the former case. Campbell
(1964: 14-18) traces those historical events which resulted in a decrease in the amount of grazing land available to Sarakatsani after
1922, and gives them causal status when he describes contemporary
social structure. Stirling, commenting on this, says 'Campbell gives us
the history; yet he presents his structural model with the implicit
synchronic assurance of permanence' – a criticism which, Stirling
would be the first to recognise, might equally well be levelled at *Turkish village*.

The way in which Pitt-Rivers and Kenny used history is no radical
departure from what had gone before. As Schapera remarked in his
reply (1962) to Evans-Pritchard, Radcliffe-Brown's work on the An-
daman Islands 'both summarized what was then known of the
people's history and in discussing their social organization repeatedly
commented on changes due to the establishment of an Indian penal

settlement on the islands in 1858.' (Shapera remarks that Evans-Pritchard had not always been so *contra* functionalism, and cites his inaugural lecture; it is therefore worth noting the circumstances in which Evans-Pritchard prepared his inaugural lecture, which are recounted in his letter to *Man* (1970).) And, just as they have predecessors so they have successors among the younger anthropologists who have followed them to the mediterranean. Typically, historical information is included in the Introduction along with a hundred years of population growth, a little rainfall and some notes on schists. For example: 'Malta's documented history stretches back over a thousand years. The summary given of it here makes no pretence of originality . . . . My sole object is to enable the reader to see the present system in its historical perspective' (Boissevain, 1965: 3). The Montevaresani are conscious of their Greek and Arab antecedents. 'These problems, however, are outside the scope of this presentation, and I only mention them as an appeal to my envied friends the archaeologist and the historian . . . as an anthropologist I have to . . . venture into the light of the social day' (Broegger, 1971: 29-30). This is what might be called the historic landscape school: it is not always unadulterated, not always without elements from other schools, but it is so unformulated and shapeless, it may be worthwhile to examine one example in some detail. Susan Tax Freeman's study of Valdemora (1970) serves well, partly because the history is fairly full, also because it is interesting and attractively presented.

Valdemora, in 1963, had a population of eighty-seven. In the grand sweep of history it leaves no trace whatsoever and Freeman therefore incorporates the village into its region for the first 1,900 years of its existence: it is near a Roman frontier post, and the supply road passed through its territory. It was occupied by Arabs for four centuries from about 712. Christians repopulated the area and re-established a bishopric from the twelfth century and a secular lord from the mid-fourteenth. Although there are spasmodic references to Valdemora in tax registers, Freeman does not get to grips with Valdemoran history until the early nineteenth century. The sale of Church lands after 1837 introduced an outsider: he bought them up, and rented them to Valdemorans. But the abolition of tithes enabled them to buy what at first they had had to rent: '. . . at last, the farmer was able to accumulate some surplus. By 1935 all of [the absentee landowner's] holdings had been purchased by farmers of the village'. The railway was built in the 1870s, and the junction and settlement for railwaymen have brought advantages to Valdemorans: they have a visiting fishmonger and grocer, which other villages do not; and the restaurant-bar at the station is a useful rendezvous from which messages and parcels may be sent along the line. Finally, the village has always been small: that has permitted its land tenure system to continue more or less unchanging, and has compelled villagers to marry people from other villages. There are no marked differences in wealth, no bitter antagonisms surviving from the civil war.

Such are the first thirty-odd pages of *Neighbours*. They are locational: Valdemora is in a region, it is 'in' a particular history. Just as she describes the region, and then the village, so the focus of the history becomes sharper as the present gets nearer. The reader is told that the place has a history of this kind or another, but that is about all that can be said. Where causes are suggested (the population has always been small) they are so interposed with graphic history it is hard to believe they are intended. It might be possible to construct an argument that this particular history defines part of the Valdemorans' identity; but then the history would have to be presented together with contemporary evidence, that Valdemorans knew their history. For example, it is interesting to be told that Valdemorans bought land when they were freed from tithes; but there is no suggestion that that hard-won land has any special status; or that the Valdemorans who bought it have wealthy descendants – or even that they claim they got it some other way (e.g. Colclough, 1971). It is interesting; but it seems that Freeman might have chosen some other process, equally substitutable for the purchase of land, and presented it with equal pleasure to the reader. That is not what history is for: it must be related in some way to the present state of affairs. It is worth noting that the abolition of feudal status provides an opportunity for anthropologists of the north-western mediterranean to contribute to the comparative sociological history of the area. The almost uniform measures to free the land from archaic rights in the early nineteenth century, inspired by Napoleonic liberalism, seem to have had rather different consequences. But no anthropologist, not one, has noted this nor, *a fortiori*, explained the varied response of different communities (Cutileiro, 1971: 16-24; Pitt-Rivers, 1963; Davis, 1973; Hansen, 1969; etc.)

III Social processes

Turn from the historic landscape school and its arbitrary charms, and consider the ethnographers who think that history is a kind of social change. This at first sight, is an unexceptionable statement: societies exist, as they say, 'in' time; societies have a sociological propensity to change; the passage of time therefore encompasses change. But consider what they actually do – consider, for example, the account of changes in the distribution of land in Pisticci (Davis, 1973). There are two sections in that book which use historical data. The first is an elaborate version – there is more detail – of what Freeman did: the land is distributed differently in 1964 from what it was 150 years before, and various things happened in the meantime. There is an attempt (1973: 86-91) to suggest that other changes were connected with these events, but there is little evidence that these changes ever occurred: in effect what is done is an imagining – an imagining that stratification, say, had not always been as it was in 1964; that it might have been different in such and such ways in 1814 – and that the redistribution of land since then is connected with the changes in stratification. That is more pretentious than Freeman's work, for there is no evidence that the concomitant changes ever occurred. The 'evidence' is little more than what might be called a sociologically plausible tale: there is a consensus among some sociologists that changes occur in stratification systems when there are changes in the distribution of property: Pisticci's property was redistributed, and so . . . . The other use of history to explain the social structure of Pisticci in the 1960s is even more specific, and it justifies the contrast between history and social change (Davis, 1973: 107-18). Figures for the distribution of a certain quantum of land in 1871 are compared with the figures for its distribution ninety years later: it is a straight case of filling the gap between state A and state B, with an attempt – from a rather more limited set of materials – to show how the change might have occurred. For the gap is not filled in at all: the change happened, things were different in the past. What that study of land tenure figures does do is show that a process – fragmentation – which is commonly thought to result from peasants' adherence to inheritance laws did not result from that only, but from other things as well. The focus of interest is a rather abstract social process; the process, it is true, can be documented only by reference to historical records and, in a limited sense, what people have done in the past has settled things for the future. But it is, in another sense, 'not history': at least, there is nothing which swells or expands the corpus of anthropological ideas: the Pisticci evidence qualifies and exemplifies a social process; but there is nothing intrinsically time-laden there – the data are old, and they must be, but that seems almost accidental. For example, the reader is unlikely to get any notion of how history (what good historians do) is to be incorporated into anthropological explanation and into anthropological comparison. If scientistic functionalism is to be undermined, if anthropologists are to be confronted with an inescapable choice between scientism and art, it will not be as a consequence of exercises such as that conducted with the Pisticci data.

IV Generations and configurations

Two anthropologists' work in the mediterranean escapes the censures levelled against the historic landscape school and the social processors. These are Lison-Tolosana (1966) and Blok (1974). Lison-Tolosana has used the parish and municipal records of Belmonte de los Caballeros extensively and in an exemplary fashion. His Introduction is fairly commonplace landscaping, though it contains unusual richness of detail. His account of stratification begins with a short passage (1966: 55-63) summarising what can be learned from the records – the sixteenth-century division into two classes and the first mention of three classes in 1879; the distinctions in ceremonial and in the social role of the classes; the absence of any political party connotation of class-membership, and the 'lexical richness' of the minutes and memorials which indicates the considerable preoccupation of the councillors with social distinctions and hierarchy. This is unexceptionable – careful and interesting social history: but it remains relatively unconnected with the present; it precedes the present but there is no connection sociological, explanatory, or causal. It is rather in his discussions of generations, of law and of religion that Lison-Tolosana makes a genuinely original contribution. His source appears to be Marias (1949); it is characteristic of Lison-Tolosana's resolute inexplicitness about theory that Mannheim (1959), who also discusses the possibilities of incorporating generations into a sociological history, is cited in his bibliography, but not in the text. The discussion of generations invokes recent history: he divides the population roughly into three sections – those who are retired, those who are in control, and those who will succeed the controllers. The experiences of the retired – selected, stored and transmitted as tradition to the generation of men who, in 1965, controlled all public office – were of extreme political conflict. They were in power in the

1930s; their successors, the present controllers aged between thirty-nine and fifty-four, had literally been warriors while their predecessors were in control – and in the process they had come to be more open to innovation and more closed to internal political conflict. The relatively highly educated youngest generation takes a lot of the experience of their elders for granted, and is rebellious, freedom-seeking but again uninterested in party conflict. They are as familiar with stable government as with piped water and electricity. Now this is a poor sketch of Lison-Tolosana's subtle and detailed analysis, but it is perhaps sufficient to show what he does: recent history is incorporated into the sociology of the village by identifying sociological categories of persons to whom it is experience, and others to whom it is tradition; and by then relating that categorisation to social roles within the community: to people's positions of power, to their responsiveness to innovation (and to the opportunities to innovate provided by other external events), and to the relations between the personnel of the various categories. This has not been done anywhere else in mediterranean anthropology, but its value is quite clear: it is a way of incorporating past events into a sociological account of the social structure of Belmonte, and of giving these events an explanatory status. He is not saying 'this is a town with an identity which is in part derived from traditions about the past'; nor is he saying 'the processes which have produced the present are examples of social change'. Rather, 'people have different experiences and receive different traditions which can be used to explain their behaviour and social relationships now'. Among other things, their experience, and the social relationships through which other people's experiences are mediated, seem to affect their attitudes to innovation: in this way, perhaps, history has a snowball effect. Covertly, it might be said, Lison-Tolosana produces an account of how people make history and consume it. It is 'living history' in the sense that it is incorporated in an analytical way into the account of a changing social structure. While the reader may be unsure what knowledge the Valdemorans or the Pisticcesi have of their history, here the facts about the past are connected with social groupings, and shown to have different significance for them. The ensemble of experience and of relations between social groups is also, further, shown to have consequences for the production of history: men's actions now are related to their experience, direct or mediated by tradition, and to their relationships with others; their actions now become part of their experience and perhaps part of the tradition which their successors will receive and interpret. In this way, history is incorporated into an account of social change. That this is not simply a matter of seeing the past through the eyes of a local community, a matter of the social reconstruction of a past reality, is sufficiently shown by Lison-Tolosana's later treatment of a larger span of time (in ch. 9): his account of relations between Belmonte and the state is located in the history of the state, and some model such as is created in the discussion of generations is used here. 'The council' he says (1966: 224) 'becomes the political cell through which the power of the State makes itself felt in the *pueblo.*' Significantly this relatively commonplace remark is immediately followed by a chronology of political change and crisis between 1812 and 1936 (ibid.: 227-8)

> In a little more than a century eight constitutions had been promulgated, there had been thirteen important revolts against the government, some dozens of pronunciamentos, absolute and moderate monarchy, democracy and absolutism, a republican dictatorship, a profusion of political parties, violent anarchy, arbitrary manipulations of power, immorality, intrigue, sectionalism, martial law, anti-clerical violence, strikes . . . murders, arson, disastrous national budgets.

At the end of this chapter (ibid.: 232-6), Lison-Tolosana again reverts to the generations, relating the minutes of the council of 1926 and earlier to the theme of the retired, the controlling and succeeding generation categories: political action at any time, he seems to say, is related to experience and to the mediation of experience by others who stand in particular relationships to the members of each successive generation.

Now this is a real advance, incorporating political and social history into a sociological theory of change – change which is produced by men in a particular web of relationships with each other. It is not social history, nor is it an anthropological study of a past condition of a particular society, nor is it a purely sociological account of social change. The essence of Lison-Tolosana's approach is to combine the succession of events with the cycle of generations: time passes – that is a constant; generation succeeds generation – and this simple, universal phenomenon can explain a large part of that history which is made locally. Undoubtedly it will be argued that other fundamental structural processes and relationships will turn out to be as important as the succession of generations and some attention will undoubtedly have to be given to explaining why some part only of experience becomes tradition. But Lison-Tolosana will have unquestionable priority in this field.

Anton Blok's book on *mafia* (1974) has no such theoretical or methodological device. What it does have – besides careful historical scholarship – is a theory of history, on a large scale, which allows the book to cover national and local processes, and to show their interdependence. This is the theory – derived from Elias – of configurations, which is the conceptual schema permitting Blok to link the oppression of Sicilian peasants to the failure of central government to gain a monopoly of violence, permitting Blok to explain the varying salience of *mafia*. A configuration is a set of relationships between various kinds of people: government officials, representatives, landlords, landlords' agents (*gabellotti*), professionals, peasants. The activities of *mafiosi* cannot be understood except in terms of the relationships between these categories of person at any given time: but the total set, the configuration, must contain tensions, perhaps even contradictions, which cause change, leading to another configuration. These notions, in Elias, are used to explain the process of state-formation; Blok, in effect, uses them to explain imperfections in that process: his account of Genuardo, and of one estate in Genuardo, is thus tied in to his account of the tensions and interdependence of categories at a regional and national level. Genuardo is only one community, and all other communities are part of the configuration. For this reason if each Sicilian community were to be studied it could be that the monographs would contain a lot of overlapping material. Nevertheless, Blok's book does substantial service in integrating local and national history on a macro-scale which is perhaps lacking in Lison-Tolosana. The cost in Blok's book is that the sources of change are located more often than not outside the community, in events which are not accessible to ethnographic inquiry, and in processes which are rather general.

It is noteworthy that Blok did fieldwork in Genuardo in 1965-7, and that his book covers the period 1860-1960. The impetus is retrospective and the method is one in which ethnographic information about the contemporary world is used, if at all, to illuminate historical data – the account of the Baronessa estate, stories of marriage and homicide, banditry and massacre – the ordinary events in a violent countryside, which are themselves recovered from documents and the careful collation of the reminiscences of survivors. It may be said with some justification that, of all anthropologists working in the mediterranean, Blok comes closest to meeting the prescriptions of Evans-Pritchard: he had done fieldwork, and he creates an ethnographic history. It should be borne in mind, however, that Blok has found it necessary to utilise a quite specific theoretical framework, a theory of configurations, which permits him to combine as it were in the same breath or paragraph, the creation of change, local events and national ones. This is scientific history, history informed by a philosophy of a kind which Evans-Pritchard's heroes, Fustel de Coulanges, Vinogradoff, Seebohm, Bloch, did not pursue. And the end result, concentrating on process, on the linkage of national and local, is very different from the tapestries of social history woven from materials gathered and assembled from sources relating to several decades or centuries by those past masters.

V Continuities and differential survival

There is one other way in which history is used and which, cleared of the sloppy thought which at present often accompanies it, promises well for the future. To distinguish it from historic landscapism, from social processism, and from the social creativism of Lison-Tolosana, it may be called survivalism. The products of this school are really rather variable, and its interest lies in its potential rather than in its achievements. The essence of survivalism is that certain institutions or customs are very ancient and can be traced in their unchangingness back to as long ago as possible. There is one good exponent of this procedure, and several others who do not pay as much attention to mental hygiene as they ought. The clean man is Levy, the husband of Professor Friedl, who accompanied his wife on her fieldwork in Boeotia in 1955-6. He has produced one article which belongs to the survivalist school (1956). It is based on an observation made in the field: brothers, when they cannot agree how to divide a property among them, cast lots. The property is divided into portions which they agree are as equal as they can be; the portions are listed on papers which are then drawn against the names of the sharers. Levy gives the example of three brothers living in one house who collaborate in building two new houses and refurbishing the old one. They each have an equal interest in the work, since the eventual division is left to chance. In this way they maintain their love, and cannot blame any discrepancy on the machinations of anybody – of themselves or their wives. Similar procedures existed in classical times, and are noted also from Byzantine and Coptic sources in the intervening period; they are also mentioned by Plutarch, himself a native of Boeotia. In this article Levy is cautious and non-commital: he has demonstrated the presence of a particular custom, always extra-legal, never formally recognised, apparently 'the same' even down to the detail of noting the composition of each share on the lot; even down to the detail that it is said to be a way to prevent envy and preserve love. He has noted it in one geographical area at intervals during a couple of millennia. He makes no further claim, although, of course, the reader of this simple recounting of the facts is swollen to bursting with guesses, suppositions, hypotheses and problems. Some of these problems are made explicit in Levy's other article – which is a straightforward account of inheritance and dowry in classical Athens; there he disclaims any intention, on that occasion, to argue for continuity: the problems are too great. Any resemblance to any living practice could be purely fortuitous: it could be a reinvention – people unconscious of the past, reinvent institutions in similar situations. It could be a reintroduction – Greeks, nationalists and philhellenes, having learned about the past, might have consciously drawn on it, to equip themselves with a tradition reaching back to classical glory. With those notes of caution he adds that the connection might also be one of continuity, of persistence. Apart from his one article, however, in which he very carefully makes no explicit claim of continuity, no one has been able to establish such persistence. There have been attempts: Hasluck tried to show that Albanian brideprice was 'Homeric' (1933). Myres (1933) pointed out that Homer provides examples of both brideprice and dowry – raising problems of explanation (why should only one 'survive'?) which effectively disposes of any simple continuity. Herzfeld (1973) has written on Greek folksongs, Casson (1938) on pottery making and distribution in antiquity and in modern times. Mirambel (1943) has a sophisticated discussion of the feud and its introduction into the Balkans which is largely based on linguistic evidence. Andromedas (1968) begins his account of the social structure of contemporary Mani with the founding of the Mycenaean kingdom of Pylos. The accolade, however, goes to Spranger (1922) whose account of a religious procession in Central Italy in which an overfed bull was required to excrete as much as possible at certain points in the ritual, combines exquisite delicacy about cowpats with extreme insensitivity towards the ordinary rules of argument: as a result the festival of San Zopito is identified with a classical fertility rite.

At this point it is regrettably necessary to examine Pitt-Rivers's later use of historical data, in which there is a heavy load of assumption about survival. Consult, for example, the sources for his influential essay on honour (1965): Hooker's essay of 1741; Montesquieu, Voltaire, Calderòn, Hobbes, the English Hymnal – all these and Goffman, Simmel, Redfield jostle together bearing insights into the concept of honour and its working-out in Alcalà. Pitt-Rivers justifies this hugger-mugger on the grounds that honour has a general structure which can be analysed 'without much concern for the local and temporal variations' (ibid.: 21). It is worth remarking that this general structure is distinguished from both 'what is honourable' and from 'what honour *is*' (his italics) on the same page: these two things do vary from time to time and place to place. It is hard to tell what honour *is*, apart from a general structure *plus* (in any given instance) what is honourable. Nevertheless, the way that evidence is used – particularly in the second part of the essay concerning 'the semantic range of the notion of honour in Andalusian society' (ibid.: 21) – does imply a continuity which is never justified: 'An earlier period of Spanish history conceptualised these notions [of honour and shame] with more clarity than today' (ibid.: 53), he writes and, later, he refers to 'the fear of ungoverned female sexuality which has been an integral element of European folklore ever since prudent Odysseus lashed himself to the mast to escape the sirens' (ibid.: 68). It is clear that when Pitt-Rivers has a problem – and there are seven pages devoted to the paradox that people with the most claim to honours are most careless of their sexual honour – he will cast around, invoking Voltaire (65), Haro (66), Lope de Vega (67), Odysseus (68), and a romantic novelist called La Picara Justina (70). The point is this: there are assumptions of continuity – historical and geographical – which are not spelled out, and which should be argued, if an impression of potpourri is to be avoided. The conceptual confusion which allows historical events, literature of the sort studied by literary critics, and folklore to *tend to illustrate* whatever real thing the general structure may be, shows little concern not only for time and place but for the status and weight of different kinds of evidence as well.

The notion that institutions or concepts have a general structure (independent of what they are) is taken up again in Pitt-Rivers's account of hospitality. So the material he uses is modern and ancient;

Homer and pre-Islamic Arabs rub shoulders with nineteenth century Eskimos and Alcaleños of the 1950s. 'There is . . .' he says, 'a "natural law" of hospitality deriving not from divine revelation . . . but from sociological necessity' (1968: 27). This adds another kind of continuity to the list – that which must be, because there is a structural necessity for it. Of course, it is not excluded that some solutions to this or to similar problems (how to treat guests, how to transmit property to succeeding generations) should have continuity, should survive. But survivals from structural necessity are of a different order from that. It appears, however, to be distinct from honour, because honour waxes and wanes in importance, and significant elements of its general structure are understood better in some ages than in others. The value of Pitt-Rivers's essay on honour is that it raises, albeit obliquely, the most fascinating question which anthropologists and historians can address themselves to. Levy has discussed survival; Pitt-Rivers causes his reader to ponder the question of differential survival. This poses problems of a high order.

Take as an example – since honour is a nebulous thing – the towers of southern Europe (another possibility is suggested by Casanova's fine essay (1966) on wine and olive presses). These at least are stone and mortar, and fall into physical decay. Towers are known to have existed in Genova, San Gimignano, Florence, Pistoia, Dubrovnik, the mountains of tribal Albania, and the southern Peleponnese. In each case they were associated with feuding clans: they were towers in which men took refuge to avoid the exercise of self-helping justice – agnates and their clients, *in each case*. But consider that Genovese towers were demolished by order of the council in the mid-thirteenth century; that Florentine towers came down after 1293; that Lineton saw the ruins of towers in the southern Peleponnese in the 1960s, and reckons that they had been in use as late as the 1830s (Lineton, 1971; Andromedas (1968) reports that there were 1,770 towers in Monemvasia in the 1930s). Margaret Durham visited people in what may have been their tower in the Gheg mountains of Albania in the 1900s:

> Life among the outlying Christian tribes is so primitive that I doubt if I can make it understood. The communal family lives in a kula, a great stone tower two or three storeys high. It has no windows only loopholes for rifles. It is often perched on a rock for better defence. The ground floor is a pitch-dark stable. The

entrance to the dwelling is by a flight of stone steps to the first
floor. An awful stench grips your throat. In pitch darkness you
climb a wooden ladder to the living room . . . . Thirty or forty
human beings of all ages and both sexes are here crowded
together (1910; cf. Cozzi 1910a, where the word is given as *kulla*).

Well – perhaps it is not a proper tower: people were born there, and
died there – it appears not to have been purely a refuge. Nevertheless,
there are documented towers from Genova to the Peleponnese which
are associated with feuding clans, and which survive differentially:
decaying or, in the case of S. Gimignano, changing from a refuge for
clans to an attraction for tourists. It may be agreed that towers provide
a sufficiently solid illustration of the problems: they exist, they are
documented. It is not known why they are where they are; nor if they
were ever anywhere else; nor why they have differentially survived.
But the possibility of a solution to these problems might justify comparison in anthropological history. That is to say, the possibility must
exist of explaining why towers, or honour, or godparenthood, which
do have a common structure, should survive in some places and not in
others. It is not necessary to posit an Ur-mediterranean social order,
eroded here, pushed to prominence by barely identifiable pressures
there. That is not necessary to the enterprise of this history which shall
be comparative, anthropological and in one sense thematic: to take
an associated set of institutions (as it may be towers, lineages, feuds;
or prestige, sexuality, wealth; or life-crisis rituals, sponsorship,
alliance) and to see what variation there may be; what changes in
context, what resulting changes in the balance of the elements there
may be – that is to apply the method of concomitant variation to a
historical process, in an area in which there is enough history, and
enough similarity, to make the enterprise worthwhile.

For while it is clear that the mediterranean presents a range of kinds
of society and is in no sense a homogeneous culture area, nevertheless
the mediterranean has produced history because, in a sense, it is a
unit: over the millennia it has proved impossible for mediterranean
people to ignore each other. They have conquered, colonised, converted; they have traded, administered, intermarried – the contacts
are perpetual and inescapable. Given this, mediterranean anthropologists should have, yes, a sense of failure – of having missed an
opportunity to be historical and to be comparative. But one of the
important characteristics of history is that, on the whole, it does not

shrink nor disappear, rather grows; and because it grows it can present an opportunity which is not always presented by the anthropologist's field – an opportunity to incorporate a historical and comparative methodology into the general stock of social anthropology. What tools are necessary? Clearly, the anthropologist must be able to show how history is made. What Marias called 'the method of generations' is a start, for as developed and utilised by Lison-Tolosana it provides an account of relationships within villages which is dynamic, productive, giving events the status of causes, suggesting ways in which certain types of social relation are interdependent with political and economic changes, so that wars, recessions, *coups d'état* are absorbed into the life of local communities, and given social meaning. This is, however, a community-centred procedure, needing to be combined with a method, such as Blok's, which identifies the part played by the community in creating those tension-bearing configurations which carry change: the community contains landlords, agents and peasants whose interests, together with those of other members of those categories in other communities, are represented at other levels in the national structure, producing that pattern, change-laden, which to some extent determines relations between classes locally. Finally, there is the work of comparison: the notion of configuration draws the ethnographer out from a village, forces him to consider national patterns, national processes, and the reciprocal relation between village and region or nation. What is then needed, it seems, is an examination of variation, of differential change, an effort to produce a comparative explanation of the differential consequences of national patterns in local communities. Contemplation of honour, of towers, of godparenthood, indicates the magnitude of the task; but it is not impossible. The materials exist in the work of historians, for example, to provide some framework for a discussion of revolutionary movements in Italy, and their various manifestations in different socio-economic settings. But the local studies have not been done, and the more general work cannot yet be integrated with an account of how history is made in villages and small communities of the kind which anthropologists study.

VI Conclusion

The combination of studies – of the creation of history locally, of its reciprocal relation to national events and processes, of concomitant variation among a number of communities is, when all is said and prospected, a far cry from Evans-Pritchard's polemic a quarter of a century ago. It is significant that when Evans-Pritchard's pupils refer to his works they tend to cite *The Nuer* and other pre-1950 books at least as often as they cite *The Sanusi* or the Marrett lecture of 1950, while later writers have introduced, along with history, some notions of methodology which identify the status they would like their evidence to have. On the whole, this has been 'scientific' rather than literary. For Lison-Tolsana the 'method of generations' divides the burden of explanation between social relationships and 'historical events'; in Blok, configurations are a device for locating local events in a framework of regional and national relationships between representatives of social categories, for giving explanatory status in part at least to the national representation of local groups. Pitt-Rivers directs attention, even if such attention is the product of exasperation, to the questions of fluctuation, of survival, or – in short – concomitant variation, and hence to quite another strand in his teacher's thought. Ironically, it is precisely the confusion caused by Pitt-Rivers's elegant use of historical and literary sources which, in a more methodology-minded age, demands careful and critical analysis of the kinds of reasoning underlying the introduction of wayward material. To cite La Picara Justina now raises precise questions about the status of her work and its contribution to explanation.

In this circumstance it is true to say that Evans-Pritchard's prediction has not been fulfilled. He suggested that fieldwork in complex and civilised societies would pose very sharply those questions about the nature of anthropological activity which, in his mind, were already resolved. Turks, Arabs, Spaniards, Greeks could have been an object-lesson to his colleagues, proving that anthropology was more like history than like a natural science. But on the whole the uses made of mediterranean history have not brought that about: rather, the tendencies have been, on the one hand, to indulge in rather patchy sketches of 'the historical background'; on the other, to create methodological devices whereby the facts about the past can be drawn into an account of changing structures. No anthropologist has undertaken research into the past societies in quite the way Evans-Pritchard intended, modelling themselves on Fustel de Coulanges or Bloch – though some historians have maintained that tradition. The only significant attempt to use historical and literary sources has resulted in confusion – an elegant one, to be sure, but one which raises

257

far more questions than it answers. The anthropological future of history lies with Lison-Tolosana and Blok.

Notes

2 Economic anthropology of mediterranean societies

1 Campbell provides his reader with much scattered information about the internal working of the sheep-herding economy: on the division of labour and its ritual reinforcement (1964: 26-31); on levels of income and indebtedness (ibid.: 250-3, 363-4), and on kinds of expenditure, on bribery (ibid.: 234-6, 240-2, 245-6), dowry (ibid.: 44-6, 302-3), clothing and food. That is not discussed here for lack of space and because there are no comparable data from elsewhere in the mediterranean.

2 In 1970 there were an estimated 3 million foreign workers in the six EEC countries. Of these, 30 per cent were workers from other EEC countries, 630,000 of them from Italy. Most of the other 70 per cent came from mediterranean countries: 441,000 from Spain; 216,000 from Greece; 298,000 from Turkey; 210,000 from Portugal; 330,000 from Yugoslavia; 244,000 from Algeria, and 120,000 from Morocco and Tunisia (EEC, 1970).

3 Samuel (1966) gives the Jewish population of Israel as 10,500 in 1865, 600,000 in 1948, 850,000 in 1949. Prag (1962) gives slightly higher figures with a total Jewish population in 1959 of 1,858,841. Anon (1966) gives the Jewish Israeli population in 1965 at 2,273,000. A. Cohen (1965: 21) gives the Arab Israeli population at 160,000 in 1949, and 229,844 in 1959, the increase being mainly due to a falling death rate.

3 Stratification

1 Lison-Tolosana (1966: 68-73): in a population of 1,300 (1958-60) some 400-odd men worked chiefly in agriculture. They were divided as follows: *braceros* (landless labourers) 16; *peones* (very small landowners, mostly supported by labouring) 117; *jornaleros* (small landowners, occasional labouring) 123; *proprietarios* (owner-cultivators, now needing machinery) 49; *pudientes* (well-off farmers) 54; *ricos-ricos* (wealthy, non-cultivating farmers) 9.

4 Politics

1 That is patronage, a term which is here used to refer to all the things which other writers have called patron-clientage or patron-client relations, dientage, nepotism, clientelism and so on. But see Weingrod, 1967-8. The people involved are either patrons or clients.
2 The locution 'no longer' is echoed elsewhere in his article: 'At this point ... kinship merges with ... friendship' (1966b: 10); 'When instrumental friendship reaches a maximal point of imbalance ... friendships give way to the patron-client tie' (ibid.: 16). It is perhaps more suitable to imagine that Wolf is running through a series of categories his analytic eye distinguishes, than that he is setting up a model of the development of a relationship. So, 'merging', 'no longer', 'giving way' 'reaches', would refer to areas of overlap between categories, not to the gradual evolution of a particular patronage tie. It is in this sense that the phrases '... in the first place ... It becomes ...' in the passage just cited from Pitt-Rivers should also be understood.

5 Family and kinship

1 cf. Wade, cited in Davis (1976a): in Italian extended families the head woman was often not the head man's wife in order to prevent the too great concentration of power in the hands of one pair of spouses.

6 Anthropologists and history in the mediterranean

1 That suggests that the priority given to Pitt-Rivers in the opening paragraphs of Davis (1969a) should perhaps be qualified. See also above, p. 94.

Bibliography

ABOU-ZEID, A. M. (1963) 'Migrant labour and social structures in Kharga oasis', in J. Pitt-Rivers (ed.) (1963), 41–54.

ABOU-ZEID, A. M. (1965) 'Honour and shame among the Bedouin of Egypt', in J. G. Peristiany (ed.) (1965b), 243–60.

ADAMS, P. (1971) 'Public and private interests in Hogar', in F. G. Bailey (ed.) (1971e), 167–87.

AITKEN, R. (1945) 'Routes of transhumance on the Spanish meseta', *Geographical Journal*, 106, 56–69.

ALBERONI, F. (1961) 'Saggio critico sulle differenze socioculturali fra due regioni meridionali', *Riv. Int. Sci. Soc.*, 69–80.

ALPORT, E. A. (1973) 'The Mzab', in Gellner, E. and Micaud, C. (eds.) (1973), 141–52.

AMBRICO, G. (1961) 'Povertà e storia nella communità di Grassano', *Boll. Ric. Soc.*, 225–34.

ANDERSON, G. (1956) 'A survey of Italian Godparenthood', *Kroeber Anthrop. Society Papers*, 15.

ANDREADIS, S. G. (1968) 'Discontinuités sociales et problèmes de développement économique en Grèce', in J. G. Peristiany (ed.) (1968b), 315–24.

ANDROMEDAS, J. N. (1968) 'The enduring urban ties of a modern Greek folk sub-culture', in J. G. Peristiany (ed.) (1968b), 269–78.

ANFOSSI, A. et al. (1961) *L'immigrazione meridionale a Torino*, Turin (Centro ricerche industriali e sociali).

ANON (1966) 'Distribution of Jews in the world', *Jewish J. Soc.*, 8, 110.

ANTOUN, R. T. (1965) 'Conservatism and change in the village community. A Jordanian case study', *Human Organisation*, 24, 4–10.

ANTOUN, R. T. (1968) 'On the significance of names in an Arab village', *Ethnology*, 7, ii, 158–70.

ANTOUN, R. T. and HAYEK, I. (eds) (1972) *Rural Politics and Social Change in the Middle East*, Bloomington (Indiana UP).

ARENSBERG, C. M. (1963) 'The Old World Peoples. The place of European cultures in World ethnography', *Anth. Q.*, 36, III, 75–99.

ARGYRIADES, D. (1968) 'The ecology of Greek administration. Some factors affecting the development of the Greek civil service', in J. G. Peristiany (ed.) (1968b), 339–49.

261

Bibliography

ASA (1969) 'Register of members of the Association of Social Anthropologists of the Commonwealth', ASA.

ASWAD, B. C. (1967) 'Key and peripheral roles of noble women in a Middle Eastern plains village', *Anth. Q.*, 40, 139-52.

AYOUB, M. R. (1959) 'Parallel cousin marriage and endogamy. A study in sociometry', *S-W J. Anth.*, 15, 266-75.

AYOUB, V. F. (1965) 'Conflict resolution and social reorganisation in a Lebanese village', *Human Organization*, 24, 11-17.

BADIAN, E. (1958) *Foreign Clientelae* (246-70 BC), Oxford (Clarendon).

BAILEY, F. G. (1966) 'The Peasant view of the bad life', *Advancement of Science*, 399ff.

BAILEY, F. G. (1971a) 'Gifts and poison', in F. G. Bailey (ed.) (1971e), 1-25.

BAILEY, F. G. (1971b) 'Changing communities', in F. G. Bailey (ed.) (1971e), 26-40.

BAILEY, F. G. (1971c) 'What are signori?' in F. G. Bailey (ed.) (1971e), 231-51.

BAILEY, F. G. (1971d) 'The management of reputations and the process of change', in F. G. Bailey (ed.) (1971e), 281-301.

BAILEY, F. G. (ed.) (1971e) *Gifts and Poison. The Politics of Reputation*, Oxford (Blackwell).

BAILEY, F. G. (1973a) 'Promethean Fire. Right and Wrong', in F. G. Bailey (ed.) (1973d), 1-15.

BAILEY, F. G. (1973b) 'Losa', in F. G. Bailey (ed.) (1973d), 164-99.

BAILEY, F. G. (1973c) 'Debate, compromise and change', in F. G. Bailey (ed.) (1973d), 309-25.

BAILEY, F. G. (ed.) (1973d) *Debate and Compromise. The Politics of Innovation*, Oxford (Blackwell).

BALIKĆI, A. (1965) 'Quarrels in a Balkan village', *American Anth.*, 67, 1456-69.

BARIĆ, L. (1967a) 'Levels of change in Yugoslav kinship', in M. Freedman (ed.) (1967), 1-24.

BARIĆ, L. (1967b) 'Traditional groups and new economic opportunities in rural Yugoslavia', in R. Firth (ed.) (1967), 253-81.

BARTH, F. (1954) 'Father's brother's daughter marriage in Kurdistan', *S-W J. Anth.*, 10, 164-71. Also in L. E. Sweet (ed.) (1970), vol. I, 127-36.

BARTH, F. (1959-60) 'The land use pattern of migratory tribes of South Persia', *Norsk Geografisk Tidsskrift*, xvii, 1-11.

BECKINGHAM, C. F. (1956) 'The Cypriot Turks', *Royal Central Asian Journal*, 43, 126-30.

BECKINGHAM, C. F. (1957) 'The Turks of Cyprus', *Journal of the Royal Anthropological Institute of Great Britain and Ireland*, 87, 165-74.

BENET, F. (1957) 'Explosive markets. The Berber Highlands', in K. Polanyi et al. (eds) (1957), 188-217.

BENET, F. (1965) 'The ideology of Islamic urbanisation', *Int. J. Comp. Soc.*, 211-26.

BENSABET, S. J. (1952) 'Los judios en Marruecos', *Cuadernos de Estudios Africanos*, 17, 37-48.

BERNARD, H. R. (1967) 'Kalymnian sponge diving', *Human Biology*, 39, 103-30.

BERQUE, J. (1955) *Structures sociales du Haut-Atlas*, Paris (Presses Universitaires de France).

BERQUE, J. (1957) *Histoire social d'un village Egyptien au xxième siècle*, Paris–The Hague (École Pratique des Hautes Études–Mouton). Partly reprinted in L. E. Sweet (ed.) (1970), vol. II, 193–221.

BIALOR, P. (1968) 'Intra-village tensions leading to conflict and the resolution and avoidance of conflict in a Greek farming community', in J. G. Peristiany (ed.) (1968b), 107–26.

BLACK-MICHAUD, J. (1975) *Cohesive Force*, Oxford (Blackwell).

BLAXTER, L. (1971) 'Rendre service and Jalousie', in F. G. Bailey (ed.) (1971e), 119–28.

BLOK, A. (1966) 'Land reform in a West Sicilian latifundo village. The persistence of a feudal structure', *Anth. Q.*, 39, 1–16.

BLOK, A. (1968) 'South Italian agro-towns', *Comp. Stud. Soc. and Hist.*, 10.

BLOK, A. (1969a) 'Peasants, patrons and brokers in western Sicily', *Anthropological Quarterly*, 42, iii, 155–70.

BLOK, A. (1969b) *Aspects of Social Ranking in a Sicilian Village*, Cyclo, University of Amsterdam.

BLOK, A. (1969c) 'Variations in patronage', *Sociologische Gids*, 16, 365–78.

BLOK, A. (1969d) 'Mafia and class struggle as contrasting factors in Sicilian latifundism', *Arch. Europ. de Sociol*, 10, 95–116.

BLOK, A. (1972) 'The Peasant and the Brigand: Social Banditry Reconsidered', in *Comparative Studies in Society and History*, 14, 4: 494-503.

BLOK, A. (1974) *The Mafia of a Sicilian Village*, Oxford (Blackwell).

BOISSEVAIN, J. (1964) 'Factions, parties and politics in a Maltese village', *American Anth.*, V, 66, 1275–87.

BOISSEVAIN, J. (1965) *Saints and Fireworks. Religion and Politics in Rural Malta*, London School of Economics Monograph on Social Anthropology, London (Athlone).

BOISSEVAIN, J. (1966a) 'Patronage in Sicily', *Man NS*, I, 18–33.

BOISSEVAIN, J. (1966b) 'Poverty and politics in a Sicilian agrotown', *International Archives of Ethnography*, 50, 198–236.

BOISSEVAIN, J. (1969a) *Hal Farrug*, New York (Holt, Rinehart & Winston).

BOISSEVAIN, J. (1969b) 'Patrons as brokers', *Sociologische Gids*, 16, 379–86.

BOISSEVAIN, J. (1970) *The Italians of Montreal. Social adjustment in a plural society*, Studies of the Royal Commission on Bilingualism and Biculturalism, 7, Ottowa (Queen's Printer, Canada).

BOISSEVAIN, J. (1974) *Friends of Friends. Networks, Manipulators and Coalitions*, Oxford (Blackwell).

BOISSEVAIN, J. (1975a) *When the Saints Go Marching Out. Reflections on the Decline of Patronage in Malta*, Cyclo, Rome (paper for AUFS conference 'Changing forms of mediterranean patronage').

BOISSEVAIN, J. (1975b) *Some Notes on Maltese Perceptions of Development and Progress*, Cyclo, University of Amsterdam and AUFS Rome.

BOISSEVAIN, J. and FRIEDL, J. (eds) (1975). *Beyond the Community. Social Process in Europe*, The Hague (Ministerie van Ouderwijs en Wetenschappen).

Bibliography

BOURDIEU, P. (1958) *Sociologie de l'Algerie,* Paris (PUF).

BOURDIEU, P. (1963) 'The attitude of the Algerian peasant toward time', in J. Pitt-Rivers (ed.) (1963), 55–72.

BOURDIEU, P. (1965) 'The sentiment of honour in Kabylie society', in J. G. Peristiany (ed.) (1965b), 191–242.

BOVILL, E. W. (1968) *The Golden Trade of the Moors,* Oxford (OUP).

BRAUDEL, F. (1972) *The Mediterranean and the Mediterranean World in the Age of Philip II,* 2 vols, London (Collins).

BROEGGER, J. (1968) 'Conflict resolution and the role of the bandit in peasant society', *Anth. Q.,* 41, 228–40.

BROEGGER, J. (1971) *Montevarese. A Study of Peasant Society and Culture in Southern Italy,* Bergen–Oslo–Tromso (Universiteits forlaget).

BROWN, K. (1973) 'The impact of the Dahir Berbère in Salé', in E. Gellner and C. Micaud (eds) (1973), 201–16.

BURKE, E. (1973) 'The image of the Moroccan state in French ethnological literature. A new look at the origin of Lyautey's Berber policy', in E. Gellner and C. Micaud (eds) (1973), 175–200.

BURNS, R. K. (1963) 'The circum Alpine area. A preliminary view', *Anth. Q.,* 36, iii, 130–55.

BUXTON, J. H. D. (1921) 'Personal and place names in Malta', *Man,* 21, 146–7.

BUXTON, J. H. D. (1922) 'The ethnology of Malta and Gozo', *Journal of the Royal Anthropological Institute of Great Britain and Ireland,* 52, 164–211.

CALIO, G. (ed.) (1964) *Famiglia e educazione oggi in Italia,* Bari (Laterza).

CALLIER-BOISVERT, C. (1966) 'Soajo. Une communauté féminine rurale de l'Alto Minho', *Bull. Etudes Portugaises,* 27, 237–78.

CALLIER-BOISVERT, C. (1968) 'Remarques sur le système de parente et sur le famille au Portugal', *L'Homme,* 8, ii, 87–103.

CAMPBELL, J. K. (1963) 'The kindred in a Greek mountain community', in J. Pitt-Rivers (ed.) (1963), 73–96.

CAMPBELL, J. K. (1964) *Honour, Family and Patronage. A study of Institutions and Moral Values in a Greek Mountain Community,* Oxford (Clarendon).

CAMPBELL, J. K. (1965) 'Honour and the devil', in J. G. Peristiany (ed.) (1965b), 139–70.

CAMPBELL, J. K. (1968) 'Two case studies of marketing and patronage in Greece', in J. G. Peristiany (ed.) (1968b), 143–54.

CAPO, E. and FABBRI-GAGGI, G. (1964) *L'exode rural et les phénomènes de feminilisation et senilization dans les campagnes Italiennes,* Cyclo, First World Congress of Rural Sociology.

CARO BAROJA, J. (1963) 'The city and the country. Reflections on some ancient commonplaces', in J. Pitt-Rivers (ed.) (1963), 27–40.

CASANOVA, A. (1965) *Marriage et communauté rurale. Exemple Corse,* Paris (Centre d'Etudes et de Recherches Marxistes).

CASANOVA, A. (1966) 'Technologie et communautes rurales. Notes sure les pressoirs pre-industriels de Corse', *Historique,* 6, xxi/xxii, 37–62.

CASSON, S. (1938) 'The modern pottery trade in the Aegean', *Antiquity,* 12, 464–73.

CHELHOD, J. (1969a) 'Les structures dualistes de la societé Bedouine', *L'Homme,* 9, ii, 89–112.

CHELHOD, J. (1969b) 'Ethnologie du monde arable et islamologie', *L'Homme*, 9, iv, 24–40.

CHEMALI, B. (1915–16) 'Mariage et noce au Liban', *Anthropos*, 10–11, 913–41.

CHIVA, I. (1963) 'Social organisation, traditional economy, and customary law in Corsica. Outline of a plan of analysis', in J. Pitt-Rivers (ed.) (1963), 97–112.

CHOURAQUI, A. (1950) *La Condition juridique de l'Israelite Marocain*, Paris (PUF).

CHOURAQUI, A. (1952) *Les Juifs de l'Afrique de Nord*, Paris (PUF).

CODD, N. (1971) 'Reputation and social structure in a Spanish Pyrenian village', in F. G. Bailey (ed.) (1971e), 182–211. See also Redclift, N. (1973).

COHEN, A. (1965) *Arab Border Villages in Israel. A Study of Conformity and Change in Social Organisation*, Manchester (University Press).

COHEN, ERIC (1968) *A Comparative Study of the Political Institutions of Collective Settlements in Israel*, Cyclo, Department of Sociology, Hebrew University of Jerusalem.

COHEN, EUGENE (1972) 'Who stole the rabbits? Crime, dispute and social control in an Italian village', *Anth. Q.*, 45, i, 1–14.

COHEN, P. S. (1962) 'Alignments and allegiances in the community of Shaarayim in Israel', *Jewish J. Soc.*, 4, i, 14–38.

COLCLOUGH, N. T. (1970) *Manfredonia Research Project. Preliminary Report*, Cyclo, UKC.

COLCLOUGH, N. T. (1971) 'Social mobility and social control in a southern Italian village', in F. G. Bailey (ed.) (1971e), 212–30.

COLE, J. W. (1969) 'Economic alternatives in the Upper Nonsberg', *Anth. Q.*, 43, iii, 186–213.

CORAM, A. (1973) 'The Berbers and the coup', in E. Gellner and C. Micaud (eds) (1973).

CORBIN, M. and STIRLING, P. (1973) *A Computer Analysis of Community Census Materials in the Comarca of Ronda*, Report to SSRC, Cyclo, UKC.

COZZI, E. (1909) 'Malattie, morte, funerali nelle montagne Albanesi', *Anthropos*, 4, 903–18.

COZZI, E. (1910a) 'La vendetta del sangue nelle montagne dell 'alta Albania', *Anthropos*, 5, 624–87.

COZZI, E. (1910b) 'Lo stato agricolo in Albania con speciale riguardo alle montagne di Scutari', *Revue d'ethnographie et de sociologie*, I, 33–49.

COZZI, E. (1912) 'La donna albanese con speciale riguardo al diritto, consuetudinario delle montagne di Scutari', *Anthropos*, 7, 309–35, 617–26.

CRONIN, C. (1970) *The Sting of Change*, Chicago (University of Chicago Press).

CRONIN, C. (1973) 'Note on Gower Chapman's Milocca', *Current Anthropology*, 14, iv, 515.

CUISENIER, J. (1967) 'Systèmes de succession et de dotation en Yugoslavie et en Turquie', *L'Homme*, 7, iii, 25–47.

CUISENIER, J. (1976) *Le Cycle domestique dans l'organization familiaire traditionale en Tunisie*, in J. G. Peristiany (ed.), *Mediterranean Family Structures*, Cambridge (UP).

Bibliography

CUTILEIRO, J. (1971) *A Portuguese Rural Society*, Oxford (Clarendon Press and OUP).

DALTON, W. G. (1972) The social structure of an oasis community in Libya, unpublished Ph.D. thesis, Manchester University.

DAVIS, J. (1969a) 'Honour and politics in Pisticci', *Proc. Roy. Anth. Inst.*, 69–81.

DAVIS, J. (1969b) 'Town and Country', *Anth. Q.*, 43, iii, 171–85.

DAVIS, J. (1973) *Land and Family in a South Italian Town*, London (Athlone).

DAVIS, J. (1974a) 'How they hid the Red Flag in Pisticci and how it was betrayed', in J. Davis (ed.) (1974b), 44–67.

DAVIS, J. (ed.) (1974b) *Choice and Change. Essays in Honour of Lucy Mair*, LSE Monographs in Social Anthropology, London (Athlone).

DAVIS, J. (1975) 'Beyond the hyphen. Notes and documents on community-state relations in south Italy', in J. Boissevain and J. Friedl (eds) (1975).

DAVIS, J. (1976a) 'Italian families', in J. K. Campbell (ed.)

DAVIS, J. (1976b) 'An account of changes in the rules for transmission of property in Pisticci 1814–1961', in J. G. Peristiany (ed.) (1976), *Mediterranean Family Structures*, Cambridge (UP).

DE BENEDICTIS, M. and BARTOLELLI, M. (1962) *Indirizzi Produttivi e prospettive di mercato per la zona di nuova irrigazione dell'arco ionico. Metaponto*, part III, vol. 2, Portici: Facoltà Agraria, Cyclo.

DE BOUCHEMAN, A. (1937) 'Une petite cité caravanière. Suhné. Institut Français de Damas', *Documents d'Études Orientales*, 6.

DESHEN, S. A. (1965) 'A case of breakdown of modernisation in an Israeli immigrant community', *Jewish J. Soc.*, 7.

DICKSON, H. R. P. (1952) *Arabs of the Desert*, 2nd ed., London (Allen & Unwin).

DIXON, J. E., CANN, J. R. and RENFREW, C. (1968) 'Obsidian and the origins of trade', *Scientific American*, March, 38–46.

DODAJ, P. (1941) *Codice di lek Dukagjini. Ossia diritto consuetudinario delle montagne d'Albania*, Rome (Reale Accademia d'Italia, Centro Studi Albania).

DOUGLASS, W. A. (1969) *Death in Murelaga*, Seattle (Washington UP).

DU BOULAY, J. (1974) *Mockery and Family Structure in a Greek village*, Cyclos, Conference on Mediterranean family structures, Nicosia.

DUCLOS, L. J. (1973) 'The Berbers and the rise of Moroccan nationalism', in E. Gellner and C. Micaud (eds) (1973), 217–30.

DUNN, R. E. (1973) 'Berber imperialism. The Ait 'Atta expansion in southeast Morocco', in E. Gellner and C. Micaud (eds) (1973), 85–108.

DURHAM, M. E. (1909) *High Albania*, London (Edward Arnold).

DURHAM, M. E. (1910) 'High Albania and its customs in 1908', *Journal of the Royal Anthropological Institute*, 40, 453–72.

DURHAM, M. E. (1928) *Some Tribal Origins, Laws and Customs in the Balkans*, London (Allen & Unwin).

DURHAM, M. E. (1935) 'Bride-price in Albania', *Man*, 35, 102.

DURHAM, M. E. (1940) 'Cowries in the Balkans', *Man*, 40, 79.

DURHAM, M. E. (1941) 'Albania', *Geography*, 26, 18–24.

DURKHEIM, E. (1898a) 'Préface', *Année Sociologique*, I, i–vii.

DURKHEIM, E. (1898b) 'Review of Kunstliche Verwandschaft bei den Sud-slaven. S. Ciszewski, 1897', *Année Sociologique*, 2, 321–3.

EBERHARD, W. (1953a) 'Types of settlement in Southeast Turkey', *Sociologus. N.F.*, 3, 49–64.

EBERHARD, W. (1953b) 'Nomads and farmers in Southeastern Turkey. Problems of settlement', *Oriens*, 6, 32–49.

EBERHARD, W. (1970) 'Change in leading families in Southern Turkey', *Anthropos*, 49, 992–1003, repr. in L. E. Sweet (ed.) (1970), vol. II, 242–56. Page references are to this version.

EEC (1970) 'La libre circulation des travailleurs', *Documentation Européenne*, n 11, Brussels (EEC).

EISENSTADT, S. N. (1953) *Absorption of Immigrants,* London (Routledge & Kegan Paul).

ERLICH-STEIN, V. (also called Ehrlich-Stein, and V. St. Ehrlich) (1940) 'The Southern Slav Patriarchal family', *Sociological Review*, 32, 224–41.

ERLICH-STEIN, V. (1966) *Family in Transition. A Study of 300 Yugoslav Villages*, Princeton (Princeton University Press).

ERLICH-STEIN, V. (1970) 'Love sentiment and love relations in rural Yugoslavia', *Anthropologica*, NS 12, 33–44.

EVANS-PRITCHARD, E. E. (1937) *Witchcraft, Oracles and Magic among the Azande,* Oxford (Clarendon Press).

EVANS-PRITCHARD, E. E. (1940) *The Nuer. A Description of the Modes of Livelihood and the Political Institutions of a Nilotic People,* Oxford (Clarendon).

EVANS-PRITCHARD, E. E. (1943) *The Place of the Sanusiya in the History of Islam,* Sidi Rafa (British Military Administration Press).

EVANS-PRITCHARD, E. E. (1949) *The Sanusi of Cyrenaica,* Oxford (Clarendon Press).

EVANS-PRITCHARD, E. E. (1956) *The Institutions of Primitive Society,* Oxford (Blackwell).

EVANS-PRITCHARD, E. E. (1964) *Essays in Social Anthropology,* London (Faber).

EVANS-PRITCHARD, E. E. (1970) 'Social anthropology at Oxford', *Man*, NS 5, 704.

EVELPIDIS, C. (1968) 'L'Exode rural en Grèce', in J. G. Peristiany (ed.) (1968b), 127–40.

FARSOUN, S. K. (1970) 'Family structure and society in modern Lebanon', in L. E. Sweet (ed.) (1970), vol. II, 257–307.

FAVRET, J. (1966) *Le traditionnalisme par excès de modernité,* Cyclo, Paper for the Sixth World Conference of Sociology, Evian.

FAVRET, J. (1968) 'Rélations de dépendance et manipulation de la violence en Kabylie', *L'Homme*, 8, iv, 18–44.

FAWCETT, C. B. (1930) 'Corsica', *Sociological Review*, 22, 72–82.

FERCHIOU, S. (1968) 'Différentiation sexuelle de l'alimentation au Djerid (sud Tunisien)', *L'Homme*, 8, ii, 64–86.

FERGUSON, A. (1966) *An Essay on the History of Civil Society,* ed. D. Forbes, Edinburgh (University Press).

Bibliography

FILIPOVIĆ, M. S. (1958) 'Vicarious paternity among Serbs and Croats', *S-W J. Anth.*, 14, 156–67.

FILIPOVIĆ, M. S. (1963) *Forms and functions of ritual kinship among south Slavs*, V Congrès international des sciences anthropologiques et ethnologiques, Tom. II, vol. I, Paris (Musée de l'Homme), 77–80.

FIRTH, R. (1967) *'Themes in Economic Anthropology'*, ASA Monographs, 8, London (Tavistock).

FLAMAND, P. (1950) 'Quelques renseignements statistiques sur la population Israelite du Sud Marocain', *Hesperis*, 37, 363–97.

FOGG, W. (1938) 'A tribal market in the Spanish zone of Morocco', *Africa*, 11, 428–58.

FOGG, W. (1939) 'The importance of tribal markets in the commercial life of the countryside of north-west Morocco', *Africa*, 12, iv, 445–9.

FOGG, W. (1940a) 'Villages, tribal markets and towns. Some considerations concerning urban development in the Spanish and international zones of Morocco', *Sociological Review*, 32, 85–107.

FOGG, W. (1940b) 'A Moroccan tribal shrine and its relation to a nearby tribal market', *Man*, 40, 100–4.

FOGG, W. (1941) 'Changes in the layout, characteristics and function of a Moroccan tribal market consequent on European control', *Man*, 41, 104–8.

FOGG, W. (1942) 'The organization of a Moroccan tribal market', *American Anth.*, NS, 44, 47–61.

FRACCARO, M. (1957) 'Consanguineous marriages in Italy', *Eugenics Quarterly*, 4, 36–38.

FREEDMAN, M. (ed.) (1967) *Social Organization. Essays Presented to Raymond Firth*, London (Cass).

FREEMAN, S. T. (1968a) 'Corporate village organization in the Sierra Ministra. An Iberian structural type', *Man* NS, 477–84.

FREEMAN, S. T. (1968b) 'Religious aspects of the social organization of a Castilian village', *American Anth.*, 70, 34–49.

FREEMAN, S. T. (1970) *Neighbours. The Social Contract in a Castilian Hamlet*, Chicago (University of Chicago Press).

FREEMAN, S. T. (1973) 'Introduction to studies in rural European social organization', *American Anth.*, 75, 743–90.

FREIDL, E. (1959a) 'Dowry and inheritance in modern Greece', *Transactions of the New York Academy of Sciences*, Series 2, xxii, 49–54.

FRIEDL, E. (1959b) 'The role of kinship in the transmission of national culture to rural villages in mainland Greece', *American Anth.*, 61, 30–8.

FRIEDL, E. (1963a) *Vasilika. A Village in Modern Greece*, New York (Holt, Rinehart & Winston).

FRIEDL, E. (1963b) 'Some aspects of dowry and inheritance in Boeotia', in J. Pitt-Rivers (1963), 113–35.

FRIEDL, E. (1964) 'Lagging emulation in post-peasant society. A Greek case', *American Anth.*, 66, 69–86.

FRIEDL, E. (1967) 'The position of women. Appearance and reality', *Anth. Q.*, 40, 97–108.

FRIEDL, E. (1968) 'Lagging emulation in post-peasant society. A Greek case', in J. G. Peristiany (ed.) (1968b), 93–106.

FRIEDMAN, F. G. (1953) 'The world of "la miseria" ', *Partisan Review*, 20, 218–31.

FRIEDMAN, F. G. (1960) *The Hoe and the Book. An Italian Experiment in Community Development*, Ithaca (Cornell University Press).

FURNARI, M. (1971) 'Industrializzazione senza sviluppo', *Giornale degli economisti e annali di economia.*

FUSTEL DE COULANGES, N. D. (nd) *The Ancient City*, New York (Doubleday).

GALT, A. H. (1974) 'Rethinking patron-client relationships. The real system and the official system in southern Italy', *Anth. Q.*, 47, 182–202.

GEARING, F. (1968) 'Preliminary notes on ritual in village Greece', in J. G. Peristiany (ed.) (1968b), 65–72.

GELLNER, E. (1958) 'How to live in anarchy', *The Listener*, 3, iv, 579–83.

GELLNER, E. (1968) 'Sanctity, puritanism, secularisation and nationalism in North Africa. A case study', in J. G. Peristiany (ed.) (1968b), 31–48.

GELLNER, E. (1969) *Saints of the Atlas*, London (Weidenfeld & Nicolson).

GELLNER, E. (1973a) 'Introduction', in E. Gellner and C. Micaud (eds) (1973), 11–21.

GELLNER, E. (1973b) 'Political and religious organisation of the Berbers of the central high Atlas', in E. Gellner and C. Micaud (eds) (1973), 59–66.

GELLNER, E. (1973c) 'Patterns of rural rebellion in Morocco during the early years of independence', in E. Gellner and C. Micaud (eds) (1973), 361–74.

GELLNER, E. and MICAUD, C. (eds) (1973) *Arabs and Berbers. From Tribe to Nation in North Africa*, London (Duckworth).

GILBERT, J. P. and HAMMEL, E. A. (1966) 'Computer simulation and analysis of problems in kinship and social structure', *American Anth.*, 68, 71–93.

GILSENAN, M. (1973a) *The Vital Lie*, Cyclo, Paper for 1973 ASA Conference.

GILSENAN, M. (1973b) *Saint and Sufi in Modern Egypt*, Oxford (Clarendon).

GLUCKMAN, M. (1971) 'Foreword', in M. Shokeid (1971).

GOLDBERG, H. (1967) 'FBD marriage and demography among Tripolitanian Jews in Israel', *S-W J. Anth.*, 23, 177–91.

GOWER CHAPMAN, C. (1973) *Milocca. A Sicilian Village*, London (Allen & Unwin).

GRAZIANI, L. (1973) 'Patron-client relationships in southern Italy', *Euro. J. Pol. Research*, 1, 3–34.

GUBSER, P. (1973) *Politics and Change in Al-Karak, Jordan*, London (OUP).

GUDEMAN, S. (1971) 'The *compadrazgo* as a reflection of the natural and spiritual person', *Proc. Roy. Anth. Inst.*, 45–71.

GUILLAUME, A. (1960) *La Propriété collective au Maroc*, Rabat (Librairie la Porte).

GULICK, J. (1953) 'The Lebanese village. An introduction', *American Anth.*, 55, 367–72.

GULICK, J. (1954) 'Conservatism and change in a Lebanese village', *Middle East Journal*, 8, 295–307.

GULICK, J. (1965a) 'Dimensions of cultural change in the Middle East. Introduction to a symposium', *Human Organization*, 24, 1–3.

GULICK, J. (1965b) 'Old values and new institutions in a Lebanese Arab city', *Human Organization*, 24, 49–52.

Bibliography

HALPERN, J. M. (1958) *A Serbian Village*, New York (Columbia University Press).

HALPERN, J. M. (1963) 'Yugoslav peasant society in transition. Stability in change', *Anth. Q.*, 3, 156–82.

HALPERN, J. M. (1969) *A Serbian Village*, revised edition, New York (Harper).

HALPERN, J. M. and ANDERSON, D. (1970) 'The Zadruga. A century of change', *Anthropologica*, NS 12: 83–97.

HAMMEL, E. A. (1957) 'Serbo-Croation Kinship terminology', *Kroeber Anthropological Society Papers*, 16, 45–75.

HAMMEL, E. A. (1968) *Alternative Social Structures and Ritual Relations in the Balkans*, Englewood Cliffs (Prentice-Hall).

HAMMEL, E. A. and GOLDBERG, H. (1971) 'Parallel cousin marriage', *Man*, NS 6, iii, 488–9.

HANOTEAU, A. and LETOURNEAUX, A. (1893) *La Kabylie et les coutumes Kabyles*, 2nd rev. ed., 3 vols, Paris (Challamel).

HANSEN, E. C. (1969) 'The state and land tenure conflicts in rural Catalonia', *Anth. Q.*, 42, iii, 214–43.

HART, D. M. (1954) 'An ethnographic survey of the Rifian tribe of Aith Waryaghar', *Tamuda*, 2, 51–86.

HART, D. M. (1957) 'Notes on the Rifian community of Tangier', *Middle East Journal*, 11, 153–62.

HART, D. M. (1958) 'Emilio Blanco Izaga and the Berbers of the Central Rif', *Tamuda*, 6, ii, 171–237.

HART, D. M. (1966a) 'Segmentary systems and the role of five "fifths" in tribal Morocco', *Revue de l'Institut de Sociologie de l'Universite de Rabat*, 5–95.

HART, D. M. (1966b) 'A customary law document from the Ait 'Atta of the Jbil Saghru', *Revue de l'Occident Musulman et de la Méditérranée*, 1, 91–112.

HART, D. M. (1970) 'Clan lineage, local community and the feud in a Rifian tribe', in L. E. Sweet (ed.) (1970), 3–75.

HART, D. M. (1973) 'The tribe in modern Morocco. Two case studies', in E. Gellner and C. Micaud (eds) (1973), 25–8.

HASLUCK, M. M. (1932) 'Physiological paternity and belated birth in Albania', *Man*, 32, 53–4.

HASLUCK, M. M. (1933) 'Bride-price in Albania. A homeric parallel', *Man*, 33, 191–5, 203.

HASLUCK, M. M. (1939) 'Couvade in Albania', *Man*, 39, 18–20.

HASLUCK, M. M. (1954) *The Unwritten Law in Albania*, Cambridge (University Press).

HERZFELD, M. (1973) 'Ritual and Textual Structures. The Advent of Spring in Rural Greece', paper for 1973 ASA conference.

HOBSBAWM, F. J. (1959) *Primitive Rebels. Studies in Archaic Forms of Social Movement in the Nineteenth and Twentieth Centuries*, Manchester (University Press).

HOBSBAWM, F. J. (1972) 'Social Banditry: Reply (to Blok)', in *Comparative Studies in Society and History*, 14, 4: 503–5.

HOFFMAN, B. G. (1967) *The Structure of Traditional Moroccan Society,* Paris (Mouton).

HOFFMAN, M. A. (1972) 'Process and tradition in Cypriot cultural history. Time theory in anthropology', *Anth. Q.,* 45, 15-34.

HUNT, R. (ed.) (1967) *Personalities and Cultures. Readings in Psychological Anthropology,* New York (Nat. Hist. Press).

HUTSON, J. (1971) 'A politician in Valloire', in F. G. Bailey (ed.) (1971e), 69-96.

HUTSON, S. (1971) 'Social ranking in a French Alpine community', in F. G. Bailey (ed.) (1971e), 41-68.

HUTSON, S. (1973) 'Valloire', in F. G. Bailey (ed.) (1973d), 16-47.

HYTTEN, E. (1966) 'Il codice etico in una zona depressa', *La Rivista da servizio sociale,* 6, i, 105-21.

HYTTEN, E. and MARCHIONI, M. (1970) *Industrializzazione senza sviluppo. Gela. Una storia medidionale,* Milan (Angeli).

KARANOVIĆ, M. (1929-30) 'Some of the large zadrugas in Bosnia and Herzegorina', *Glasnik zemaljskog Muzeja u Bosni i Hercegovini,* 41, 63-77; 42, 133-56, (French résumé of Serbo-Croat text).

KASPERSON, R. E. (1966) *The Dodecanese. Diversity and Unity in Island Politics,* University of Chicago, Department of Geography, Research Paper 108.

KASTRATI, Q. (1955) 'Some sources of the unwritten law in Albania', *Man,* 55, 124-7.

KAVADIAS, G. B. (1963) *Les Structures familiales chez les Saracatsans de Grèce,* Vie Congrès international des sciences anthropologiques et ethnologiques, tom 2, vol. 1, 156-8, Paris (Musée de l'Homme).

KAYSER, B. (1968) 'Les migrations interieures en Grèce', in J. G. Peristiany (ed.) (1968b), 191-200.

KENNA, M., (1971) Property and ritual relationships on a Greek island, unpublished Ph.D. thesis, University of Kent.

KENNA, M. (1974) *A Study of Permanent and Temporary Island Migrants in Athens,* Report to SSRC on project HR2445/2 lodged in BLL.

KENNY, M. (1960) 'Patterns of patronage in Spain', *Anth. Q.,* 33, 14-23.

KENNY, M. (1961) *A Spanish Tapestry,* London (Cohen & West).

KENNY, M. (1963) 'Europe. The Atlantic fringe', *Anth. Q.,* 36, iii, 100-19.

KENNY, M. (1968) 'Parallel power structures in Castille. The patron-client balance', in J. G. Peristiany (ed.) (1968b), 155-62.

KEYSER, J. M. B. (1973) 'The middle-eastern case. Is there a marriage rule?', *Ethnology,* 293-309.

KHALAF, S. G. (1965) 'Industrial conflict in Lebanon', *Human Organization,* 24, 25-33.

KHURI, F. L. (1967) 'A comparative study of migration patterns in two Lebanese villages', *Human Organization,* 26, 206-13.

KHURI, F. L. (1970) 'Parallel cousin marriage reconsidered. A Middle Eastern practice that nullifies the effects of marriage on the intensity of family relationships', *Man,* NS 5, iv, 597-618.

KHURI, F. L. (1976) 'Family associations in Beirut', in J. G. Peristiany (ed.) (1976), *Mediterranean Family Structures,* Cambridge (UP).

Bibliography

KIRAY, M. B. (1970) *Squatter Housing. Fast Depeasantization and Slow Work-erization in Underdeveloped Countries,* Cyclo, Technical University of the Middle East, Ankara.

KRADER, L. (1960) 'The transition from serf to peasant in eastern Europe', *Anth. Q.,* 33, 76–90.

LAMBIRI, J. (1968) 'The impact of industrial employment on the position of women in a Greek country town', in J. G. Peristiany (ed.) (1968b), 261–88.

LA PALOMBARA, J. (1964) *Interest Groups in Italian Politics,* Princeton (UP).

LAPHAM, R. J. (1969) 'Social control in the Sais', *Anth. Q.,* 42, iii, 244–62.

LEE, D. D. (1953) Greece, in M. Mead (ed.) (1953), 77–114.

LEMARCHAND, R. and LEGG, K. (1971–2) 'Political clientelism and develop-ment', *Comparative Politics,* 4, 149–78.

LEVY, H. L. (1956) 'Property distribution by lot in present day Greece', *Trans-actions of the American Philological Association,* 87, 42–6.

LEVY, H. L. (1963) 'Inheritance and dowry in classical Athens', in J. Pitt-Rivers (1963), 137–44.

LINETON, M. J. (1971) *Mina. Past and Present. Depopulation in a Village in Mani, Southern Greece,* thesis submitted for the degree of Ph.D. in Social Anthropology, UKC.

LISON-TOLOSANA, C. (1966) *Belmonte de los Caballeros. A Sociological Study of a Spanish Town,* Oxford (Clarendon Press).

LISON-TOLOSANA, C. (1968) 'Social factors in economic development', in J. G. Peristiany (ed.) (1968b), 325–37.

LITTLEWOOD, P. (1974) 'Strings and kingdoms. The activities of a political mediator in southern Italy', *Arch. Europ. Sociol.,* XV, 33–51.

LOIZOS, P. (1974) 'The progress of Greek nationalism in Cyprus 1878–1970', in J. Davis (ed.) (1974b), 114–33.

LOIZOS, P. (1975) *The Greek Gift. Politics in a Cypriot village,* Oxford (Blackwell).

LOMBROSO, G. (1896) 'Sulle condizioni sociale economiche degli operai di un Sobborgo di Torino', *La riforma sociale,* III, 316–30.

LOPREATO, J. (1962) 'Interpersonal relations in peasant society. The peasant's view', *Human Organization,* 21, 21–4.

LOPREATO, J. (1967) *Peasants No More. Social Class and Social Change in an Underdeveloped Society,* San Francisco (Chandler).

MACDONALD, J. S. (1963) 'Agricultural organisation, migration and labour militancy in rural Italy', *Ec. Hist. Review,* second series, 16, 61–75.

MAHER, V. (1975) *Women and Property in Morocco,* Cambridge (UP).

MANNHEIM, K. (1959) *Essays on the Sociology of Knowledge,* London (Rout-ledge & Kegan Paul).

MARAIS, O. (1973) 'Berbers and the Moroccan political system after the coup', in E. Gellner and C. Micaud (eds) (1973).

MARASPINI, A. L. (1968) *The Study of an Italian Village,* Paris (Mouton).

MARIAS, J. (1949) *El metodo historico de las generaciones,* Madrid.

MARX, E. (1967) *Bedouin of the Negev,* Manchester (UP).

MATARUS, R. (1963) *Le Mariage des cousins parallèles chez les Arabes,* Vie congrès international des sciences anthropologiques et ethnologiques, tom 2, vol. 1, Paris (Musée de l'Homme), 185–9.

MAUNIER, R. (1927) 'Recherches sur les echanges rituels en Afrique du Nord', *Année Sociologique* NS 1,924–5, 11–97.

MAUNIER, R. (1937) 'Les groups d'interest en Afrique du Nord', *Annales Sociologiques*, fasc. 2, 35–61.

MAUSS, M. (1930) 'Voyage au Maroc', *L'Anthropologie*, 40, 453–6.

MEAD, M. (ed.) (1953) *Cultural Patterns and Technical Change*, Paris (UNESCO).

MEDICI, G. et al. (1962) *Polyverizzazione e frammentazione della proprieta fondiaria in Italia*, Milan (Feltrinelli).

MIKESELL, M. W. (1958) 'The role of tribal markets in Morocco. Examples from the northern zone', *Geographical Review*, 48, 494–511.

MIKESELL, M. W. (1960) 'Market centres of northeastern Spain. A review', *Geographical Review*, 50, 247–51.

MINTZ, S. W. and WOLF, E. R. (1950) 'An analysis of ritual godparenthood (compadrazgo)', *S-W J. of Anth.*, 6.

MIRAMBEL, A. (1943) 'Blood vengeance in southern Greece and among the Slavs', *Byzantion* (American series), 2, 381–92.

MOHSEN, S. K. (1967) 'Aspects of the legal status of women among Awlad 'Ali', *Anth. Q.*, 40, 153–66.

MONTAGNE, R. (1930a) *Les Berbères et le Makhzen dans le sud du Maroc*, Paris (F. Alcan).

MONTAGNE, R. (1930b) *Villages et Kasbas Berbères. Tableau de la vie sociale des Berbères sedentaires dans le sud du Maroc*, Paris (F. Alcan).

MONTAGNE, R. (1931) *La vie sociale et la vie politique des Berbères*, Paris (Soc. de l'Afrique Fr.). Tr. J. D. Seddon (1973), *The Berbers. Their social and political organisation*, London (Cass).

MONTFERT, P. (1934) 'Essai sur la propriété paysanne au Maroc', *Renseignements Coloniaux*, 8, 148–52; 9, 165–74.

MOORE, C. H. (1963) 'Politics in a Tunisian village', *Middle East Journal*, 17, 527–40.

MOSELY, P. E. (1943) 'Adaptation for survival. The Varžić zadruga', *Slavonic and East European Review*, 21, 147–73.

MOSS, L. and CAPPANNARI, S. C. (1960a) 'Folklore and medicine in an Italian village', *Journal of American Folklore*, 73, 85–102.

MOSS, L. and CAPPANNARI, S. C. (1960b) 'Patterns of kinship. Comparaggio and community in a south Italian village', *Anth. Q.*, 33, 24–32.

MOSS, L. and CAPPANNARI, S. C. (1962) 'Estate and class in a south Italian hill village', *American Anth.*, 64, 287–300.

MOSS, L. and THOMSON, W. H. (1959) 'The Southern Italian family. Literature and observation', *Human Organization*, 18, 35–41.

MUENSTERBERGER, W. and AXELRAD, S. (eds) (1964) *The Psychoanalytic Study of Society*, New York (International Universities Press).

MURPHY, R. E. and KASDEL, L. (1959) 'The structure of parallel cousin marriage', *American Anth.*, 61, 17–29.

MYRES, J. L. (1905) 'The evil eye of the camera', *Man*, 5, 12.

MYRES, J. L. (1933) 'Homeric and Albanian bride-price', *Man*, 33, 204, 195–6.

NADER, L. (1965a) 'Communication between village and city in the Modern Middle East', *Human Organization*, 24, 18–24.

Bibliography

NADER, L. (1965b) 'Choices in legal procedure. Shia Moslem and Mexican Zapotec', *American Anth.*, 67, 394–9.

NIMKOFF, M. F. (ed.) (1965) *Comparative Family Systems,* Boston (Houghton Mifflin).

PARSONS, A. (1962) 'Autorità patriarcale e autorità matriarcale nella famiglia napoletana', *Quad. Sociologia,* 4, 416–52.

PARSONS, A. (1964) 'Is the Oedipus complex universal? A south Italian "nuclear complex" ', in Muensterberger and Axelrod (eds) (1964), 3, 278–301, 310–26.

PATAI, R. (1951) 'Nomadism. Middle Eastern and Central Asian', *S-W J. Anth.*, 7, 401–14.

PATAI, R. (1965) 'The structure of endogamous unilineal descent groups', *S-W J. Anth.*, 21, 325–50.

PAULSON, B. and RICCI, A. (1966) *The Searchers. Conflict and Communism in an Italian Town,* Chicago (Quadrangle Books).

PERISTIANY, J. G. (1965) 'Honour and shame in a Cypriot village', in J. G. Peristiany (ed.) (1965b), 171–90.

PERISTIANY, J. G. (ed.) (1965b) *Honour and Shame. The Values of Mediterranean Society,* London (Weidenfeld & Nicolson).

PERISTIANY, J. G. (1968a) 'Introduction to a Cyprus highland village', in J. G. Peristiany (ed.) (1968b), 75–91.

PERISTIANY, J. G. (ed.) (1968b) *Contributions to Mediterranean Sociology,* The Hague (Morton).

PETERS, E. L. (1960) 'The proliferation of segments in the lineage of the Bedouin of Cyrenaica', *Journal of the Royal Anthropological Institute of Great Britain and Ireland,* 90, 29–53. Repr. in L. E. Sweet (ed.) (1970), vol. I. Page references are to this version.

PETERS, E. L. (1963) 'Aspects of rank and status among Muslims in a Lebanese village', in J. Pitt-Rivers (1963), 159–200.

PETERS, E. L. (1965) 'Aspects of the family among the Bedouin of Cyrenaica', in M. F. Nimkoff (ed.) (1965), 121–46.

PETERS, E. L. (1967) 'Some structural aspects of the feud among the camel-herding Bedouin of Cyrenaica', *Africa,* 37, 261–82.

PETERS, E. L. (1968) 'The tied and the free. An account of a type of patron-client relationship among the Bedouin pastoralists of Cyrenaica', in J. G. Peristiany (ed.) (1968b), 167–88.

PETERS, E. L. (1972) 'Shifts in power in a Lebanese village', in R. Antoun and I. Hayek (eds) (1972), 165–97.

PETRULLO, V. M. et al. (1937) 'A note on Sicilian cross-cousin marriage', *Primitive Man,* 10, 8–11.

PHOTIADIS, J. D. (1965) 'The position of the coffee-house in the social life of the Greek village', *Sociologia Ruralis,* 5, 45–56.

PITKIN, D. S. (1959a) 'A consideration of asymmetry in the peasant-city relationship', *Anth. Q.,* 32, 161–7.

PITKIN, D. S. (1959b) 'The intermediate society. A study in articulation', *Proc. Am. Ethn. Soc.,* spring, 14–19.

PITKIN, D. S. (1959c) 'Land tenure and family organisation in an Italian village', *Human Organization,* 18, 169–73.

274

PITKIN, D. S. (1960) 'Marital property considerations among peasants. An Italian example', *Anth. Q.,* 33, 33-9.

PITKIN, D. S. (1963) 'Mediterranean Europe', *Anth. Q.,* 36, iii, 120-9.

PITT-RIVERS, J. (1960) 'Social class in a French village', *Anth. Q.,* 33, 1-13.

PITT-RIVERS, J. (1961) *The People of the Sierra,* Chicago (UP) (First edition 1954).

PITT-RIVERS, J. (1963) *The Egalitarian Society,* VIe Congrès international des sciences anthropologiques et ethnologiques, tom 2, vol. 1, 229-33, Paris (Musée de l'Homme).

PITT-RIVERS, J. (1965) 'Honour and social status', in J. G. Peristiany (ed.) (1965b), 19-78.

PITT-RIVERS, J. (1968) 'The stranger, the guest and the hostile host', in J. G. Peristiany (ed.) (1968b), 13-30.

PIZZORNO, A. (1960) Familismo Amorale e marginalitá storica, ovvero perchè non c'è niente da fare a Montegrano, *Quad. di Sociol.,* 2.

PLOTNICOV, L. and TUDEN, A. (1970) *Essays in Comparative Social Stratification,* Pittsburg (UP).

POLANYI, K. et al. (eds) (1957) *Trade and Market in the Early Empires,* Chicago (Free Press).

POWELL, J. D. (1970) 'Peasant society and clientelist politics', *Am. Pol. Sci. Rev.,* 64, 411-25.

PRAG, A. (1962) 'Some demographic aspects of Kibbutz life in Israel', *Jewish J. Soc.*

PRICE, C. A. (1963) *Southern Europeans in Australia,* Melbourne (OUP and ANU), 2 vols.

PRICE, R. (1967) 'Un Barbier-aracheur de dents en Andalousie', *l'Homme,* 7, i, 97-102.

PRICE, R. and PRICE, S. (1966a) 'Stratification and courtship in an Andalusian village', *Man,* NS 1, 526-33.

PRICE, R. and PRICE, S. (1966b) 'Noviazgo in an Andalusian pueblo', *S-W J. Anth.,* 22, 302-32.

PRINS, A. H. J. (1965) 'The modified Syrian schooner. Problem formation in maritime change', *Human Organization,* 24, 34-48.

REDCLIFT, M. (1973) 'Gema', in F. G. Bailey (ed.) (1973d), 120-34.

REDCLIFT, N. (1973) 'Saburneda', in F. G. Bailey (ed.) (1973d), 99-119. See also Codd, N. (1971).

REIMANN, H. (1967) *Sicily. Sociological and Anthropological Research in an Underdeveloped Region. A Preliminary Report,* Paper to sixth World Congress in Sociology, Evian, Cyclostyle.

REITER, R. R. (1972) 'Modernization in the south of France. The village and beyond', *Anth. Q.,* 45, 35-53.

REIGELHAUPT, J. F. (1967) 'Saloio women. An analysis of informal and formal political and economic roles of Portuguese peasant women', *Anth. Q.,* 40, 109-26.

ROSEN, L. (1968) 'A Moroccan Jewish community during the Middle Eastern crisis', *The American Scholar,* 37, iii. Repr. in L. E. Sweet (ed.) (1970), vol. II, 388-404.

Bibliography

ROSEN, L. (1972) 'Rural politics and national political structure in Morocco', in R. T. Antoun and I. Hayek (eds) (1972), 214–35.

ROSEN, L. (1973) 'The social and conceptual framework of Arab-Berber relations in central Morocco', in E. Gellner and C. Micaud (eds) (1973), 155–74.

ROSENFELD, H. (1958) 'Processes of structural change within the Arab village extended family', *American Anth.*, 60, 1127–39.

ROSENFELD, H. (1968) 'The contradictions between property, kinship and power, as reflected in the marriage system of an Arab village', in J. G. Peristiany (ed.) (1968b), 247–60.

ROSENFELD, H. (1972) 'An overview and critique of the literature on rural politics and social change', in R. T. Antoun and I. Hayek (eds) (1972), 45–74.

ROSSI, E. (1965) *Viaggio nel feudo di Bonomi*, Rome (Rivniti).

ROSSI-DORIA, M. (1956) *Riforma agraria e azione meridionalista*, Bologna (Agricole).

ROSSI-DORIA, M. (1963) *Rapporto sulla Federconsorzi*, Bari (Laterza).

SAMUEL, VISCOUNT (1966) 'Where did Israel put its million Jewish immigrants?' *Jewish J. Soc.*

SANDERS, I. T. (1953) 'Village social organization in Greece', *Rural Sociology*, 18, 366–75.

SANDERS, I. T. (1954) 'The nomadic peoples of northern Greece. Ethnic puzzle and cultural survival; *Social Forces*, 33, 122–9.

SANDERS, I. T. (1955) 'Selection of participants in a mutual aid group in rural Greece; *Sociometry*, 18, 581–5.

SANTANGELO-SPOTO, H. (1892) 'Paysan-agriculteur de Torremaggiore (Foggia). Ouvrier-tenancier dans le systeme des engagements momentaries', in Le Play (ed.), *Les Ouvriers des deux mondes*, series 2, vol. 3, 213–68.

SCHAPERA, I. (1962) 'Should anthropologists be historians?', *J.R.A.I.*, 92, 144–56.

SCHNEIDER, J. (1969) 'Family patrimonies and economic behaviour in western Sicily', *Anth. Q.*, 42, iii, 109–29.

SCHNEIDER, J. (1971a) 'Of vigilance and virgins', *Ethnology*, 9, i, 1–24.

SCHNEIDER, J. (1971b) *Friends of Friends*, Cyclo.

SCHNEIDER, P. (1969) Honour and conflict in a Sicilian town, *Anth. Q.*, 42, iii, 130–54.

SCHNEIDER, P., SCHNEIDER, J. and HANSAN, E. (1972) 'Modernisation and development. The role of regional elites and noncorporate groups in the European Mediterranean', *Comp. Stud. Soc. Hist.*, 14, 328–50.

SCHORGER, W. D. (1969) 'The evolution of political forms in a northern Moroccan village', *Anth. Q.*, 42, iii, 263–86.

SEDDON, J. D. (1970) *Economic Change and Family Structures in a Moroccan Rural Commune*, Cyclo, Paper for Mediterranean Family Structures Conference, Nicosia.

SEDDON, J. D. (1973a) 'Local politics and state intervention. North-east Morocco from 1870–1970', in E. Gellner and C. Micaud (eds) (1973), 109–40.

SEDDON, J. D. (1973b) 'Introduction', in R. Montagne (1931).

SEDDON, J. D. (1974) 'Aspects of underdevelopment in north-east Morocco', in J. Davis (ed.) (1974b).

SHOKEID, M. (1971) *Dual Heritage,* Manchester (UP).

SILVERMAN, S. F. (1965) 'Patronage and community – nation relationships in central Italy', *Ethnology,* 4, ii, 172–89.

SILVERMAN, S. F. (1966) 'An ethnographic approach to social stratification. Prestige in a central Italian community', *American Anth.,* 68, 899–921.

SILVERMAN, S. F. (1967) 'The life crisis as a clue to social functions', *Anth. Q.,* 40, 127–38.

SILVERMAN, S. F. (1968a) 'Agricultural organisation, social structure, and values in Italy. Amoral familism reconsidered', *American Anth.,* 70, 1–20.

SILVERMAN, S. F. (1968b) 'The Italian land reform. Some problems in the development of a cultural tradition', *Anth. Q.,* 41, 66–77.

SILVERMAN, S. F. (1970a) 'Stratification in Italian communities. A regional contrast', in L. Plotnicov and A. Tuden (eds) (1970), 211–99.

SILVERMAN, S. F. (1970b) 'Exploitation in rural central Italy. Structure and ideology in stratification study', *Comp. Stud. Soc. Hist.,* 327–9.

SILVERMAN, S. F. (1974) 'Bailey's politics' (review article), *J. Peasant Studies,* 2, 111–20.

SPENSER, R. F. (1958) 'Culture, process and intellectual current. Durkheim and Ataturk', *American Anth.,* 60, 640–57.

SPENSER, R. F. (1960) 'Aspects of Turkish kinship and social structure', *Anth. Q.,* 33, 40–50.

SPENSER, R. F. (1961) 'The social context of modern Turkish names', *S-W J. Anth.,* 17, 205–18.

SPRANGER, J. A. (1922) 'The festival of San Zopito and the ox at Loreto Aprutino', *Journal of the Royal Anthropological Institute of Great Britain and Ireland,* 52, 306–19.

STAHL, P. H. (1974) *Ethnologie de l'Europe du sud-est. Une anthologie,* Paris (Mouton).

STIRLING, A. P. (1953) 'Social ranking in a Turkish village', *British Journal of Sociology,* 4, 31–44.

STIRLING, A. P. (1957) 'Land, marriage, and the law in Turkish villages', *International Social Science Bulletin,* 9, 21–33.

STIRLING, A. P. (1958) 'Religious change in Republican Turkey', *Middle East Journal,* 12, 395–408.

STIRLING, A. P. (1960) 'A death and a youth club. Feuding in a Turkish village', *Anth. Q.,* 33, 51–75. Repr. in L. E. Sweet (ed.) (1970), vol. II, 169–92.

STIRLING, A. P. (1963) 'The domestic cycle and the distribution of power in Turkish villages', in J. Pitt-Rivers (ed.) (1963), 201–13.

STIRLING, A. P. (1965) *Turkish Village,* London (Weidenfeld & Nicolson).

STIRLING, A. P. (1968) 'Impartiality and personal morality', in J. G. Peristiany (ed.) (1968b), 49–64.

STIRLING, A. P. (1969) 'Honour, culture, theory and some doubt', *Bijdragen tot de Taal – land – en Vokenkunde,* 125, 118–33.

STIRLING, A. P. (1974) 'Turkish village revisited', in J. Davis (ed.) (1974b).

Bibliography

STIRLING, A. P. and ROWLAND, R. (1973) *Economic Development and Social Structure in Apulia,* Cyclo, University of Kent.

SUZUKI, P. (1960) 'Village solidarity among Turkish peasants undergoing urbanization', *Science,* 132, 891–2.

SUZUKI, P. (1964) 'Encounters with Istanbul. Urban peasants and village peasants', *International Journal of Comparative Sociology,* 5, 208–15.

SWEET, L. E. (1960) *Tell Toquaan. A Syrian village,* Anthropological papers of the Museum of Anthropology of the University of Michigan, 14.

SWEET, L. E. (1967) 'The women of 'Ain ad Dayr', *Anthropological Quarterly,* 40, 167–83.

SWEET, L. E. (ed.) (1970) *Peoples and Cultures of the Middle East,* 2 vols, New York (Natural History Press).

SYLOS-LABINI, P. (1964) 'Precarious employment in Sicily', *International Labour Review,* 89.

TANNOUS, A. L. (1941) 'Social change in an Arab village', *American Sociological Review,* 6, 650–62.

TANNOUS, A. L. (1942) 'Emigration. A force of social change in an Arab Village', *Rural Sociology,* 7, 62–74.

TANNOUS, A. L. (1949) 'The village in the national life of Lebanon', *Middle East Journal,* 3, 151–63.

TENTORI, T. (1964) 'Appunti sulla famiglia Italiana e sul rapporto genitori-famiglia', in G. Calio (ed.) (1964), 93–112.

VALENTINI, G. (1945) 'La famiglia nel diritto tradizionale albenese', *Annali Lateranerisi,* 9, 9–212.

VINCENT, J. (1973) 'St. Maurice', in F. G. Bailey (ed.) (1973d), 200-18.

VINOGRADOFF, A. R. (1973) 'The socio-political organization of a Berber Taraf tribe, pre-protectorate Morocco', in E. Gellner and C. Micaud (eds) (1973), 67–84.

VINOGRADOFF, A. R. (1974a) 'French colonialism as reflected in the male-female interaction in Morocco', Trans. *New York Acad. Sev.,* series 2, 36, 192–9.

VINOGRADOFF, A. R. (1974b) *The Ait Ndhir of Morocco. A Study of the Social Transformation of a Berber Tribe,* Museum of Anthropology, University of Michigan Research Paper, no. 55, Ann Arbor (University of Michigan Press).

WADE, R. (1971) 'Political behaviour and world view in a central Italian village', in F. G. Bailey (ed.) (1971e), 252–80.

WADE, R. (1973) 'Colombaio', in F. G. Bailey (ed.) (1973d), 219–52.

WATERBURY, J. (1970) *The Commander of the Faithful. The Moroccan Political Elite. A Study of Segmentary Politics,* London (Weidenfeld & Nicolson).

WATERBURY, J. (1972) *North for the Trade. The Life and Times of a Berber Merchant,* London (University of California Press).

WATERBURY, J. (1973a) 'The coup manqué', in E. Gellner and C. Micaud (eds) (1973), 397–423.

WATERBURY, J. (1973b) 'Endemic and planned corruption in a monarchical regime', *World Politics,* XXV, 533–55.

WEINGROD, A. (1960) *Reluctant Pioneers. Village Development in Israel,* New York (Cornell UP).

WEINGROD, A. (1967-8) 'Patrons, patronage and political parties', *Comp. Stud. Soc. Hist.,* X, 376-400.

WEINTRAUB, D. (1964) 'A study of new farmers in Israel', *Sociologia Ruralis,* 4, 3-51.

WEINTRAUB, D. and LISSAK, M. (1961) 'Absorption of north African immigrants in agricultural settlements in Israel', *Jewish J. Soc.,* 2.

WESTERMARCK, E. (1914) *Marriage Ceremonies in Morocco,* London (Macmillan).

WESTERMARCK, E. (1920) 'The belief in spirits in Morocco', *Acta Academiae Aboensis, Humaniora,* 1, 1-166.

WESTERMARCK, E. (1926) *Ritual and Belief in Morocco,* London (Macmillan), 2 vols.

WHITAKER, I. (1968) 'Tribal structure and national politics in Albania 1910-50', in I. M. Lewis (ed.), *History and Social Anthropology,* ASA Monograph 8, London (Tavistock).

WHYTE, W. F. (1944) 'Sicilian peasant society', *American Anth.,* NS 46, 65-74.

WILLEMS, E. J. (1962) 'On Portuguese family structure', *Int. Jnl. Comp. Soc.,* 3, 65-79.

WILLIAMS, H. H. and WILLIAMS, J. R. (1965) 'The extended family as a vehicle of culture change', *Human Organization,* 24, 59-64.

WILLNER, D. (1970) *Nation Building and Community in Israel,* Princeton (UP).

WILLNER, D. and KOHLS, M. (1962) 'Jews in the Atlas mountains of Morocco. A partial reconstruction', *Jewish J. Soc.,* 4, 207-41.

WOLF, E. R. (1962) 'Cultural dissonance in the Italian alps', *Comp. Stud. Soc. Hist.,* 5, 1-14.

WOLF, E. R. (1966a) *Peasants,* Englewood Cliffs (Prentice-Hall).

WOLF, E. R. (1966b) 'Kinship, friendship and patron-client relations in complex societies', in M. Banton (ed.), *Social Anthropology of Complex Societies,* ASA Monograph, 4, London (Tavistock), 1-22.

WOLF, E. R. (1969) 'Society and symbols in Latin Europe and in the Islamic Near East. Some comparisons', *Anth. Q.,* 42, iii, 287-301.

WYLIE, L. (1963) 'Demographic change in Roussillon', in J. Pitt-Rivers (ed.) (1963), 215-36.

WYLIE, L. (1964) *Village in the Vaucluse,* New York (Harvard UP), rev. ed.

Index